THE RISE OF THE JAPANESE CORPORATE SYSTEM

married and has one son. At present he is
Professor, Graduate School of Policy Science,
Saitama University.

Japanese Studies
General Editor: Yoshio Sugimoto

THE RISE OF THE JAPANESE CORPORATE SYSTEM

The Inside View of a MITI Official

Koji Matsumoto

Translated from the Japanese by Thomas I. Elliott

KEGAN PAUL INTERNATIONAL
London and New York

First published in Japanese in 1983

This revised and updated edition
first published in English in 1991 by
Kegan Paul International Ltd
PO Box 256, London WC1B 3SW, England

Reprinted 1993
Further revised and first published in paperback 1994

Distributed by
John Wiley & Sons Ltd
Southern Cross Trading Estate
1 Oldlands Way, Bognor Regis,
West Sussex, PO22 9SA, England

Columbia University Press
562 West 113th Street
New York, NY 10025, USA

© Koji Matsumoto 1991, 1994

Set in Times 10 on 12 point
by Input Typesetting Ltd., London

Printed in Great Britain by T. J. Press, Padstow, Cornwall

                                                         Data

                                                       ne inside

                                                    yu. *English*

Library of Congress Cataloging in Publication Data
Matsumoto, Koji, 1944–
    [Kigyo shugi no koryu]. English
    The rise of the Japanese corporate system: the inside view of a
MITI official/Koji Matsumoto
        276pp. 220cm.– (Japanese studies series)
    Translation of Kigyo shugi no koryu
    ISBN 0–7103–0488–9
        1. Industrial management–Japan.   2. Corporate planning–Japan.
3. Entrepreneurship.   4. Comparative management.   I. Title
II. Series: Japanese studies series (Kegan Paul International)
HD70.J3M3413   1991
658.4'00952–dc20   90–38467
                                                             CIP

Contents

Contents

Preface

In general, Japan's economic system is viewed as being capitalism, and there seems to be no room for doubting otherwise. If one glances at the many subsystems that form the Japanese economy's foundation, for example, such as private ownership of property, joint stock companies and well-developed markets, one is forced to conclude that yes, indeed, Japan belongs to the group of highly developed capitalist nations.

But just as democratic government is possible within the framework of, say, a monarchy, with the external monarchal form being maintained even as the government becomes democratic over a lengthy period of political evolution, we know there are times when a country's internal mechanism can differ from the system seen externally. The contemporary Japanese situation can be viewed as a noteworthy example of such a case.

Although not widely recognized yet, a new economic system has developed and been nurtured in Japan inside a shell of capitalism. The new system differs greatly from traditional capitalism, but that does not mean to say it has drawn close to socialism. Nor can the newness of this system be understood by viewing it as depending principally on either market or planning principles, or on the two in combination.

The issue in the new system is not the degree of government interference in the economic process, or the relationship between government and corporations. Rather, it is the new elements that have appeared in the structure of corporations – the basic units of the economy – and the economic conclusions those elements have brought about. More specifically, the issue is the essential breaking away from a capitalistic corporate structure and, related to that, the disappearance of many capitalistic characteristics from the overall economy.

This new corporate system is the source of the might of the Japanese economy. It provided the propulsive energy that enabled the Japanese economy to expand fifteen-fold between the mid-1950s and the mid-1980s, and to this day it remains the source of the Japanese economy's strong vitality.

This book discusses the new corporate system in specific terms, explaining how it differs from the system of orthodox capitalist corporations, in being both more progressive and more fitting for meeting the various conditions of contemporary industrial society. It also explains the circumstances, in the context of the new corporate system, that brought forth powerful corporations for which it is difficult to find comparisons in other countries.

It may seem to some that the interpretation of the contemporary Japanese economy that this book offers contains some quite bold assertions. But the author feels that, if anything, this book should have been written sooner in Japan. And yet it is not as if there were not reasons for the new corporate system not having been recognized sooner.

One is that the system gradually took form over a long period directly from the everyday business reality, in a process of much trial and error. It was not created artificially on the basis of a specific theory or thought system. And during its development, nothing particularly dramatic occurred to attract attention to it.

Another reason it was not recognized sooner was the general mind-set of the Japanese intelligentsia.

Since the second half of the nineteenth century, Japan has continually imported aspects of Western civilization. And although there have been exceptions, most members of the Japanese intelligentsia in every period since then tended to view the special features of Japan's economic society that could not be found in the West simply as reflections of Japan's backwardness. As Japan 'progressed', they said, those special features would be absorbed into the Western model, and that was the best thing that could happen.

While aspects of Western civilization had universal value, they said, aspects of Japanese culture were 'special'. Their way of thinking seemed to be the natural approach to interpreting the situation, and it led those people to believe that the distinctively different aspects of Japan's economy were diversions from the ideal form, temporary deviations which would disappear with Japan's modernization. At the very least, those people did not make the effort needed, based on the Japanese reality, to encourage the creation of a conceptual framework, say, or a system with universal appeal.

This type of thinking is truly trying to gain power with those studying Japan, which is one of the psychological reasons that prevented the 'discovery' of the new economic system.

At any rate, Japan is now approaching the end of a period. In global terms, many Japanese corporations have moved to the forefront of their industries, and although – when viewed from the overall economy – one can still pinpoint various inefficiencies in many areas, the mechanism that moves Japanese industry today is powerful almost beyond comparison. Given these circumstances, the concept that the special aspects of the Japanese situation will be absorbed into the Western model together with Japan's modernization is highly unrealistic.

Whether they like it or not, the Japanese are now having to reinterpret their country's economy. And apart from whether or not it succeeds, this book is an attempt at such an interpretation.

Let me briefly discuss the contents of this book by chapter. The first chapter describes how the collective of what can be called 'corporate employees' exercise control in the medium-size and larger corporations that comprise the nucleus of Japan's economy, and explains how the joint stock company system has been reduced to a shell. It demonstrates that Japanese corporations have a structure and behavioral pattern that are different from those of corporations that exist in a situation of orthodox capitalism.

The second chapter looks closely at American, Chinese and Yugoslavian corporations as representatives of capitalism, collective socialism and self-management socialism, respectively, and compares their special features to those of Japanese corporations.

Based on the comparison in the second chapter, the third chapter explains in specific terms the efficiency and progressiveness of the new corporate system.

In the fourth chapter, the author explains that the Japanese economy, consisting of cells of corporations with unique systems, is shifting to a new economic system, i.e., 'kigyoism'. The chapter describes the essential features of this new system.

The fifth chapter describes the 'kigyoistic' society, whose features are a remarkable degree of equality, vertical mobility, cohesiveness and unity, and which consists of a multitude of small and large corporations, as a social system with unique aspects.

The sixth chapter, in a summation discussion, propounds that the 'corporate revolution' which took place in Japan after the Second World War was the basic factor behind Japanese industry's tremendous global performance. It analyzes the significance of this revolution in the light of world history.

The original version of this book was written in Japanese during 1981 and 1982 when the author was in the Ministry of International Trade and Industry, first in the Industrial Policy Bureau and then in the International Trade Policy Bureau. It was published in Japan in February 1983 under the title *Kigyō Shugi no Kōryū* (The Rise of Kigyoism). Four years later, in 1987, the book was chosen as a special aid project for translation into English by the Foundation for Asian Management Development, headquartered in Tokyo. Mr Thomas I. Elliott, president of Dynaword Incorporated in Tokyo, and a foremost translator of Japanese to English, was asked to translate the book. He was assisted by Mr Hiromitsu Tanaka. Except for adding some updated data and deleting some small parts, including an introduction in the original Japanese that reflected on Japan's postwar economic development, the English version is a complete and accurate rendition of the original Japanese-language book. Also, I want to thank the staff of Dynaword Incorporated for their fine help in editing and proofing this book.

Finally, in terms of ordering my thinking into unified concepts, I am very grateful to Professors Ryushi Iwata and Tadanori Nishiyama of Musashi University in Tokyo. And regarding publication of my book in English, I want to express my appreciation to Professor Yoshio Sugimoto, who teaches at La Trobe University in Melbourne.

In closing, I must state that nothing I have written in this book should be construed as reflecting the opinions of the Japanese government or the Ministry of International Trade and Industry.

K.M.

1 Corporations for Corporate Employees

1 Independence from Shareholder Control

Under commercial law, a corporation is defined as an incorporated association with shareholders as its corporate members. Corporations in countries like the United States announce general shareholders' meetings by sending letters to shareholders that normally open with the phrase, 'Your company is pleased to report . . .'.

The circumstances in Japan differ greatly from that depiction, and the concept of 'your company' or 'my company' applies to the company for which a person works rather than a company in which a person owns shares. It is commonly accepted in Japan that the word *shain* (corporate member) refers to an employee of a company. The fact that a *shain* is actually a shareholder in Japan has clearly degenerated into a mere legal concept, and it is far closer to the truth to say that, as a social reality, the business corporation in Japan is a body of its employees.

1 Few family-owned companies; mutual shareholding

In developing countries, although it may be natural that ownership and management of companies are not often clearly separated, it is not uncommon even in advanced capitalist nations to see corporations controlled by those who own the capital stock.

A look at selected Western nations shows that there are large percentages of family-owned companies among the leading corporations. Some of the following figures are slightly outdated, but in England the figure was 29 percent of the top 116 companies, in France, 50 percent of the top 200 companies, and in West Germany, 48 percent of the top 150 companies. From the standpoint of family ownership of more than 51 percent of the outstanding shares of a company, the number of family-owned companies was 49 of the top 72 companies in West Germany and 30 out of the top 100 in France.[1] It cannot be denied, therefore, that colorings of family ownership are still a strong factor among European companies.

In contrast, if the discussion is limited to larger corporations, family ownership is rare in Japan, with the exception of a few industries – construction and foodstuffs for example.

Table 1.1 shows the leading shareholders of companies listed in the First Section of the Tokyo Stock Exchange. Notice that no individual owns 40 percent or more of the shares in any company, and only about 4 percent of all companies have individuals owning 10 percent or more of their shares. Notice, too, in Table 1.2, that although individuals held the majority of shares of listed companies in 1955, the figure fell steadily until in 1987 it was only 23.6 percent.

But there are persons such as Konosuke Matsushita of Matsushita Electrical Industrial Co., Ltd., founders of large companies who appear to have a strong personal influence on those companies but whose shareholdings are small. Matsushita, for example, before his passing owned only about 2.1 percent of the shares of the company he founded, so he was not even the principal shareholder. Although Matsushita clearly had a strong influence on the company he founded, the influence was due entirely to his achievements as a successful manager and certainly cannot be

Table 1.1 *Shareholdings of leading individual and corporate shareholders in selected Japanese companies*

Share (%)	Corporate		Individual		Total	
	No. of companies	%	No. of companies	%	No. of companies	%
Under 10	660	57.3	65	5.6	725	62.9
10–19	133	11.5	33	2.9	166	14.4
20–29	112	9.7	8	0.7	120	10.4
30–39	54	4.7	2	0.2	56	4.9
40–49	38	3.3	–	–	38	3.3
50% or more	47	4.1	–	–	47	4.1
Total	1,044	90.6	108	9.4	1,152	100.0

Source: Compiled from *Nikkei Kaisha Joho* (Nikkei Company Information), published by Nihon Keizai Shimbunsha, Fall 1989. Covers corporations on First Section of Tokyo Stock Exchange.

Table 1.2   *Percentage of shares held by selected shareholders in companies listed on first section of Tokyo Stock Exchange, 1955–87*

	1955	1965	1975	1979	1987
Government & local public bodies	0.4	0.2	0.2	0.2	0.8
Financial Institutions	19.5	24.5	35.6	38.2	42.2
Investment trusts	4.1	6.2	1.7	2.0	2.4
Securities companies	7.9	6.1	1.5	2.1	2.5
Other corporations	13.2	17.3	25.5	25.3	24.9
Foreign corporations	1.5	1.6	2.5	2.4	3.6
Individuals, others	53.4	44.1	33.0	29.7	23.6

Source: Compiled from *Kaīsha Nenkan Jojo Kaishaban, 1990* (Corporate Year Book, Listed Companies Edition, 1990), and materials from Nomura Securities.

thought of as deriving from his position as a shareholder, based on the capital stock he owned.

In this way, Japan differs considerably from Europe in terms of there being very few family-controlled enterprises in Japan.

What, then, is the comparison between Japan and the United States? There are a number of powerful families in the United States, including the Du Ponts, the Mellons and the Rockefellers who exercise great control over industry. The information is dated somewhat, but even the maximum estimate concerning family-owned businesses shows that out of the top 500 American corporations, about 30 percent are family-owned.[2] Compared to Europe, however, there are fewer family-owned corporations in the United States, and institutional investors such as pension funds, the trust departments of commercial banks, investment banks and life insurance companies are becoming increasingly important.

Among these institutional investors, pension funds have become the world's largest investors. By the end of 1980, total investments of pension funds exceeded 700 billion dollars, which made them direct or indirect owners of one-third to two-fifths of the outstanding shares of all American companies.[3] This money is nothing other than money accumulated from workers and set aside for their pensions in the future, and most of the other funds are money created for financing public and semi-public projects. In that context, it is clear that the structure of American capitalism has moved considerably away from traditional capitalism.

3

Although institutional investors may be operating funds for

Table 1.3 *Negative replies in proxies and written votes returned by corporate shareholders (with total shares held by corporate stockholders taken as 100%)*

No. of negative replies	0	1 or less	2–5	Over 5	No reply	Total
No. of companies	892	57	2	1	74	1,026
%	(86.9)	(5.6)	(0.2)	(0.1)	(7.2)	(100)

Source: Prepared from Figure 56 in the 1983 White Paper on General Shareholders meetings by the Economic Research Center of Daiwa Securities.

the public good, viewed from a company's eyes they are still shareholders who strictly monitor performance and apply pressure to protect the profits from their investments. In that sense, institutional investors are more severe and devoid of personal feelings than individual investors, for the professional managers entrusted to manage these funds are selected for their ability as securities analysts and are readily dismissed if profits are not satisfactory.

In American companies, performance is evaluated principally in financial terms, such as through Return on Investment (ROI; i.e., the percentage of profit on gross sales multiplied by the percentage of capital turnover; expressed as percentage of annual gross profit against amount of investment), etc., and management is conducted while receiving pressure from cold, calculating 'capitalists'. The standards for evaluating performance extend into a company's internal operations, so that evaluations are made mainly on those standards, not only concerning management's performance, but also concerning decisions on corporate strategy and whether to accept or reject individual investment plans. For that reason, American companies adopt managerial policies that pursue all-out rationalization from the standpoint of the capital invested by the shareholders.

As already mentioned, about three-quarters of all shares in Japan are owned by legal entities that are organizations. Although the Japanese situation viewed from this point closely resembles the one in the US, the resemblance is superficial. The internal circumstances of companies in the two countries are totally different.

A unique feature regarding shares held by legal entities in

Japan is the mutual holding of shares among companies that have business relationships and among companies and financial institutions. The top shareholders of Toyota Motor Corporation and their holdings of outstanding shares, for example, include the Mitsui Bank, the Tokai Bank and the Sanwa Bank, all of which hold 4.8 percent, and Toyota Automatic Loom Works, Ltd., which holds 4.6 percent. Conversely, Toyota is a principal shareholder in the same companies and banks, holding 4.2 percent in the Mitsui Bank, 5.2 percent in the Tokai Bank, 2.2 percent in the Sanwa Bank and 24.8 percent in Toyota Automatic Loom Works (*Source*: Toyo Keizai, Japan Company Handbook, Fall Edition, 1989).

The practice among companies in Japan of mutually holding each other's shares did not arise as a result of viewing such action as a way of effectively managing assets, as in the United States. Rather, one company having another acquire some of its shares, is a move to have 'stable' shareholders, or, as clearly seen from the expression 'to inlay shares', the actual situation regarding the mutual holding of shares in Japan should be called an 'interlocking' of companies.

Ordinarily, it is the shareholder who selects a company whose shares he wants to acquire, but in Japan it is the reverse, and the company selects shareholders it wants to have acquire its shares.

And, as shown in Table 1.3, close to 100 per cent of all institutional shareholders submit blank proxies to general shareholders' meetings. (It appears that corporations holding each other's shares mutually exchange blank proxies.)

The results of proxy voting at general shareholders' meetings are the same as if candidates in an election were allowed to fill in their own names on ballot slips. Also, institutional shareholders in Japan, unlike those in the United States and other countries, do not send representatives to board meetings or financial committee meetings to monitor or participate actively in the company's operations. Even if they tried to do so, the other company could do the same and interfere with the management of the first company, so the influence based on holding shares is balanced out.

Also, except for instances when companies dissolve the relationship of mutually holding each other's shares, such as when the business relationship between them ends, they will continue as shareholders as long as the other company feels it is necessary and regardless of whether dividends are earned.

5

In this way, corporate shareholders that have a relationship of mutually holding another company's shares show almost no interest in the management of the other company or even in whether they will receive dividends. They faithfully follow the wishes of management in the company of which they supposedly own a part.

Regardless of the subjective motive a company may have for promoting a move toward having stable shareholders, it is clear what the results will be if the majority of a company's issued shares are held by such shareholders. This practice is a de facto total separation of management from the wishes of the owners, which is exactly what has happened in Japanese corporations.

Although the fact that Japanese companies consider dividends to be de facto cost items is also quite strange in terms of a capitalist company supposedly being organized for the profit of its shareholders and the results of its activities being distributed to shareholders as dividends, viewing dividends as cost items, can be understood on the premise of the foregoing situation. As well, the yield on shares has tended to drop continually after reaching a peak of just under 12 percent in 1951, and, in 1986, yield fell as far as 0.78 percent, less than one-quarter of the interest of 3.76 percent on one-year time deposits.

It is no exaggeration to say that such a status is the exact opposite of that found in American corporations, where the main direction of management responsibility is toward shareholders and where managers keep or lose their positions depending on how well they perform in terms of producing a high ROI.

2 Various systems becoming vacuous

Incorporated associations have established various systems, based on the premise of the separation of ownership and management, that let shareholders control the companies. The general shareholders' meeting, for example, the board of directors, the system of chartered accountants and the system of statutory auditors all monitor corporate management from the shareholders' standpoint, checking the behavior of managers who act contrary to the best interests of the shareholders and making certain the wishes of the shareholders are reflected accurately in the company's management.

Such legislation also exists in Japan, but the systems are not functioning in the manner intended. Taking the general shareholders' meeting as an example, it is not uncommon for meetings in the US to last three hours or more and to have shareholders ask tough questions on all phases of management. In fact, managers are often judged by the quality of their responses to these questions.

In Europe, especially with large West German corporations, general shareholders' meetings are day-long affairs. When a problem is on the agenda they sometimes last into the small hours of the morning.

Investment clubs organized by private shareholders are also quite popular, and an organization called The Federation for Protecting Owners of Securities sends delegates to general meetings on behalf of shareholders to participate actively in discussions and to see that their statements are presented in a positive manner.[4]

The situation is quite different in Japan, where general shareholders' meetings are short and ceremonial. A look at the time required for companies listed on the Tokyo, Osaka, Nagoya and the other five stock exchanges to hold their general shareholders' meetings shows that 76 percent finish their meetings in 30 minutes or less. As to the agenda, at 90 percent of the meetings there is only an explanation by management and no questions at all (*White Paper on General Shareholders' Meetings, 1989*, p. 87).

From the standpoint of voting, in 57 percent of all companies that responded in a survey, proxies or written votes returned by shareholders to management represented more than 50 percent of the total votes held by all shareholders (same source). Almost all of these proxies were blank powers of attorney, making approval of the agenda items foregone conclusions. It is possible to say that general shareholders' meetings in Japan are conducted through blank powers of attorney.

Board of directors' meetings in Japan have also been reduced to mere formalities. Legally, board meetings are carried out on behalf of shareholders and the board has the responsibility to protect the interests of shareholders by monitoring activities carried out by the representative director and his staff. The representative director has the ultimate responsibility for carrying out decisions made by the board; he directs internal operational policies and represents the company regarding external matters. This basic form of the board of directors' system is the same in most American and European companies as well.

In the United States, about 80 percent of all companies have more external directors nominated by major institutional shareholders than internal directors.[5] These external directors are empowered to make independent checks on management on behalf of shareholders, and there have been quite a few cases where presidents have been fired by the board of directors. Of course, among the external directors, there are some with wide expertise in making financial evaluations who may be weak in corporate management. There are also directors given appointments as an honor and those selected by internal management and placed under their effective control. There are also cases where corporate executives are able to establish strong private power bases against shareholders on the basis of their business acumen and achievements.

One must be careful, therefore, about oversimplifying the situation in the United States, but a comparison, especially with the Japanese situation, illustrates, as will be shown later, that American managers have much less independence *vis-à-vis* shareholders than their Japanese counterparts. In fact, recently the trend is strengthening for boards of directors to interfere in the management in American companies. According to *Business Week*, 10 September 1979, the number of companies setting up committees comprised of external directors, such as audit committees and business activity review committees, increased dramatically compared to five years earlier, and the number of top executives who have had their authority revoked and been dismissed because external directors questioned their responsibility for managerial failures has increased markedly.

Previously in the United States, corporate authority was concentrated in the company president, but as the powers invested in the board increased, the authority of the board chairman, who heads the board of directors, also increased to such an extent that today the rank of president is generally accepted to be below that of vice-chairman.[6]

There have also been an increasing number of cases where shareholders have taken company management to court, charging them with negligence and errors in management policies. To protect themselves, 95 percent of the executives in 1,000 major American companies carry Officer Liability Insurance. The total amount of insurance premiums paid is said to be about 125 million dollars per annum.[7]

When one considers the situation in the United States, it is quite easy to see that corporate executives in Japan are placed in quite a different environment in terms of the degree of pressure exerted by shareholders.

The board of directors in a Japanese company is comprised almost solely of internal directors who have risen through the company's ranks. Besides being directors, these men usually also have functions in daily company operations. This is indicated in how they are addressed, such as 'Director and Manager of such and such a department'. As those titles indicate, in the operation of everyday business they are subordinates of the president, who essentially controls personnel matters related to them.

The board system, in principle, provides equal rights to all board members to voice their opinions in board meetings; but, in Japanese reality, it is inconceivable to think that a subordinate could have equal say with the company president. And, of course, it is unlikely that a president could be removed from office because the company's business performance did not improve. If, by chance, some director made such a proposal, the situation would be reversed in that it would be the director who would be removed from office.

The authority of company president who is a representative director is great, but his role inside the company does not derive from his representative position. The original role of the director with representative authority is that he is supposed faithfully to put into effect the board's decisions, even as the board supervises his activities. In reality, however, that is nothing but a fabrication in Japan.

In large Japanese companies, there are many instances where a vice-president, senior managing director or managing director will be representative directors, but even though they are all directors, any authority they may have does not derive from their directorial positions. According to the common sense prevailing in Japanese companies, those men remain nothing more than subordinates of the president.

Concerning this point, the same holds true for company auditors. They are usually chosen from among people inside the company, and are either men who could not be promoted to director or men who have completed their tenure as senior managing directors or managing directors. In short, auditors are also nothing more than subordinates of the president. Since the situation is like one in which the person being audited is choosing the person doing the auditing, it is natural to say that the auditors' functions have become almost entirely nominal and devoid of content.

In this manner, various systems stipulated in the Commercial Code, namely, board of directors, representative directors and corporate auditors become devoid of content,[8] whereas, the fact cannot be denied that positions not mentioned in the Code, such as president, vice-president, senior managing director and managing director in a company's 'bureaucratic structure' have come to possess overwhelming importance and reality within the company.

Inside a company, the positions of representative director or director and member of the board are rarely associated with their roles under commercial law, and the actual situation is probably that the people in these positions are looked at as 'important' people.[9] It is often stated in the articles of incorporation of a Japanese company that the 'Chairman, President, Vice-President, Senior Managing Director and Managing Director each represent the company'. This confirms that, in fact, 'representative authority' is a mere appendage to corporate positions that do not have any legal grounds at all.

These systems were established originally to protect the interests of shareholders through the monitoring of management acivities within the company. Consequently, it may only be natural that as shareholders' control regressed and the possession of shares was rendered impotent, the positions established by these systems simply degenerated into internal status symbols.

3 Corporate liberation from shareholder control

As the foregoing shows, one can only say that major Japanese businesses, as stock corporations, have evolved into something unique. The relationship between company and shareholder among companies mutually holding each other's shares has become quite different from the original intent. Some of these differences follow:

1 The corporation selects the shareholders rather than vice versa
2 The shareholders do not control the corporation. Rather,

the corporation has real control over the wishes of shareholders

3 The corporation has gained almost complete independence
from its owners.

4 Japanese enterprises consider profits to be of secondary
importance and dividends an element of capital cost

5 Internally, the various corporate systems have become
almost completely devoid of content.

In particular, when one reviews the relationship that has evolved in Japan between a corporation and its shareholders and
compares it to that envisaged under the corporate concept, one
finds that a totally different form has emerged in Japan which
has, in fact, reversed the old order. As this line of thinking is
followed, one can see that although large Japanese corporations
have the structural and legal forms of a stock corporation, one
begins to wonder when one looks at their economic reality if they
can really be called a stock corporation.

Since such relationships cannot be found in the United States,
the capitalist countries of Europe or elsewhere, it is fair to say
that the Japanese corporation, as a capitalist enterprise, has taken
on an absolutely unusual form.

From such observations, several concepts and theories have
been presented to explain the special characteristics of Japanese
companies and the unique Japanese economic structure on which
they are based. Tadanori Nishiyama holds one of the most
extreme opinions: he says an analysis of the corporate control
structure shows that the Japanese economic system is no longer
a capitalist system.[10]

One of the objectives of this book is to try to give a new
interpretation to the realities that exist within Japanese corporations. The analysis will not necessarily be limited to the mechanism of the control structure. Although it is true that the special
characteristics of the control structure most clearly express the
features of the Japanese corporate system, they do not go so far
as to form the system's foundation. The special characteristics are
more a result than a cause.

It cannot be stated that the progress in achieving stable shareholders and mutual holding of shares among legal persons was
the cause which led to the creation of a mutated form of capitalist
enterprise in Japan. If Japanese enterprises are unusual, the seeds
of their uniqueness most likely existed before then. This is because

if they were the traditional form of capitalist enterprise, the idea of gaining independence from shareholder control could never have occurred.

Therefore, the motive force that brought about this situation has to be sought elsewhere. At the very least, one should ask about the background circumstances. If one does not, then even if it can be clearly shown that the Japanese system has become something that is quite different from traditional capitalism or that it is no longer capitalism, that will still not be sufficient for understanding intrinsically and positively what exactly that something is or what exactly the dynamics are that move enterprises having such unusual systems.

2 Qualitative Changes in Workers

In sharp contrast to the poor treatment of shareholders and their limited say in managing Japanese corporations, the situation regarding employees is quite the opposite. In fact, it can be stated that employees replaced shareholders as the main structural elements in larger Japanese corporations.

Japanese corporations have a system of career employment in which once a person is hired, he remains in the company until he reaches retirement age, usually between 55 and 60. Only under an extreme situation such as the bankruptcy of the corporation would such a scenario not occur. Also, the treatment of employees in terms of salary and job position is improved gradually, according to the number of years of employment. This is the seniority system.

Of these two systems, both management and labor are agreed on retaining the career employment system, and there has been no attempt as yet toward effecting any basic change. During the severe recession from 1974 to 1976, related to the first oil crisis, some corporations carried out designated dismissals, especially targeted against senior employees, resulting in the companies themselves becoming the subject of discussion. But a survey covering 943 companies listed on the First and Second Sections of the Tokyo Stock Exchange revealed that the major policies taken during the recession of 1974–76 took the form of cutbacks in the number of new employees hired, non-replacement of retiring employees, job reassignments and seconding. Designated dismissals accounted for only about one percent of the change in the labor force, consistently the lowest percentage throughout the period. (*Report on Movements of Labor Force: 1974–76*, survey commissioned by Ministry of International Trade and Industry (MITI), 1976.)

The results of that survey, then, showed that the principle of non-dismissal was, in general, rigidly followed even during the period of severe recession in the mid-1970s, when minus economic growth was experienced.

With regard to the seniority system, it is quite difficult to clarify its existence in quantitative terms. By that, it is meant that even if a direct relationship could be found between an employee's degree of seniority in a company and his salary, it would be difficult to determine whether such a relationship was the result of a clear-cut practice or the natural result of the employee's long service. It is rather easy to expect that the longer a person is employed, the more capable he becomes because of the experience he gains, and his salary will therefore increase regardless of whether the seniority system exists or not.

At the same time, however, it is widely recognized that differences in the salary levels of production line workers, supervisory, clerical and technical workers directly attributable to seniority are much higher in Japan than in other countries. This fact would indicate the existence, to some degree, of such a special system in Japan.

The career employment and seniority systems are not stipulated by law and are not items that are put in contracts between companies and employees; they are nothing more than practices. But just as happens with most practices that develop after spontaneous generation, they have today become types of social norms.[11]

Japanese corporations always seek to avoid dismissing employees except when the company is facing bankruptcy or some other crisis. And when large-scale dismissals are forced on a corporation, the company's managers often become the targets of social criticism, and they are considered somewhat irresponsible. Worker layoffs are usually considered the last resort by Japanese managers who are searching for ways to survive in a difficult business situation.

13

From the employee's viewpoint, moving from one company to another is generally considered as not very desirable. People who move are often thought of as being unable to hold a job, or as psychologically incapable of getting along with other people in an organization. There is, of course, realistic support for such a social consciousness, and most people who quit a company in Japan usually end up losing.[12]

The direct results brought about by these two employment practices and their support by the social consciousness that developed as a result of their widespread diffusion throughout society in general led to a long-term, stable relationship between Japanese companies and their employees.

1 Employee sharing of corporate risk

Under such labor practices, the grounds for a fundamental agreement of mutual interests between company and employees were born. For its part, the company cannot replace employees easily, like it can other production factors, such as land and raw materials. The company, therefore, had to concern itself with maintaining and developing employee abilities and morale.

In reverse, viewed from the employees' standpoint, they knew that if the company were to prosper they would benefit economically from higher salaries, promotions, improved health and welfare benefits as well as socially from the company's higher prestige.

Concerning this point, the role played by the seniority system is also quite important. In a completely competitive environment, persons who have confidence in their ability will probably be able to improve their positions regardless of whether the company prospers or not, and they will still find satisfaction. In that same situation, however, there is a strong possibility that employees who lack confidence will think they will be left behind even if the company prospers.

The seniority system promises a degree of equality in treatment and thus has the function of directly relating the fortunes of the company to the fortunes of each employee. From the employees' viewpoint, this relationship can be construed as a sharing of corporate risk.[13]

Since, if the practices of career employment and seniority did not exist, employees who had recently entered a company, i.e., employees with little seniority, would probably have been able, on the average, to get more money and a higher position, the two practices can be viewed as systems that allow an employee to win back gradually, as his years with a company increase, the losses in pay and position he suffered because of his lack of seniority at the start. In short, these systems are, in effect, a means of making employees invest their wages and positions in the company as 'savings'. If a company should become bankrupt, the employee will have lost his 'savings' because his seniority would be almost valueless in another company. Even if the person found employment in another company, he would have to start on the low rung of the seniority ladder and begin accumulating his 'savings' once again.[14]

For employees, therefore, the continued existence of a company means that their seniority 'assets' are being protected. Even if a company did not deteriorate to the point of bankruptcy, if its business situation worsened and it was seriously considering a cut in pay, its employees would have to accept the pay cut, as long as it was not too large, because changing jobs means losing all the seniority earned to that point.

The corporate risk borne by employees is made heavier through other types of internal systems as well.

One of these is the retirement allowance reserve system. Many major companies have a retirement allowance reserve that is larger than their paid-in owned capital, and since most of those companies are investing the reserves in equipment and machinery, Japanese workers, unlike American workers whose retirement allowance reserve is in a pension fund set up outside their company, even face the possible danger of not being paid a retirement allowance if their company goes bankrupt.

Also, the larger a Japanese company becomes, the more attention it pays to health and welfare measures for its employees, and as long as an employee is affiliated with a company, he receives a variety of benefits related to daily living that persons outside the company cannot receive. If his company goes bankrupt, he loses all such benefits.

Another Japanese system is bonus payments, made to employees during the summer and at the year-end as their allocable share of business results. The total amount of such bonuses is, on average, equal to about five months of basic salary. Basic monthly salary is normally not affected by business results very much, but bonuses, from the nature of their payment, can become proportionately larger as profits increase or smaller or paid in installments as business takes a poor turn. Bonuses, therefore, can be considered as specific ways in the wage system to express the risk-sharing function of employees.[15]

Employees in Japanese companies are also placed in a position where they must share some of the risk concerning managerial positions. As a company's busines expands, the number of supervisory positions available for employees increases, but if business becomes poor, fewer such positions become available. In an American corporation, although the number of managerial positions increases when business expands, it is not certain that new positions will be filled from the ranks of current employees.

It is quite normal for American companies to search outside their own company for executives, and there are even companies that specialize in executive searches. In Japan, however, a company will not generally search for outside personnel to fill positions even if the number of available positions increases in a company. At the same time, even if the number of available positions decreases, it would present problems if the company moved to decrease the number of supervisory personnel. Therefore, employees in a rapidly expanding Japanese company are promoted early, but those in slower growing companies are generally promoted at a corresponding pace. Although some of Japan's larger companies have been large for many, many years while others were medium-sized or smaller companies that developed rapidly in fairly recent years into large companies, one need not study a company's history to categorize it but can tell to a certain degree what category it is in by looking at the academic backgrounds of the company's top managers.

The real nature of the allegiance a Japanese employee feels toward his company, or what is called his feeling of belonging, derives from objective conditions such as those described above. It is nothing more than employees being in a situation where they are forced into sharing corporate risk and taking on such feelings as an extension of their personal best interests.

In the systems in the West, there is a lack of the kind of conditions that would tie the fate of a corporation to the fortunes of its employees. The only relationship employees have with a corporation is providing part of their occupational functions in return for a salary, and, in a sense, rather than receiving economic compensation from their company, one can say they receive it from their functions. In this kind of environment, employees will constantly be led to believe that working in a company is the same as taking some product and selling it. Workers need only concentrate on their labor, and just as there is no need for someone who sells something to worry about the state of health or the everyday livelihood of the purchaser, so also is it unlikely for workers to have a positive interest in the management of their company.

The differences in the attitude of a worker and the ties binding him to his company in Europe or the United States compared to those of a worker in Japan arise from differences in the objective conditions of his employment, i.e., whether workers share corporate risk. It is not necessary to search for answers in differences in national mentalities, represented by such concepts as Western 'individualism' or Japanese 'group mentality'.

2 Corporate control by employee groups

Through their assumption of sharing corporate risk, Japanese employees have come to possess (or have been 'forced' to possess) a direct and personal interest in corporate management. It is this fact which has created the basis for Japanese corporations to recognize and sanction the extensive participation of employees in management.

In the first place, the management itself in Japanese companies is comprised of men who have come up through the ranks. Among top executives in the United States, there are many cases, of course, where a longtime employee of a company became president, but there are also a great many examples where persons outside the company were scouted and selected to be president on the basis of their established reputation as an effective manager. In family-controlled corporations, persons who have never participated in a company's operations are sometimes chosen to become president purely on the basis of their blood relations. (In China, where the socioeconomic system is quite different and where perhaps a comparison may not be appropriate, the plant director – who is also the chief executive officer – is usually a member of and appointed by the Party.)

When considered on a global scale, it is unusual to find a country where employees begin their career in the lower echelons of a company and, after many years of service, are selected for supervisory positions, even sometimes rising as high as president, while, at the same time, people are very seldom hired from external sources.

According to the results of a survey conducted on corporations listed in the First Section of the Tokyo and Osaka Stock Exchanges, only about 12 percent of all top managers were hired from outside the company. (*Comprehensive Managerial Capabilities Indices for 1988*, compiled by the Business Behavior Division, Industrial Policy Bureau, MITI.)

Compared to managers of companies in the developing countries, who almost always own the companies as well, and managers of companies in the West, who defer to the companies' stockholders, Japanese managers, with the kind of background just described, have no basic gap in experience or interests between themselves and ordinary employees in their companies.

It is, of course, natural for a certain degree of conflict in interests or differences in opinion to arise between executives looking at the total management picture and ordinary employees, but when observed from an overall standpoint, a feature of Japanese executives is that they have been selected from and represent the general body of employees.

Another factor leading to Japanese employees extensively participating in management is the wide dispersion of leadership controls over the entire employee organization in Japanese corporations. American executives are appointed to look after shareholders' interests and are often placed in a position where they must object to pressing demands from employees for higher wages, on the one hand, and move, on the other, to maintain high and stable dividends for the shareholders. In such an internal structure of corporate control, American management must be a system of authoritative top down decision-making, with authority concentrated at the top.

In a Japanese corporation, the employees themselves are a part of the internal corporate structure and have a direct interest in management. It would present little or no problem, therefore, to provide them with initiatives to determine company policies. Not all decision-making in Japanese corporations is conducted from the bottom up, of course, and many decisions are made on the initiative of top management. Top down or bottom up in Japan is merely a matter of determining which procedure is better for decision-making; it is not, as in the United States, required because of the characteristics of the control structure.

Participation by employees in a wide range of decision-making processes can be seen not only in clerical functions but also in plant operations. In plants, as will be related later, a large number of workers participate in production control, a phenomenon rarely seen outside Japan.

A third factor is the spread of the joint labor–management consultation system. This system calls for consultation by both labor and management on such important matters as modifications of production lines, establishment of new plants and direct foreign investment, other major and minor management policy problems, and matters where the interests of both labor and management tend to converge, such as the working environment, work safety and health, and worker benefits and welfare. According to a survey conducted by the Japan Productivity Center, over 90 percent of Japan's large corporations have a labor–management consultation system.

With regard to the range of issues covered by this system, recent trends show that problems that had been major issues for collective bargaining in the past, such as wages and working hours, are now being covered by labor–management consultation. This type of management participation system is today becoming more and more firmly entrenched as a way of Japanese corporate life. Management participation in Europe, such as the procedure in West Germany which relies on legal enforcement, can lead to inflexibility in management and opposition from company executives. Generally speaking, such systems cannot be considered as functioning smoothly. More European corporations are now energetically evaluating the Japanese system in which management absorbs the opinions of the workers and incorporates them into its management policies.

Although participation in management by shareholders – 'members' of the corporation – receives all kinds of support from the legal system in Japan, such participation has, in effect, degenerated into a mere formality. On the other hand, the fact that management participation by 'employees' has developed as a normal practice rather than as a response to external pressure can be considered as resulting from the basic nature of the Japanese corporation, that is, a collective body of worker employees.

When considered from such a viewpoint, one can see that, in a sense, employees of Japanese corporations have been forced to share corporate risk mainly through the unique Japanese employment practices, and that they are actually running the corporations, autonomously, as a collective body. Despite external appearances, then, actual controlling authority has moved from shareholders to employees in Japanese corporations.

In this manner, the points of difference between a Japanese corporation and an 'orthodox' capitalist corporation can be summarized for now as follows:

Whereas the normal capitalist corporation is controlled by shareholder capitalists who have laid out the risk capital, a Japanese corporation is controlled by labor-providing employees who each share part of the corporate risk.

3 From 'worker' to 'corporate employee'

On the basis of analyses made on control structures within Japanese corporations, Tadanori Nishiyama claims that the Japanese economic system has already been transformed into a system that might be called 'laborism', where corporations are under the control of workers, or, perhaps, supervisory workers.[16] Aside from the question of what to call the resultant Japanese economic system, it is questionable whether one can say its principal feature is that it is 'under the control of workers'. The reason is that workers who share corporate risk can no longer be called workers in the traditional sense.

As described earlier, and at least as far as large corporations are concerned, capitalists have, in effect, already lost actual controlling power over corporations. But it would not be adequate to describe this situation simply as a loss of management control by capitalists. A capitalist is a capitalist because of his corporate controlling power and because he possesses such power through his ownership of shares. A capitalist who has lost control of a corporation is still an investor and has assets, but it would be difficult to call him a capitalist in the true sense of the word.

In the same way, a worker is a worker because he exists outside the corporation and sells his labor to the corporation. A Japanese 'worker' who shares corporate risk, thereby assuming a real part of the responsibility of corporate management, and who, to that extent, controls the corporation, is very hard to describe as a 'worker' in the traditional sense.

It would be quite a different story if a working person could simply be called a 'worker'. If one ignored the many different conditions under which a person works, for example, and called every working person a worker, a politician would become a 'political worker', an artist an 'art worker' and so on, in the same sense that farmers in the medieval age were also workers. It can readily be seen that such nomenclature is meaningless.

According to economic doctrine, a worker is described as a person who sells his working capabilities in the labor market and receives payment in return. In Marxist theory, 'a worker belongs to the class of people that possesses neither the means of production nor the money with which to procure those means but instead sells its labor to capitalists. In return, the workers receive wages with which they buy the items they need to sustain their livelihood and that of their families'.[17]

Japanese workers, however, clearly do not fit into this category. Among American and European workers, there are actual situations where those concepts apply, but the same concepts hardly apply to the Japanese work scene. The gap between the actual labor situation existing in Japan and the theoretically accepted situation cannot be explained away simply by defining it as a separation of theory and reality.

When a Japanese worker seeks a job position, he places much greater emphasis on the management status of a company than on the conditions for which he will sell his labor. According to Figure 1.1, however, which compares British and Japanese workers' motives for choosing to work in the plants of large corporations, British workers place the most importance on wages and working conditions and the least importance on the stability of the company. In Japan, the motives are exactly the opposite. Thus, the two groups of workers have different attitudes in that area, and it is the attitude of British workers that should be defined as traditional. Japanese 'workers' pay less attention to the conditions for which they sell their labor, and more attention to the status of the company that seeks to employ their services. This can only be termed unique when considered in relation to the traditionally accepted behavior of workers around the world.

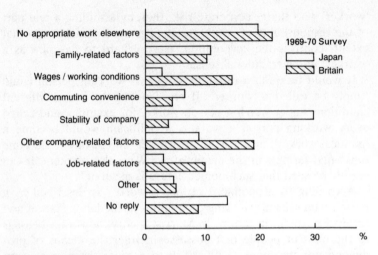

Figure 1.1   Comparison of motivations among British and Japanese factory workers for joining large companies

Source: Daily life and awareness of British and Japanese workers by Group for Comparative Research on Labor-Management Relations in Japanese and British Companies 1970

In addition, Japanese workers are not overly concerned with the amount of pay they receive per hour, nor with the standard workload they are required to perform per hour, but they are very interested in the actual amount of 'take-home' pay.

In labor–management negotiations in Europe and the United States, wages and work norms are discussed and decided together, for these two factors comprise the basic conditions for which workers sell their labor. Japanese workers do not place much emphasis on these two factors because of their apparent lack of interest in the price for their labor. This thinking, in terms of what workers traditionally are supposed to be interested in, is strange. Also, a wage system that pays workers commuting, family and other allowances cannot be understood if one considers labor simply a commodity.

In the West, too, wages are basically simple mathematical results achieved by multiplying the hourly wage rate by the number of hours worked. Such a method of computation follows naturally when labor is considered a commodity, and such factors as commuting expenses and number of family members have no relationship whatsoever to the value of the labor provided. Cer-

tainly, a wage system that includes commuting and family allowances is difficult to explain when labor is considered a commodity
to be sold. (In the West, the pay received by those in middle
management or above is not strictly tied to the amount of labor
provided, and thus differs in this sense from the wages paid to
workers; their wages are called 'salaries'. In Japan, however, no
one can say there is absolutely no awareness of any essential
difference between wages and salaries; essentially, almost all such
remuneration is considered as salary).

In the West, moreover, the wages workers receive are uniformly
decided through negotiations between the company and labor
unions organized by industry and trade. It is normal practice that
those wage levels rarely reflect how well or poorly the individual
companies are doing. To illustrate, the situation in West Germany
(and probably in most Western countries) can be described as
follows:

> In West Germany, a company that cannot provide its workers
> with wages on a par with the standard level paid by other
> companies in the same field cannot survive. The level of
> standard wages is a matter that supersedes labor–management
> relations in individual companies. No difference in standard
> wages exists, regardless of the size of the enterprise or
> subcontractor. Any labor–management relationship must
> consider this principle as a basic premise.
>
> Even if business operations become unfavorable, this is not
> an excuse for any unilateral lowering of standard wages or
> for not implementing an increase in the wage scale decided
> between federations of labor unions and management. Wages
> belong to a 'sacred area' beyond the manipulation of
> labor–management organizations within a company. A
> company that cannot provide its employees with the same
> standard of basic wages paid by other companies in the same
> or related fields, even during periods of economic recession,
> is no longer socially worthy to continue existing.[18]

In terms of the principles of a market economy, it is absolutely
inconceivable to sell machinery and materials at higher prices to
more profitable companies and at lower prices to less profitable
ones, whether in Japan, in West Germany or elsewhere. But those
principles are not applied in Japan in terms of labor.

In the West, moreover, wages differ according to the type of work and degree of responsibility, and do not relate to such matters as number of years of employment, sex, etc. In effect, workers in the West wear labels saying they can perform a certain job. They register themselves with those labels in the labor market and try to sell themselves to companies.[19] A worker is primarily connected to his particular job, and via his job he is connected only indirectly to the company. And it is exactly because of such circumstances that one can say workers are selling their labor to companies.

The situation is completely reversed with Japanese workers. Their ties are primarily with the company, not with their jobs. When a Japanese worker seeks employment with a company, he is not too concerned about his job assignment; at the very least, he will not cling to a desire for a particular job. He knows his job will be defined after he is assigned to a specific work site and that his duties will change quite often, sometimes completely. This is especially true with clerical workers. But is it possible, after all, to negotiate the selling of labor, when one does not know what the contents of the labor will be from the start?

As these interrelated facts are reviewed, one must conclude that, in Japan, labor as a commodity or the essence of what makes a worker a 'worker' has been lost.

The thinking of workers in Japan conforms to this. After analyzing the results of an awareness survey conducted among members of the Federation of Electrical Workers' Unions, a well known scholar of Japanese labor economics reached the following conclusion:

> Japan's 'well-off workers', even if one focuses on blue-collar workers, are relatively free from the idea that their labor is a means to an end. In fact, if one were to say it boldly, blue-collar workers in Japan have followed the white-collar class in strongly integrating the bureaucratic labor mentality, as defined by John H. Goldthorpe.[20]

Labor as a means to an end refers to the thinking that the central interests in life for workers exist outside their job and work site and that labor is a necessary evil to acquire the economic rewards to sustain such interests. The bureaucratic labor mentality, on the other hand, refers to the belief that the central concern of workers is their work. The latter defines position and promotion within the company as the source of social identity, and labor thus becomes aware that it is rendering a necessary service to the organization, an awareness that had hitherto been the realm of the white-collar class.[21]

Even among factory workers, it has become difficult in Japan to find a labor mentality that looks at work as a means to an end. Perhaps this is a natural result of the situation where the external conditions necessary for considering labor as such a means have all but disappeared from the work environment.

In this way, Japanese workers have become somewhat different from those elsewhere in terms of their environmental conditions and attitude toward work. In drastic terms, because of their relationship with the corporation, Japanese workers have deviated from the original concept of a worker. Viewing Japanese company employees as 'workers' is no more than a conceptualized viewpoint disunited from reality.

The fundamental concept of capitalists and workers can exist only when the traditional structure of capitalist corporations, in which capitalists control the corporations and workers remain on the outside selling their labor, is taken as the premise. The reality in Japan differs from that traditional structure. In the situation where the risk-sharing and control functions have shifted from the capital to the labor side so that capitalists have been forced outside the organization, and, in reverse, workers are held inside, capitalists are no longer capitalists and workers are no longer workers.

In effect, Japan's 'capitalists' have lost their control over corporations, have the same kind of awareness of the company as those investing in it through the stock market, and 'workers' are no longer actually or consciously selling their labor to the company, but have been integrated into the company.

Looked at another way, why is it that in Japan the word *rodosha* (worker) is not used as a common expression as much as the word 'worker' in the United States or the word *Arbeiter* in West Germany?

In Japan, factory workers think of themselves as *shain*, which translates literally as 'corporate member'. Why did this combination of words, not found in any other advanced capitalist country, come to have such an overwhelming reality and daily usage in Japan?

The reason is that there is a corresponding reality to support their use. In Japanese corporate society, there is a tenuous existence that is neither capitalist nor managerial, nor can it be accurately defined by words like 'employee' or 'worker'. The reality found in Japan is the existence of a category called 'corporate member' that corresponds to 'worker' in Europe and the United States but which has mutated into something quite different in Japan.

In order to keep definitions straight, throughout the rest of this book, employees who have been integrated into a corporation through their sharing of corporate risk will be called 'corporate employees'. The term 'corporate member' is more commonly used, but because it is also widely used to signify a person being in a specific company, it is more appropriate to use the term 'corporate employee', which is almost synonymous with 'corporate member'.

Using the words 'corporate employee' instead of 'worker' is a very natural step to enable the reader to look squarely at the real situation, for those words relate directly to the real situation in Japan and provide a basis for understanding the structure of Japanese corporations.

Some may say using the word 'corporate employee' in place of 'worker' is only a matter of preference and vocabulary, but when words or expressions that do not accurately reflect reality are used, one is apt to be influenced by old connotations that are inevitably attached to the words, thus making it difficult to look squarely at the situation as it really is.

In the West there is the West's reality, and in Japan there is Japan's reality. It is about time to graduate from the approach of taking theories born of the West's reality, attributing to them a universality, and merely labeling as peculiarly Japanese the features in Japan that differ from them and then discussing at length what those peculiarities have brought about. The time has come to have concepts that conform to reality.

3 Corporate Employees and the Corporation

As seen in the foregoing, employees share corporate risk in a Japanese corporation, and a degree of authority is also transferred to them. In that sense, labor has become an integral part of the organization, playing a principal role in management, whereas capital has lost almost all of its controlling functions and management has been separated from capital. This hollowing out of capitalist control, therefore, and the Japanese system of employment, should not be treated as separate matters related to, respectively, the control structure and labor economics, but should be grasped overall within the same framework. Capital and labor have each interpreted differently the fact that authority and the sharing of risk have shifted from capital to labor.

In this way, Japanese corporations have aimed for growth with the united body of employees playing a prominent role, and have allowed employees to participate in various levels of the decision-making process while rejecting interference by investors who do not possess interests in common with the company. Although there is some danger of oversimplification in making such a statement, the most direct description of this situation is that Japanese corporations 'are controlled by, and exist for, their employees'. Japanese corporations are thus united bodies of corporate employees.

1 Homogeneity within the body of employees

The distinctive corporate system described above is reflected in the inner structure of Japanese corporations. One of their unique features lies in the high level of homogeneity and equality that exists within the body of corporate employees. The wide dispersion of decision-making authority, and uniformity in personal careers, have already been mentioned. There is also a high level of uniformity in wages and other amenities.

As shown in Table 1.4, the monthly salary of a 50-year-old department manager who is a university graduate, is only approximately three times that of a factory worker in his 20s who is a high school graduate. According to studies by the Japan Federation of Employers' Associations (Nikkeiren), the annual income of a company president in pre-war days was about 100 times that of a newly hired employee. Today, on the basis of take-home pay, the difference is only about seven to eight times (Table 1.5).

If one considers that the president is usually an older person and that the seniority system is at the base of Japan's wage system,

Table 1.4   *Wage comparison by selected positions, age and type of duties*

Category	Age						
	25–29	30–34	35–39	40–44	45–49	50–54	55–59
University graduates							
Dept. gen. mgr.	350	383	405	419	471	487	483
High school graduates							
Dept. gen. mgr	225	322	341	367	394	404	39
Manager	233	252	319	327	344	359	323
Asst. manager	209	248	290	308	320	312	297
Production	188	224	251	262	259	247	–
Administration	192	234	277	297	313	317	–

Source: Ministry of Labor, Research into Basic Statistics of Wage Structure, 1981; unit is thousand yen.

Table 1.5   *Annual income of presidents and new employees of private companies (male college graduates including bonuses)*

		Presidents (a) (¥)	New employees (b)	(a) vs. (b)
1927	Pre-tax	165,000	1,500	110.0-fold
	Post-tax	151,000	1,500	100.7
1963	Pre-tax	6,082,000	257,900	23.6
	Post-tax	3,013,500	252,500	11.9
1973	Pre-tax	15,676,700	825,500	19.0
	Post-tax	7,181,400	797,400	9.0
1979	Pre-tax	22,018,000	1,462,900	15.1
	Post-tax	10,913,000	1,407,000	7.8

Source: Survey by Nikkeiren.

it can be said that the difference will, in effect, be even less. As shown in Table 1.5, a president's salary is about seven-fold that of a new employee. The salary of an employee without director-ship status approaching retirement, meanwhile, is about 1.7-fold that of a new employee. Since a president is usually as old or older than a person approaching retirement, his salary is thus actually about four times that of employees with equivalent seniority.

That type of difference is much less noticeable in Japan than in the United States or other capitalist countries. And there are other differences as well, aside from salaries, when Japanese and Western companies are compared. In Japanese companies, for example, it is not customary to make any distinction between managers and regular employees in the use of dining rooms, washrooms, uniforms, etc. Also, in terms of vacation time off, Japanese managers are rather at a disadvantage over other employees. According to a comparison study by Ronald P. Dore, the annual paid vacation time available to senior managers in British companies is about twice that of ordinary employees, and the allowance given managers when on sick leave, compared to their regular salary, is four times the allowance given ordinary workers. In Japan, on the other hand, pay raises are sometimes suspended for managers on sick leave, and the number of paid days off for managers, unlike factory workers, is restricted.[22]

As demonstrated, the level of equality existing today within Japanese corporations is unique compared to the situation in the rest of the world. This exists not only in comparison with companies in the capitalist countries, but also with those in socialist countries, as will be illustrated later on.

The greater amount of equality and uniformity seen in Japanese corporations, compared to corporations in other countries, cannot be explained as a matter of simple differences in degrees of level or intensity. Rather, at the base are changes in the so-called corporate concept, brought about by the formation of a unique corporate system.

2 Mutation of corporate concept

According to Robert J. Ballon, if a Western manager is asked to illustrate the average corporate structure, he will probably produce a drawing much like the one in Figure 1.2.[23] The main role

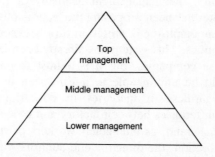

Figure 1.2   Diagram to illustrate the average company structure

of top management in that structure is to determine basic policies; the main responsibilities of middle management are to direct the supervisory staff in the execution of policies and strategies established by top management; lower management supervises the work sites.

As the above figure shows, a European or an American sees a corporation as a structure divided into three levels: top, middle and lower management. Factory workers are not included in that structure; they are outside the corporation, united and organized into labor unions for regulating the sales conditions of their labor and protecting their many interests. White-collar workers in the lower stratum may also be 'workers', but because of their relationship with the corporation, they are placed in a position substantially different from blue-collar workers, and a wide chasm separates them.[24] With the exception of West Germany, white-collar workers are not united in any labor unions.

In contrast, blue-collar workers in Japan are very much a part of the corporation, and, excluding temporary and seconded workers, are integrated within the corporate structure. The difference beween Japanese blue-collar and white-collar workers lies mainly in their work site or in their future potential for promotion arising from differences in their educational backgrounds. There is no 'chasm' as seen in the West.

As the educational levels of workers rise and automation and robotization develop in factories, and as office automation progresses, university graduates will have to be used in the factories and the work processes in both factories and offices will become more comparable and similar. This will cause distinctions between blue- and white-collar workers to lose much of their significance. In recent years, the management academy of the Japan Productivity Center has been proposing the 'zebra-collar worker concept', where an employee is shifted in turn between factory work and clerical duties. This system has already been introduced into some Japanese companies, but it is almost certain that such a venture would be unthinkable in a European or an American company, regardless of increases in educational levels and decreases in differences between factory and office work.

On the other hand, as blue-collar workers became integrated into the corporation, the directors and auditors who should have been looking after the interests of the shareholders instead became representatives of the united body of employees, to look after their interests.[24]

Together with this integration of blue-collar workers into the corporation, systems originally established to serve the interests of capital have lost their justification to exist and have been absorbed into the body of employees that has collectively assumed the sharing of corporate risk.

The company president is, essentially, no more than the highest-ranking employee, while the newest worker is the lowest-ranking one. In a giant corporation, although the differences between the highest and lowest positions are by no means small, they are only differences in degree; there are no qualitative distinctions.

Confrontations between management, which incorporates the collected interests of shareholders, and labor unions representing the interests of the workers, are a special feature of the capitalist economic system, but from the observations made, it is obvious that this feature is no longer applicable under the Japanese corporate system. It would be closer to the truth to say that the congregation of employees in a Japanese company is united in its opposition to any external force that threatens the collected interests of the group of corporate employees. Under such circumstances, it is difficult for any labor consciousness to develop along horizontal multi-company lines beyond the framework of the company. This is the reason why labor and management at a company in Japan may join together in privately exulting over a strike that occurs at a competitor's plant. This is also the reason why feelings of solidarity are not transmitted to temporary workers, even those at the same work site in the same company.

Also, the reason that Japanese companies make forceful efforts to prevent shareholders from interfering in management relates to their basic nature of being coalitions of corporate employees. And the move by Japanese companies to promote stable shareholders can be compared to the move by Western companies, troubled so much by unions, to nurture tractable company unions.

Institutional shareholders with mutual holding of shares are essentially 'company capital'. Also, attempts to stifle the voices of shareholders at general shareholders' meetings through the use of *sokaiya*[25] can be compared to the use of strikebreakers and lockouts by Western companies.

The fact that measures Japanese companies take to protect their managerial authority are not aimed at employees but are, rather, a precaution against stockholders, can be understood only when based on the premise that the concept of the corporation in Japan has changed from that of a corporation of stockholders to that of a corporation of corporate employees.

3 Changes in the concept of corporate responsibility

There is a theory that the mutual holding of shares by institutional shareholders has hollowed out the rights of individual shareholders. Because it has become impossible to conduct checks on management from the capital side, the theory says, Japanese corporate management has turned into an irresponsible system. There are many opinions concerning this theory, of which the following is representative:

> The authority embodied in company shares is implemented on behalf of shareholders by the corporate management, but a check function is completely missing from the process. Mutual interdependency between companies as seen in mutual holding of corporate shares has trasmuted the checks functions into a status of mutual unaccountability from which any sense of responsibility has disappeared. Any factor of responsibility must be accompanied by some system to check such responsibility, but when companies hold each other's shares such a checking system is nonexistent.[26]

Assertions by proponents of this theory emphasize in particular that the system of checks by the capital side do not function effectively, but one wonders if it's proper to jump directly from that observation to the conclusion that managment has become irresponsible. If, in fact, it is said that Japanese companies are being managed entirely irresponsibly, that means there is no self-control on management. This seems highly improbable inasmuch as the high efficiency and vitality found in Japanese companies today could never be maintained under such disorderly conditions. As Okumura pointed out, it is clear that Japanese corporate management does not feel a strong sense of responsibility toward shareholders, but this does not necessarily mean that managment lacks a sense of responsibility. It is there, but facing a different direction.

As explained in the foregoing sections, the main objective of Western management is to guarantee high dividends for its shareholders, and its sense of responsibility is directed mainly toward these shareholders. Consequently, when recessions occur, no matter what else, management moves to protect dividends, corporate executives' salaries, and cope with the costs by dismissing or laying off workers. In fact, dismissals and layoffs are employed not only in times of business recessions, but are sometimes used even for maintaining high dividend payments.

Japanese management, in general, has a much higher sense of responsibility toward its employees as opposed to its shareholders. If forced to choose between skipping dividends and laying off personnel, almost all Japanese managers will choose the former – indeed, the situation is such that they would have to choose the former. Likewise, if the situation demands that employee wages be cut back, managers will also be obliged to reduce their own remuneration.

If Japanese managers did not have to answer to anyone for their responsibilities and were free to pursue their private interests, they would dismiss as many people as necessary when times were bad and feel no qualms about raising their pay whenever they wanted. In fact, however, such actions are not generally possible even if managers wanted to do so.

Compared to companies in other industrialized capitalist nations, there is much less of a deviation in pay levels between ordinary employees and company executives, including the company president, in Japanese companies. And although management in Japan has the authority to dismiss personnel, they cannot freely do so. These facts indicate that some form of responsibility is clearly at work.

A sense of responsibility is born not only out of a system arranged to guarantee responsibility. The theory propounded by Okumura appears to focus mainly on systems analysis, but economic realities do not always express themselves through systems. It is especially necessary to keep that in mind when analyzing the circumstances in a country like Japan, where, although an existing system may be imported *in toto*, the underlying social nexus of relationships is completely different. Even though there is no clear system in Japan through which employees can ensure that managers live up to their actions, Japanese managers are always under pressure, from economic and social relationships, to perform responsibly.

For example, although the remuneration of managers must also be cut if a company faces a situation so serious that it must cut the wages of its ordinary employees, this action is not taken because of any pressure in the system. Rather, if it were not taken, a strong feeling of unfairness would spread among the employees, creating difficulties in upholding company morale. The reason that feeling would arise is closely related to the sense of homogeneity that exists between managers and employees. A Japanese, for example, does not have any feelings of unfairness concerning Arab kings and the luxurious lives they lead because he cannot identify with them. A sense of unfairness only arises from actual differences in treatment when one feels a degree of homogeneity with the object of comparison.

In Western companies, management exists in a separate world from the general employees, and there is almost nothing to suggest homogeneity. The pay of a company president is incomparably larger than that of an ordinary worker, and in bad times, even if the salaries of managers continue as they are while the wages of workers are cut and personnel are dismissed, the workers might protest, but generally speaking, unfairness would not be one root of their objection. If the managers of a Japanese company tried to do something similar, however, there is no question that the employees would criticize the managers, asking how the president can worry about his own income while everyone in the company should be united in an effort to overcome the existing crisis. Such a reaction is an expression of the feeling that the president in a Japanese company is not a ruler existing apart from ordinary employees but is thought of as the person standing at the apex of the group of employees and of the fact that a base exists for a corporate system supporting that thinking.

Where European and American companies tend to be abstract economic structures, Japanese companies are communal congregations of corporate employees and therefore have a much higher degree of reality as social structures. In American corporations, which are lacking in terms of their employees coming together that way, and especially where many managers often move from one company to another, if there were nothing in the system for holding them responsible, they might not even develop a sense of responsibility. It would be quite reckless to use the same yardstick when measuring the Japanese situation.

4 Corporate employee unions

Labor unions in Western countries are organized by industry and by trade, whereas labor unions in Japan are organized in units based on individual enterprises. Thus, there are more than 70,000 labor unions in Japan compared to, for example, 16 in West Germany. It can be readily understood from a comparison of these figures alone that Japanese unions are of an entirely different breed.

It has already been generally recognized that Japanese enterprise unions have the following characteristics:[27]

First, union members in the West retain their membership and their rights and privileges when they change companies – even if they become unemployed. If a Japanese employee leaves his company, however, he automatically loses his membership rights. Furthermore, temporary workers and subcontract laborers are not eligible for union membership.

Second, white-collar workers usually do not join unions in the West, whereas in Japan, all regular employees, regardless of job category, must belong to the enterprise union.

Third, officers of labor unions in the West are completely independent of any company, and work full-time on union business. In Japan, union officers retain their positions as corporate employees, maintaining their union offices as temporary jobs.

And lastly, union fees in Western industrial labor unions are collected uniformly from all members and allocated to the individual factories and local union offices. In Japan, unions in individual enterprises collect their dues and conduct all other administrative work on their own, and they contribute money to support the activities of the national labor federations and labor centers. (The amount is usually limited to no more than 10–20 percent of the total collected dues.) Not only do Japan's enterprise unions have financial independence, but they also have a high degree of independence from the supervision and control of the headquarters of a higher-level union. For example, almost all collective bargainings are internal negotiations between the enterprise union and company management. It is only in extremely rare instances that a high-level union organization would interfere.

It is generally understood that the enterprise union, career employment and the seniority system constitute the 'three pillars' supporting the Japanese employment system. But enterprise labor unions should not be viewed as having an independent base as a system; rather, they should be viewed as reflecting the concept that 'a company is organized by and for corporate employees'.

Japanese labor unions are organized by enterprise, and they have to conduct their activities on an enterprise basis, because the interests of all regular employees working in the company are concentrated in the company and those interests differ from the interests of employees of other companies. There are also horizontal labor organizations in Japan, like the national labor federations and labor centers, and if the interests of the workers cannot be protected unless there is a horizontal joining of forces that rises above the individual enterprise, it is only natural for the decision-making authority and initiative to shift to the higher organization. Nonetheless, unions in Japan are organized on an individual enterprise basis and national labor federations are nothing other than federations because the related interests of the workers differ by company. In other words, because corporations became corporations of corporate employees, labor unions, too, became unions of corporate employees.

Some aspects of the special features of Japanese labor unions can be considered strange when compared to the original concept of labor unions, but only when one thinks of unions as organized by workers. If they are considered as unions of 'corporate employees', all of those features can be understood as natural developments. Although supervisory employees above a certain level are usually not in the union, that is mainly for the sake of convenience, and, in terms of the way Japanese unions are, it would not be strange at all even if they were union members. This is also seen when decisions are made concerning the boundaries of membership.

From the nature of labor unions in Western countries, it must appear strange to know that decisions concerning from which level of job gradings (administrative supervisors) should be included in the union are a matter for negotiation between the union and the company. Labor unions try to include as high a level of supervisors as possible as members, and the company tries to keep the rank as low as possible. The actual levels at which employees become union members, as stated earlier, are decided through negotiations and differ according to company.[28] Negotiations, such as those to decide on the boundaries of union membership, are probably unthinkable in the West because in Western countries the thinking is that the workers were there first, then came the workers' interests to be protected, and then from there unions were created. This point again emphasizes how unique Japanese labor unions are and clarifies the fact that there is no gap between supervisors and clerical workers within the job system. When viewed in terms of the actual situation in Japanese companies, in job positions from the president down through directors, department managers, deputy managers, section chiefs, foremen, team leaders, etc., it is almost meaningless to try and determine the position above which employees are on 'the company side'.

In the West, once a factory worker becomes a foreman, he almost always resigns from the union and switches over to management. Such a rigid separation is virtually non-existent in Japan. Each position is a continuous line from top to bottom, without any breaks where a clear line can be drawn. And yet, while the union is eager to recruit members from supervisory positions, it does not try to recruit temporary or subcontract workers, distinguished in the plants by the color of the hats they wear. The labor union clearly distinguishes between regular workers and temporary personnel. It seldom presses for improvements in the compensation for workers who are not corporate employees when conducting negotiations for wage increases, and even when it does, the demands are always lower than those for corporate employees.[29] Why do Japanese unions take such a cold attitude toward temporary workers? Because their relationship with the company is literally temporary and they do not qualify for application of Japanese employment rules. They do not participate in corporate risk sharing and, in effect, exist 'outside' the company. In a word, they are workers, not corporate employees. On the other hand, temporary and subcontract workers are perhaps, from the common definition of a worker, the most worker-like of all. (Incidentally, there is no exact equivalent in the West of the concept of temporary and subcontract workers because the relationship of Western workers to the company resembled that of Japanese temporary and subcontract workers from the start.)

If Japanese labor unions were unions of workers, it would be strange, in terms of their original nature, if they did not try to have temporary and subcontract workers join as full union members. But since the unions are essentially unions of corporate employees, it is again only natural for them to 'discriminate' against or differentiate between those who belong to a category of workers which differs from corporate employees, regardless of whether such an action is right or wrong.

The form of union activities used by Japanese labor unions is naturally different from that of Western ones. In the West, labor unions focus on the improvement of wages and other working conditions, but because the interests of corporate employees are centralized in the company that employs them, and because those interests are so highly dependent on the ups and downs of the

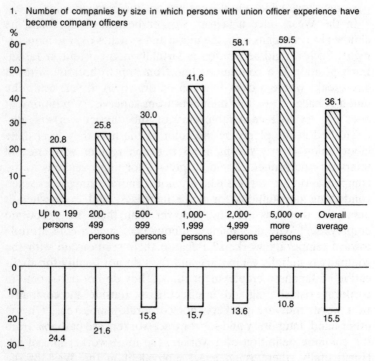

1. Number of companies by size in which persons with union officer experience have become company officers

2. Number of company officers who have union officer experience

Figure 1.3   Situation regarding advance to company officer positions by persons with experience as one of top three company union officers

Source: Japan's labor–management relations, Shakai Keizai Kokumin Kaigi, 1977

company, the principal concern of Japanese unions thus has to be directed toward management policies rather than current wages. That is how they most effectively protect the interests of the employees. Japanese unions thus pay total attention to company development, which nullifies any possibility of a basic conflict of interest with management. For that reason, the majority of workers in Japan consider labor–management to be a relationship of mutual cooperation (Table 1.6.) It is also not uncommon to find ex-union members becoming company directors.

Smooth Japanese labor–management relations were brought about by this kind of structure rather than because Japanese workers, compared to Western workers, essentially have a different corporate loyalty or group mentality, and those relations came about quite naturally.

In the West, labor–management confrontation refers to a confrontation between the company and the labor union. In Japan, however, it is merely a confrontation between management and 'companified' workers within the framework of the company. Herein lies the reason why strikes in Japan are uncommon, why any strike that would drive company management into a crisis situation would be highly exceptional, and why restrictive work practices so common in the West are almost never seen in Japan.

It is not surprising that Marxist thinking cannot easily penetrate labor unions in the private sector because there is no confrontation, at least in the principal part of the Japanese economic structure, between capital and labor – the basic ingredient needed for the introduction of Marxism. The few persons who advocate Marxism attribute this to the influence of a *kigyoistic* ideology (translator's note: *kigyo* means 'corporation' or 'company') which has moved Japanese workers and labor unions from the normal type of activities and consciousness that are originally associated with workers and unions.

Hiroshi Arabori, a member of the Japan Communist Party Council of Governors, describes the situation as follows:

Another matter is the problem of overcoming *kigyoism*. The idea that workers exist because the company exists was quite easy for workers to understand and accept and was the basic element that transformed labor unions into enterprise unions. The concept of career employment, however, on which this idea is founded, is showing signs of crumbling. But thinking

Table 1.6 *Thinking of workers concerning selected questions related to labor–management*

1 How do you view the labor–management relationship?

(a)	(b)	(c)	(d)	(e)
It's like a parent–child relationship, and therefore workers should trust management and leave such matters up to them.	Labor and management are a single, cooperating unit and should therefore understand each other's position and work well together.	Because labor and management stand on equal terms and barter concerning labor, it's natural to have a conflict of interests and natural to struggle when the need arises.	Because labor and management are basically in conflict, in an antagonistic relationship, workers should engage in all-out struggles.	Don't know.
6.5%	55.1%	19.3%	2.5%	16.7%

2 How do you view strikes?

(a)	(b)	(c)	(d)	(e)	(f)
Workers have the right to strike, so it's all right to strike.	Workers have the right to strike, so going on strike is inevitable.	Even though workers have the right to strike, strikes should be avoided as much as possible.	Even though workers have the right to strike, strikes should be avoided.	Can't make a blank statement.	Don't know.
9.5%	29.3%	32.4%	14.3%	10.4%	4.2%

3 In recent years, labor unions have begun to stress discussions with management. What do you think about that trend?

It's a good thing	It's not a good thing	Don't know
83.0%	5.6%	11.5%

Source: 'Survey Regarding Worker Awareness', Public Affairs Section, Secretariat, Prime Minister's Office, March 1978 for 2 and 3; December 1982 for 1

that has been cultivated for a long time will not collapse naturally. It is impossible for *kigyoism* to be overcome spontaneously and for workers to stand firmly with a class awareness. That is exactly why, despite the intensification of the various contradictions between capital and workers and the fact that conditions are improving for consolidation of the working class, that there actually has been no progress. *Kigyoistic* thinking is the principal factor obstructing progress in the consolidation of the working class and we must move all out to overcome it.[30]

But the reason Japanese 'workers' do not have the established worker-like awareness is not because that awareness was distorted by an ideology, whether *kigyoism* or some other 'ism', and the belief that 'workers exist because the company exists' is certainly one way of thinking. As the above quote dejectedly points out, there is a realistic foundation for it. Frankly speaking, employees do not have a worker-like awareness because they have already lost the essence of being workers in their relationship with the company. In Marxist parlance, in other words, 'existence determines awareness'.

5 The company as a group of people

The basic nature of Japanese companies should be seen as that of a congregation of highly homogeneous corporate employees having strong psychological ties and united through common interests. Inasmuch as Japanese corporations are 'unified groups of humans', they have to some degree taken on a type of commonality with other non-economical organizations. On this point, Dore asserts that 'the singularity of Japanese firms lies in their adoption of organizational systems that many Western nations would consider appropriate only for military and administrative applications to industry' and goes on to point out the similarities between Japanese companies and the British military.[31]

In Japanese companies, the 'human factor' occupies an overwhelmingly important position. And rather than saying they provide investment opportunities to risk capital, it is more accurate to say they are a venue where corporate employees combine various elements and the necessary capital for corporate activities. Furthermore, corporate employees are not elements which need to be united, and they comprise the main body. The inner structure and operations of a company reveal a number of special features that would be impossible to comprehend under normally accepted concepts of traditional capitalist enterprises. Let us look at four of them.

(a) The importance of personnel management

It is also a reflection of the special form of Japanese companies that tremendous emphasis is placed on personnel management as a means of internal control.

In Western companies, financial management occupies a position of overwhelming importance as a means of corporate control, and personnel management is relegated to a position of lesser importance. For example, when positions open, they are advertised and filled through public recruitment, a highly unplanned approach.[32] In a Japanese company, personnel management occupies a position of equal, and in some cases even higher, importance than financial management, and the post of personnel director is a weighty one in every organization. Personnel recruitment also follows the general routine of hiring university and high school graduates each spring. Personnel transfers are also conducted periodically each year when employees in various positions are moved around simultaneously. Conducting personnel policies under a highly controlled and consolidated program, similar to the drafting of annual budgets, is a typical feature of Japanese companies.

Because they are essentially congregations of humans, Japanese companies carry out effective control through human ties rather than through capital-based relations in their policies toward subsidiary organizations. Even when capital control is not sufficient, as long as persons placed in important positions in the subsidiary are within the framework of the parent company's career employment and seniority systems and follow unified personnel policies, the parent company can control them and therefore, in effect, control the subsidiary.

Another expression of such an approach concerns overseas subsidiaries. In contrast to American multinationals, which make efforts to have either 100 percent ownership or an overwhelming majority of the capital in subsidiaries they set up overseas, Japanese companies are not as concerned with capital control of such subsidiaries but often have a policy of placing Japanese in important positions in the subsidiaries so that, in effect, by 'occupying' management they have control.[33]

(b) Excessive competition

The objective of a capitalist corporation is said to be the pursuit of profits, but when applied to contemporary operations, particularly to the specific activities of oligopolistic corporations that have a wide range of policy options, this objective can be more effectively explained through hypotheses such as 'assurance of suitable profits' or 'maximum expansion of total sales or share'.

When the special characteristics of the Japanese corporate structure are considered, it seems natural that the corporate objective, used as a guideline for selecting practical corporate policies, would be long-range development as expressed by sales and market share. For corporate employees, career income is more important than current monthly salary, and career income depends on the company's long-term development. The long-term development of the company also brings about the increasing possibility of promotions and better posts and an improvement in the company's social prestige, which increases the social position of each corporate employee.

That is also one reason why competition among companies relates more to sales, production volume and equipment capacity, or to the shares of each of those three, rather than profits, and why there is frequently a tendency toward excessive competition that ignores short-term profits.

Under the Japanese corporate system, although a company may become more cost efficient because of new technology or a new production system, workers in other companies will not move to the more promising company. The employees in the company with the cost disadvantage, in the same way that soldiers who materially are inferior will fight by depending on their superior spiritual strength, will compete with the more efficient company by accepting worsened working conditions, such as longer working hours, the forgoing of regular pay increases or pay cuts.

The most direct confrontation for the body of corporate employees of one company is with the body of corporate employees of the competing company, who will threaten the profits of those in the first company in such ways as decreased real income, worsened working conditions and reduced possibilities of promotion.

If the Western type of competition can be called a functional competition, the Japanese one can be described as a struggle between human groups that can, for this reason, lead to exceptionally fierce competition. This is one of the factors obstructing the horizontal consolidation of corporate employees belonging to different companies in the same industry, and it cultivates even stronger ties between corporate employees and the company for which they work.

(c) Emergence of feeling of belonging

The feeling of belonging that Japanese have toward their company emerged as a so-called by-product of the forgoing type of corporate system. Common interests, homogeneity within the corporate employee group, and similarities in thinking and behavioral patterns from working together over a long period of time in the same company are factors that have served to promote the feeling that corporate employees are fellow passengers in the same boat. It is not necessary to try and find any special mental feature in the Japanese nature to explain this feeling. The feeling is common with the people of any country, the workings of a psychological mechanism universal to all humans.

The answer to why Japanese have feelings of belonging to a company resembles the answer to the question of why Americans, for example, or Chinese or Frenchmen came to have feelings of belonging to their country. Such items as the feeling of sharing the same fate and the homogeneity of patterns of thinking and behaving cultivate a national consciousness. For those who agree that it would be extremely difficult to cultivate the type of patriotism and national consciousness seen today if the world developed so that people generally were able to choose whatever country they wanted and freely move from one to the other – 'country-hopping', much as some people job-hop – it is not so difficult to appreciate why Japanese corporate employees have a feeling of belonging to their company while the workers of other countries do not necessarily have the same feeling. That feeling has absolutely nothing at all to do with feudalistic or any other traditions.

This is also clearly seen by comparing the situation existing during the Meiji Era, when relationships between workers and the company were cold and calculating, to the present situation, when, with the spread of career employment, such a feeling of belonging to the company formed and developed.[34]

(d) Difficulty of buy outs and mergers

The reason why much more difficulty accompanies the buy out or merger of companies in Japan compared to those in the West derives from the fact that Japanese corporations are organizations of corporate employees who have a feeling of belonging to their company.

In the West, the buying and selling of companies is a common occurrence. Companies are collective bodies of assets that are evaluated on the market, and if a buyer appears with an attractive offer to buy, even an outstanding company will respond energetically. In Japan, however, one will very seldom see even a business division of a company, let alone an entire company, up for sale.

To the Japanese, a buy out has an immoral overtone. In Japan, a corporate buy out is often referred to as a *nottori* (takeover), which is definitely not a neutral value judgement. The word has the connotation of something owned fairly being seized by unfair means.

Most people know that Keita Goto, former president of the Tokyu Railway Corporation, who during his lifetime had a hundred or so companies under his control, was called 'Keita the Bandit'.[35] The reason Japanese think this way is not because the Japanese spiritual make-up is particularly special, but because Japanese corporations are organized as aggregate bodies of corporate employees, and in effect the buying and selling of a company takes on a semblance of buying and selling a group of human beings.

Another feature of Japanese companies is the difficulty in accomplishing mergers. Whether the merger is to be on equal terms or constitutes an absorption of one company by the other – whether 'his' company is absorbing or being absorbed – is a serious matter for the employees in the companies involved. This concern results from the fact that mergers are also a matter, not of capital, but of human factors, and they signify an amalgamation of two different groups of corporate employees into one.

According to the financial magazine *Diamond*, it was not until June 1981, 11 years after the merger of Yawata Steel and Fuji Steel to form Nippon Steel Corporation, that it became possible to implement personnel policies of appointing supervisors from the level of foreman and above on the basis of ability and experience within the new company. In the interim, staff appointments were made on the basis of maintaining a balance between ex-Yawata people and ex-Fuji people. Another case is the merger between the Daiichi Bank and the Kangyo Bank in 1971, to form the Daiichi Kangyo Bank. There is still today a First Personnel Department to look after the concerns of ex-Daiichi and a Second Personnel Department to take care of ex-Kangyo personnel.[36]

These examples show the difficulty in 'merging' people in Japanese companies.

In Europe before the modern age, states were considered the property of monarchs. Monarchs sometimes divided up their territory among their children or exchanged territory with other monarchs for part of their territory. In the modern age, however, after the establishment of nations for the people, the inhabitants themselves came to constitute the nation and such division or exchange of territory became impossible. And because companies moved from being the property of capitalists to being companies of corporate employees integrated in a closely knit association, it becomes extremely difficult to carry out volitional divisioning, merging or selling of companies, a situation among Japanese corporations that somewhat resembles that concerning nations in Europe. In a sense, it may only be natural that in Japan, where corporate employees and their families account for the majority of Japanese citizens, the thinking evolved that the *nottori* of companies were unscrupulous acts.

Notes

1   Ken Yoshimori, *Seiyokigyo no Hasso to Kodo* (Thinking and Behavior of Western Corporations). Tokyo, Daiyamondosha, 1979, pp. 86–108.
2   Survey by *Fortune* magazine, 1967.

3　Peter F. Drucker, *Managing in Turbulent Times*. London, Heinemann, 1980, pp. 182–3.

4　'Shoji Homu' (Legal Affairs in Business Matters), *Shoji Homu Kenkyukai*, October 5–15 (1980), p. 22.

5　Akihiro Okumura, *Nihon no Toppu Manejimento* (Top Management in Japan). Tokyo, Daiyamondosha, 1982, p. 30.

6　Kyoichi Matsui, 'Shuso Retsujitsu: Amerika Daikigyo no Kokeisha Erabi' (A Tough Decision: Choosing a Successor in an American Corporation), *President*, Vol. 18, No. 8 (July, 1980), p. 136.

7　'Shoji Homu', 11/5 (1979), p. 35.

8　For reference on how Japan's boards of directors have been stripped of all their contents, see Nikkei Bijinesu ed., *Torishimariyaku no Kenkyu* (Study of Boards of Directors). Tokyo, Nihon Keizai Shimbunsha, 1981, pp. 35–52.

9　Ibid., pp. 20–1. The following conversation is given as an example of how even a member of the president's secretariat in a Japanese corporation does not readily know who has representative authority.

　　Q. How many persons have representative authority?

　　A. Managing directors and above.

　　Q. Does the chairman have representative authority?

　　A. Just a minute, let me check . . . yes, the chairman also has representative authority.

　　If those in the president's secretariat are not certain about who has representative authority in the company, there is even less chance of other employees' knowing.

10　Tadanori Nishiyama, *Shihai Kozo Ron* (Theory of Control Structure). Tokyo, Bunshindo, 1980, pp. 49–68.

11　'Henbosuru Roshikankei' (Changing Labor/Management Relations), *Shakai Keizai Kokumin Kaigi*, (1977), p. 123. This survey shows that concerning the leaders in management and labor (common whether in Sohyo or Domei groups), 90 percent feel that the career employment system should be continued.

12　Kiichi Kageyama, *Kigyo Shakai to Ningen* (Human Beings and Corporate Society). Tokyo, Nihon Keizai Shimbunsha, 1976, pp. 216-17. What most affects people at all levels in a Japanese corporation is the closed nature of the country's labor market. White-collar workers, for example, get hemmed in a complicated system of promotions and pay increases, including longevity considerations, which makes it almost impossible for them to change jobs.

　　A worker may be dissatisfied with his job and have great confidence in his ability to do better work, but quitting his company is difficult because he is not certain how much his past experience will be evaluated by the company to which he would move. Refer also to: Kensuke Nakayama, *Donna ni Tsurakutemo Kaisha o Yameruna*

– *Tenshoku Seiko, Datsusara Seiko wa Genso ni Suginai* (No Matter How Bitter Your Experience, Don't Quit Your Company – Success in Changing Jobs or Starting Your Own Business Is Nothing but Fantasy). Tokyo, Eru Shuppansha, 1981. This book gives specific examples of how most white-collar workers who quit their companies end up failing in their new jobs.

13   Tamotsu Yamada, *Nihonteki Keiei no Keizaigaku* (The Economics of Japanese-Style Management). Tokyo, Chuo Keizaisha, 1980, pp. 29–33.

14   Drucker, p. 237. Drucker points out that the right of workers in Japanese companies to keep their jobs closely resembles the definition of an 'asset'. He explains that the system of career employment means that Japanese companies are operated for the welfare of employees, and the right of Japanese workers to keep their jobs is considered more important than any of their other rights – and any right held by any other person. Thus, in the most correct sense career employment very closely resembles the definition of an 'asset'.

In Japanese tradition, the only instances in which the right of Japanese employees to keep their jobs is violated are bankruptcy and a company's inability to settle its debts. This tradition is the same as rules up to now governing 'asset rights'.

15   Yamada, pp. 30–2. Generally, American workers do not receive bonuses the size of Japanese bonuses. A 'gift' of money might be paid to American workers at Christmas, but this gift would be a small amount. On the subject, see: Toshio Shishido, *Nihon Kigyo in USA* (Japanese Companies in the U.S.). Tokyo, Toyo Keizai Shinposha, 1980, p. 63.

16   Nishiyama, pp. 64–8.

17   Kozo Kuruma, et al., *Shihonron Jiten* (Dictionary of Capitalism). Tokyo, Aoki Shoten, 1961, pp. 451–2.

18   Yoshitoshi Mabuchi, *Hadaka no Nishi Doitsu Keizai* (West Germany's Economy without Adornment). Tokyo, Nihon Shoseki, 1979, pp. 174, 206. For examples in the U.S., see Shishido, p. 62.

19   Hirohide Tanaka, *Gendai Koyoron* (Modern Theory of Employment). Tokyo: Nihon Rodo Kyokai, 1980, p. 367.

20   Takeshi Inagami, *Roshi Kankei no Shakaigaku* (Sociology of Labor/ Management Relations). Tokyo: University of Tokyo Press, 1981, p. 40.

21   Inagami, pp. 11–12.

22   R. P. Dore, 'Nihonteki Keiei Shisutemu no Iso' (Topology of Japanese-Style Management), *Keizai Hyoron*, 7 (1981), p. 19.

23   Robert J. Ballon, *Nihongata Bijinesu no Kenkyu* (Study of Japanese-Type Business). Tokyo: President Publishing Co., 1978, pp. 60–3.

24   Ningen Noryoku Kaihatsu Senta, (ed.), 'Rodosha o Toshite Mita

Eikokubyo' (The British 'Sickness' Seen through Workers), *Ningen Noryoku Kaihatsu Shiriizu*, 51 (1978), p. 20.

Managerial participation at the shop level does not work well in the West largely because of the gap between blue- and white-collar workers.

Both management and labor have extremely negative attitudes toward such participation. The labor side believes that if it is not careful in getting involved with the way the white-collar side manages things, it can get swept away and only end up getting hurt. Labor does not understand white-collar thinking and feels that all the managers want to do is wring from the workers whatever can be wrung.

Management, on the other hand, says blue-collar workers do not know anything anyway, and even if both parties sit down to negotiate, the blue-collar workers will not understand.

25 A *sokaiya* is a person who owns a small number of shares in a number of companies, expedites proceedings at the general shareholders meetings of these companies at the request of management and receives payment for such services in the form of transportation expenses. For additional information, see Koji Matsumoto, *Seisanseikojo no Himitsu* (Organizing for Higher Productivity), p. 14. Tokyo, Asian Productivity Organization, 1981.

26 Hiroshi Okumura, 'Hojin Shihonshugi to Kabunushi Sokai' (Juridical Person Capitalism and Annual Shareholders Meeting). *Shoji Homu*, (Dec., 1978), p. 11.

27 For reference on the characteristics of enterprise unions, see *Nihon Keizai Jiten* (Dictionary of Japanese Economic Terms). Tokyo, Nihon Keizai Shimbunsha, 1981, pp. 887–8.

28 Yoshinobu Matsuzaki, *Rodo Kumiai no Ura Omote* (Front and Back of Labor Unions). Tokyo; Daiyamondosha, 1977, pp. 33–4.

29 Matsuzaki, pp. 41–4.

30 Hiroshi Arabori, 'Kakushin Toitsu Sensen to Rodo Kumiai Undo' (The Labor Union Movement and Unification of Progressive Elements), *Rodo Undo*, 10 (1978), pp. 88–9.

For statements about *kigyoism* by other proponents of Marxism, see Ryoichi Mukasa, Yoshihisa Tokita, Shin'ichiro Kimoto and Tokuo Takagi, (eds.), *Kojo Chosa: Kyodai Kojo to Rodosha Kaikyu* (Factory Survey: Huge Factories and the Working Class, Tokyo, Shinnihon Shuppansha, 1980, pp. 104, 114, 118.

31 Dore, p. 18.

32 Ku Tashiro, *Nihonjin no Mita Yoroppa no Jinji Fudo* (Japanese View of European Personnel Management Practices). Tokyo, Nihon Keiei Shuppankai, 1981, p. 32.

In Europe, managers are involved in all personnel matters, including the selection of staff members, distribution of duties, evaluation of performance, promotions and pay increases. In short, decisions on personnel matters are made by managers rather than by members of the personnel department, who merely advise and support the managers concerning personnel affairs.

For a systematic comparison of personnel management in Japanese and Western corporations, refer to Ryushi Iwata, *Nihonteki Keiei no Hensei Genri* (Structural Principles of Japanese-Style Management). Tokyo, Bunshindo, 1977.

33 Nobuaki Takakura, *Nihon no Kaigai Kigyo Keiei* (Japanese Management of Overseas Companies. Tokyo, Toyo Keizai Shinposha, 1979, p. 171.

A survey of 10,118 multinational corporations with American affiliations shows that 72 percent of the American parent companies hold 95 to 100 percent ownership while a mere nine percent hold 51 to 94 percent ownership. Only 13 percent of the corporations surveyed show a minority interest for the American parent companies.

In comparison, Japanese corporations have a minority interest of 49 percent or less in only 40 percent of the companies in which they invest, but their majority interest in such companies averages around 51 to 60 percent.

For further discussion of Japanese-style management, see Takakura, pp. 171–3.

34 Bureau of Commerce and Industry/Ministry of Agriculture and Commerce, *Shokko Jijo* (Condition of Workers, Vol. 2). Tokyo, Shinkigensha, 1976, p. 122.

In a publication of the same name, produced by the Ministry of Commerce and Industry in the late 1890s, the relationship between companies and workers is described as follows:

'In the relationship between companies and their workers, it is difficult to see any of the feelings of fellowship so common in the old family industry system. The present relationship has the employers against the workers, with the latter paid for work the former assign them. Japanese industry is thus in a period of transition, where you can find neither the old feelings of fellowship between employers and workers, nor any clear definition of the legal relationship between them as seen in other nations. The situation has led to concern on the part of employers regarding the irresponsibility of workers, and to complaints from workers about employers being heartless.'

35 Yonosuke Miki, *Goto Keita Den* (Biography of Keita Goto). Tokyo, Toyoshokan, 1955, p. 2.

36 'Gappei Jinji Gonengo Junengo no Meiun – Mentsu no Taito ka Hiai Umu Kyushu ka' (What Happens to Personnel Five and 10

Years after Merger – Balance of 'Face,' or Acquisition Leading to Grief?), *Shukan Daiyamondo*, 2–20 (1982), p. 16.

2 Comparison with Foreign Corporations

Part I: *Comparison with Capitalist Corporations*

Japan has a unique system in which employees sharing corporate risk control their companies. Compared with companies in the Western nations, therefore, Japanese companies have extremely few management constraints from shareholders, horizontally organized labor unions, or other external influences, and have almost complete freedom in corporate management. Also, because there is no structure in Japanese companies like the duality of interests that leads to confrontations between management and labor and divides Western companies, corporate employees are able to unite in the pursuit of corporate growth and development.

1 Management Policies in American Companies

It would not be easy to find examples anywhere else in the world of companies that have the freedom of Japanese companies to pursue their growth exactly along the planning lines which they themselves set. In socialist societies, of course, the State completely controls companies, giving them little autonomy and making them readily subject to intervention from political sources. But even in capitalist societies, particularly in companies where ownership and management are not separated, policies to deter corporate growth are sometimes intentionally introduced if it is forecast that a situation could develop that might endanger family control. When it appears as if a company may not earn sufficient profits for them, moreover, the family owners may sacrifice the company by moving their capital to other investment opportunities.

Even in the United States, where the separation of corporate ownership and management is advanced, shareholders have a strong influence on management, leading to financial affairs being given precedence over other matters due to shareholders' demands for a generation of high dividends over the short term. It is said, as a result, that it is not easy for top management to introduce bold capital investment programs or daring innovations which will bear fruit over the long term but which do not tie to short-term profits.

The results of analyses by two Japanese scholars who estimated and compared the Abelian type of investment function of Japan and the United States, also provided proof of the negative attitude of American companies toward capital investment. In comparing the parameters of the estimated investment functions of the two countries, the subjective discount rate of entrepreneurs for the future was 14.4 percent for Japan and 19.2 for the US. The elasticity of capital investment with the marginal Q-ratio (Increment of <Corporate Value/Replacement Cost of Capital Equipment>) was 1.4 for Japan and 0.6 for the US. These studies concluded that the relatively low level shown in the subjective discount rate of Japanese entrepreneurs indicates that compared with American companies Japanese concerns have a background supporting positive moves to make investments that may be unprofitable in the short term but will be profitable in the long term. They also concluded that the higher elasticity of the marginal Q-ratio indicates that Japanese companies react quickly to investment opportunities, while American companies, although favored with the same type of investment opportunities, cannot take full advantage of them because something in their system prevents it.[1]

Voices have grown stronger even in the United States in recent years, criticizing the passive attitude of American corporations toward innovation and capital investment, saying that the management philosophy that emphasizes ROI causes harm.

Certain studies that compared the focus of management objectives in Japanese and American corporations, show that while American companies emphasize objectives such as ROI and higher stock prices, they do not emphasize market share, percentage of new products, rationalization of production and distributions systems, or other items that can be considered as tying to their long-term growth, as much as Japanese companies do.[2] The ROI concept American companies emphasize is a healthy concept and does not by itself cause any problems, but serveral problems surface when ROI becomes the sole or dominant guideline for management policies or the standard for evaluating management results.

One problem is that overemphasizing ROI will cause managers to disregard business projects with highly unpredictable outcomes. The larger the scale of an innovation being contemplated, the greater the risks involved, including risks related to technology, the difficulty of forecasting demand and introducing new factors into policies such as those for sales and distribution. Among economic risks, there are those for which probabilities can be measured and insurance taken and those for which they cannot. The latter is the area of risk where entrepreneurial functions are in demand. Such risks are effectively difficult to evaluate quantitatively and therefore do not fit into evaluation systems based on ROI.

Companies that consider ROI as nothing more than one of many standards for evaluating the potential profitability of a project are also able to view the project from other evaluative angles. But companies that view ROI as the ultimate standard for preliminary evaluation of a project are naturally highly likely to drop risky undertakings that fail to meet ROI evaluation standards. And, generally speaking, since the longer the gestation period for an investment, the greater a project's uncertainty, this tendency results naturally in management's perspective being limited to the short term.

According to a study done in the United States on eight specific cases of technological innovation, an average of 19.2 years was required to move a product from the drawing board to the marketplace.[3] For example, the home-use video tape recorder (VTR), a representative product of innovation in Japan, took 25 years to move from the research stage to the marketplace. The more creative an innovation, the more risk present in the initial research stage. Rather than calling it high risk, in fact, the initial stage is usually more like shooting for the moon. As long as evaluation is limited to satisfying ROI standards, management will tend to avoid projects with a high level of uncertainty and large-scale projects that have the potential of being tied to truly creative innovations, and will instead choose safer projects with an assured investment return. At such times, management reacts positively toward actions that respond in a rational manner to known and certain conditions and reacts negatively toward actions that attempt to change such conditions.

To cite an example, let us look at how American companies selected their systems for producing integrated circuits (IC). One of the essential work operations in IC production is bonding, an extremely labor-intensive process. In order to carry out more effective production, American companies built plants in Southeast Asian countries and hired low-cost female workers to perform this process. Japanese companies, on the other hand, concentrated their efforts on developing automated facilities at home, which would make their operations profitable even though they paid high wages. Together with advances in factory automation technology, their success led to speedy operations and high product quality, and resulted in a large productivity gap in Japan's favor.[4]

The response of the American companies was rational, but it was a 'short-term rationalism'. Had the companies considered that the existing technical conditions might change or be overcome, their response might not necessarily have been considered rational. At any rate, the only reason major American electrical equipment manufacturers such as General Electric and Westinghouse stopped producing semiconductors in the 1960s was because they determined that purchasing them from vendors rather than producing them in-house would mean a higher ROI.

Another example of 'short-term rationalism' is the way American steel companies were lax in modernizing their production facilities, thereby losing their competitiveness vis-à-vis Japanese steel imports. Although there were other reasons as well, that loss of competitiveness seems to have been one result of management that emphasized ROI.[5]

A second problem is the possibility that, regardless of whether management is ROI-oriented or not, the very process of rationalizing decision-making itself may result in a dampening of the vitality of the overall economy. Although there is no doubt about the desirability of rational decision-making from the standpoint of individual companies, this is not necessarily true when viewed from the standpoint of providing innovations to the overall economy.

55

Suppose, for example, there is a Country A with companies that carry out highly rationalized decision-making and a Country B with companies that are fired with an animal spirit but manage themselves, based largely on intuition. Further suppose that companies in both countries are faced with deciding whether or not to put into effect business plans for which there is only a 10 percent chance of success. The managers of the companies in Country A study their projects carefully, analyzing all factors, and manage to conclude correctly that they have only a 10 percent chance of success. The managers of the companies in Country B, meanwhile, have neither the staff nor the personal capability to carry out such analyses, and, instead, relying on experience and intuition, decide that their projects have an adequate chance of success and immediately begin investing in them.

What would happen in the foregoing situation? First of all, the companies in Country A would make no investment and thus would face no risk; of the companies in Country B, however, 90 percent would meet with failure. Some of them, in fact, could face bankruptcy because of their decisions to invest. Even the managers of the 10 percent of the companies that were successful through good luck would realize afterward how rash and reckless they had been. They would reflect deeply on their actions and vow that had they known the risks involved beforehand they would never have undertaken such a project.

Clearly, from the standpoint of individual companies, the managers of the companies in Country A were much wiser and more rational than the managers of the companies in Country B. Viewed from the standpoint of the national economy, however, one must evaluate the situation somewhat differently. Country A saw no change at all in its economy and gained nothing. Country B experienced violent changes in its economic environment, accompanied by considerable friction and capital losses, but definitely gained an innovation, and its industry progressed a step forward.

For numerous innovations to be introduced in a country, it is important for companies to believe that the apparent risk is less than the actual risk. Even though from the standpoint of a particular company such risk-taking might involve mistakes in judgment, from the standpoint of the overall economy the diversity of trials is increased and the possibility of creative destruction is raised.

Of course, if a company makes a mistake as a result of its trials, the marketplace will judge it sternly.

In effect, rationalization of the decision-making process that exists in management that emphasizes ROI transfers an innovation's evaluation as much as possible from the marketplace to a prior in-house screening. In fact, the pre-market screening by such rational methods probably provides most innovations with a built-in success factor. It is also true, however, that many innovations were marketed after completely erroneous, even misdirected, evaluations, but were successful eventually because of purely coincidental changes in the external environment.

The American managerial posture emphasizing ROI may be rational in the context of individual companies, therefore, but viewed in terms of the overall economy this posture clearly reduces the overall number of attempts to introduce innovations and results in sapping the economy of its vitality.

A third problem is that because the aptness of many project strategies tends to be evaluated by taking the financial index ROI as the ultimate standard, the potential hidden behind ROI's abstract figures, in areas such as production technology and market development, is often far removed from top management's purview. Those companies that make repeated and daring challenges in unknown areas in technology and marketing probably concentrate their main decision-making efforts on unearthing the potential in those areas. But financially oriented companies, apart from whether they view such potential as high or low, accept it as a given factor and concentrate their thinking on the financial aspects of their task. Capable management is based on a general perspective that covers not only financial matters but all other areas, such as production, technology, marketing and labor. And that general perspective is not just a collection of indices; it is based on factual – not necessarily expert – knowledge across a wide spectrum. Premised on such knowledge, management's success or failure ultimately depends on deep insight backed by experience.

Theories and general knowledge are useful, therefore, but by themselves are insufficient to make a superior manager. History shows that outstanding managers and persons who developed new management concepts were not always well-educated. Henry Ford, for example, graduated only from grade school, as did both Konosuke Matsushita and Soichiro Honda. American management today, however, with its strong financial orientation, effected a change in the qualities required of top managers, as seen in comments such as the following by American researchers. One result is that American corporations today are controlled by financial experts (Figure 2.1).

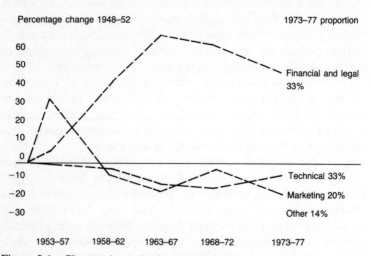

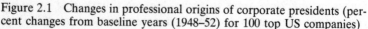

Figure 2.1   Changes in professional origins of corporate presidents (percent changes from baseline years (1948–52) for 100 top US companies)

Source: Robert H. Hayes and William J. Abernathy, 'Managing Our Way to Economic Decline'. *Harvard Business Review* (November–December 1980): p. 75.

'Of greater importance is the fact that the quality of ambitious executives with the best qualifications for top management positions has undergone a general change. Neither can the great change that has taken place in the attitude of executives, stimulated and cultivated by such trends, be overlooked. Universities and business circles have become obsessed with an erroneous and bigoted bias toward something called 'professional managers'. But professional managers in this context should actually be referred to as 'pseudo-professional managers'. These pseudo-professionals, despite having no professional knowledge whatsoever in industrial or technological fields, boldly join organizations which they know nothing about and try to manage them by strict application of market penetration strategies founded on theories of financial control and details concerning the organization's negotiable securities.

In recent years, the idealism fostered by these pseudo-professionals has grown to achieve a status akin to a corporate religion. The primary principle of such a religion naturally rests on downgrading the importance of experience in the industry as well as technical knowledge of the work site.[6']

2 Restrictions on Management

Leading American executives also realize that management attitudes in the US may sap corporate vitality and even endanger future growth. For example, former Chairman of the Board of General Electric (GE), Reginald H. Jones, who retired in 1981, opined as follows for a newspaper interview:

> The biggest problem in American business today is the sharp decline in the quality of US-produced goods, attributed largely to a management malaise that has permeated corporate suites in recent years. The only hope for correcting it is to revamp the thinking in corporate boardrooms so directors and stockholders recognize they sometimes must forgo short-term profits to make the kind of needed investment that will enhance the long-range opportunities of the corporation. What we have today is a bunch of money managers who are under tremendous pressure from Wall Street to have every quarter a little bit better than the last. American industry also can learn a lot from the Japanese about improving quality and productivity, particularly in doing more to involve employees more directly.[7]

As Jones aptly pointed out, a short-sighted management philosophy and a management attitude that gives priority to financial control are not matters of policy. Rather than freely choosing that approach, American managers had it forced on them as a result of 'pressures from Wall Street'. Worded another way, that approach is a natural consequence of American corporations being subordinated to earning profits for capital; it is thus a problem related to the system rather than to policy.

For American industry today to regain its former vitality, it appears that even if companies do not achieve independence from capitalistic control, they should at least introduce measures to ease the overly intense pressure from investors seeking short-term profits. There are probably many other American businessmen who feel as former GE Chairman Jones does, but the general trend of corporate society in the US seems headed in the opposite direction.[8]

In recent years, in an increasing number of American companies a majority of their directors are brought in from the outside, and in major corporations the percentage of outside directors on boards of directors is becoming larger than the percentage of internal directors. Also increasing is the number of companies with audit committees that are composed entirely of outside directors as well as ad hoc committees with a majority of outside directors.[9] Some companies have even experimented with having representatives, not only of investors, but also of consumer organizations and minority groups, participate in board meetings. Although such moves may enhance the public nature of corporations, they could also make it difficult to avoid the further deterioration of managerial autonomy.

Konosuke Matsushita said the following concerning such moves:

I believe that Japanese boards of directors will not, nor should they, change along the same lines as some American boards. Frankly, I was surprised to learn that the percentage of outside directors was so high in the US. And when I think of our own experience and try to imagine the ideal management formula for the future, I worry that having a large number of outside directors on the board may place overly confusing demands on those engaged in day-to-day management, maybe causing them to lose their interest and enthusiasm.

The United States has always been the most liberal nation, and freedom in economic activities is highly respected. In fact, when Chrysler Corp. faced a managerial crisis a number of years ago and asked the US government for a billion dollars in tax relief, people in business circles and the mass media, such as *The New York Times*, were overwhelmingly opposed, insisting that Chrysler's difficulties were its own responsibility and that government aid would be contrary to the free enterprise concept.

Such opposition confirms that, on one hand, support of laissez-faire thinking is still very much alive in the US. Why, on the other hand, I wonder, are companies moving toward more restrictions on managerial freedom?[10]

There is no question that the American economy is a free economy, and a free economy guarantees freedom of choice in the market to all individuals. When one considers the extent to which shareholders and workers as individuals in the United States are free to select a company in which to invest their money or to which to sell their labor and compare this with the situation in Japan – where extensive restrictions exist in the capital market through the system of institutional mutual holding of shares, and in the labor market through career employment practices – one readily sees that the degree of freedom in the economy is much greater in the US. The point, however, as asserted by Matsushita, is that there are really two separate questions: whether or not a nation follows a liberal economic system differs greatly from whether or not a company has freedom of corporate management.

Companies may be free from government controls but that does not necessarily free them from shareholder controls.

When seen from this perspective, it must be agreed that the separation of ownership and management has clearly produced negative effects on corporate vitality and freedom. This is because responsible corporate control by entrepreneurs, who tie a corporation's destiny to their own profits and who directly develop the corporation, has been replaced by outside control by investors.

In other words, while keeping control, capitalists moved outside the corporations. It is difficult to believe that such a development is unrelated to what seems like a decline in the vitality of American capitalism in the twentieth century as compared with that in the nineteenth.

Besides shareholder controls, companies in the West are also restricted by another outside force: labor unions set up along industry and trade lines.

Unions were organized originally to bargain with management on labor's behalf to gain the best possible working conditions for labor. Today, however, their functions have exceeded that objective. From a power base built on control of the labor supply, unions now exert strong restrictive influences even on decisions related to management policies, such as those concerning the introduction of new technology or the making of new capital investments.

As is well-known, these trends are especially strong in Britain. British labor unions today are able to veto managerial moves that concern even the most trivial of matters.

> This is a problem that depends on how one interprets the phrase 'managerial authority'. Matters normally carried out based on managerial authority in Japan may become, in England, matters that cannot be unilaterally carried out by management. They may have to be negotiated with the union or subjected to labor–management council reviews. To give a simple example, we encountered the following situation when we made a study of British steel workers. Management wanted to establish a regulation whereby workers would be required to wear protective helmets, but the matter first had to be presented to the labor union for approval. Management wanted every worker to wear a helmet for safety reasons, but with strong opposition to the proposal from within the union, the union could not approve it. A rule requiring every worker to wear a helmet could not materialize and the use of helmets would be left to the discretion of the individual.[11]

No matter how strongly a labor union influences corporate management, it will not solely – just as capitalist control, by itself, will not – diminish management autonomy. If an increase in responsibility accompanies an increase in union influence, i.e., if the union is integrated into corporate management and achieves corporate control from within, then a situation will emerge in which workers become the main element responsible for the autonomous development of the company's management.

Since Western workers share almost none of the corporate risk, Western labor unions tend to avoid taking any responsibility for management. The unions pursue their special interests related to matters such as wages, intensity of labor, and other demands for union members, while remaining outside the companies and trying to assert control from there.

For corporate employees in Japan, meanwhile, it is not easy to change jobs, even if their company is facing financial difficulties.

There is no way for these employees to protect their interests, other than making a group effort to rehabilitate the company. Also, the reason Japanese corporate employees tend to emphasize stability and corporate growth over temporary rewards they might receive as workers, and why they seem to feel more responsibility toward their company than their counterparts in Western countries is not because they have a keener sense of responsibility, but because they have been placed in a position where, as an actual fact, they must share the corporate risk.

In the West, companies are settings where capital and labor – two forces that are external to the companies but make decisions which influence and restrict internal management policies – confront each other to defend their special interests.

In Japan, because companies are under the control of corporate employees who are integrated into the organization, a high degree of autonomy in exercising corporate control and great freedom for executing management policies have been achieved.

It can probably be said that corporations in Japan have succeeded in recreating the situation that existed during the formative years of capitalist companies, when entrepreneurs integrated authority and responsibility, only this time on a much wider scale, extending literally to the masses. This is clearly one of the important factors that led to the rapid increase in the productivity of Japanese corporations. A corporation has the chance to be managed better when, viewing the interests involved objectively, the authority to control the corporation is in the hands of the persons who must accept the responsibility for exercising that authority.

3 'Freedom of Management' in Corporations in Japan

In general, Japanese corporations up to now have continually shown great vitality and noteworthy results as innovators. But saying so does not hide the fact that the level of achievement of Japan in developing truly creative and fundamentally innovative technologies has not been at all satisfactory. For instance, if one looks at the areas of technology in which Japan today is showing outstanding results and traces their origins, one finds that most of the technology came from the West, particularly from the United States.

This fact demands serious attention. Although there is a problem of inadequate funding, tied to, for example, the low level of government investment in basic research and development, there is also a need to review the Japanese educational system, the social organization and other areas such as national psychological traits.

Such problems exist, but they are separate from the fact that Japanese corporations are outstanding innovators. Actually, the creation of unprecedented theories in the natural sciences is not something for which one should rely on corporations. By their nature, research activities and innovations are different, and the latter are purely matters to do with industry. Creativity in corporations is realized during the process of innovation, and at least as far as this point is concerned, Japanese corporations have been more than sufficiently creative.

Although Americans invented the transistor, Japanese industry developed its latent potential and delivered the transistor to consumers in the form of small radios. And when American corporations were faced with strict government regulations related to pollution, they devoted all their efforts to strong lobbying to have the standards eased; Japanese corporations, in the same situation, moved to find solutions through technology.

Numerical Control (NC) machine tools, too, were first developed in the United States, but American efforts to supply low-priced products to the general market were unsuccessful. If left as they were, these machine tools would have ended up as high-cost, high-precision machines used only in special applications. Japanese industry moved in, however, and developed NC technology as the central labor-saving and automatic technology, and then succeeded in producing and supplying low-cost practical NC machine tools to the marketplace.[12]

There are also products like the rotary engine and home-use VTRs, as well as continuous casting technology for steel production. These were all originally conceived in other countries, but efforts there to commercialize them or to develop related technology further ended in failure, or, in some cases, no effort was made to bring the products along in the market. These and numerous other examples can be found where Japanese corporations took concepts or products developed elsewhere and turned them into practical and commercial successes.

Viewed globally, the Japanese corporation can be called an outstanding creator of industrial innovation, with a robust, active industrial spirit. It also seems clear that a considerable portion of such vitality is derived from the high degree of management autonomy held by the Japanese corporation.

Japanese corporations are free not only from external controls from shareholders, but also from pressures from national industrial and trade/labor unions. When compared with companies in most of the other industrially advanced nations (explained in a later chapter), they are also relatively free from government constraints. Such constraints reach extreme levels in socialist countries.

In many nations, although the particular influence may differ, management autonomy is weakened to a considerable degree by external influences such as *zaibatsu*-type family ties, shareholders, labor unions and the government.

Corporations in Japan, however, given their final authority, are exposed to extremely little pressure from other interest groups and can freely pursue their own objectives, i.e., growth and development. At the very least, this feature cannot generally be found elsewhere, either in capitalist or socialist countries.

4 Consolidation of Corporate Objectives Among Employees

Japanese corporations are able to consolidate the total energy of their employees toward corporate objectives, a feature not found elsewhere. They can do so because of the special corporate system found in Japan, wherein corporate employees are integrated into the corporate structure and assume shares of the corporate risk to become the main standard-bearers for carrying out company operations.

There are two aspects to this sharing of corporate risk. First, the career employment system binds the individual's destiny, in terms of his working life, to the rise and fall of the company's fortunes. Second, the seniority system diminishes individual risk by assuring a degree of equality in treatment, thus again directly binding the individual's future to that of the company's. In that situation, corporate employees are actually forced to become interested in corporate management as an extension of their personal interests. Most of the working characteristics of Japanese corporate employees can be explained from these two aspects.

As is well known, Japanese workers have a reputation for being diligent. If, however, one looks closely at the actual working characteristics of, say, production line workers in Japanese plants, one sees that while the reputation the workers have is not completely off the mark, neither does it present a completely true picture. The working characteristics of line workers cannot be explained simply by saying they work long hours or work without complaining.

Rather, the basic characteristic of Japanese workers is that they think about what is most needed by their company and then personally take the initiative to promote it. They do not work passively, in other words, bound by rules and regulations, but instead view their work from a corporate perspective, working closely together, participating in production control and generally becoming the standard-bearers for technological innovations.

In an overall comparison with Western workers, the principal characteristic of Japanese workers lies in their desire to play an active part in corporate operations. One cannot say that Western workers are not diligent. When compared with Japanese workers, however, it must be admitted that Western workers tend not to work unless ordered to do so and tend not to apply much thought to their jobs. They appear to be concerned solely with performing their jobs according to predetermined work procedures. And they do not seem to think very much about the reason for such work procedures or give much thought to resolving problems, such as malfunctions, when they occur. A job manual, for example, may instruct a worker to 'tighten the screw two and a half turns'. But there may be times when two and a half turns are not enough to tighten the screw properly. In this situation, a Japanese worker will usually confirm whether the screw is sufficiently tightened, and, if it is not, tighten it as much as necessary. Such voluntary behavior may appear trivial, but similar behavior is not often seen in the West.

That seemingly trivial difference in the voluntary behavior of Japanese workers became a major point of departure. Japanese corporations adopted the general philosophy of placing the responsibility for product quality directly on the shoulders of the line workers, having them build quality directly into the product. This move greatly simplified the inspection process and caused a marked drop in the frequency of faulty items, and became possible only because management was able to place complete trust in the initiative of the worker.

Western workers are not particularly irresponsible, but there is a difference in how they interpret responsibility. For example, they consider that their work-site responsibility is ended when they turn the wrench two and a half times as per instructions in the manual. If a faulty item is produced because the worker followed instructions, it is not the worker's responsibility, because the production of a certain percentage of faulty products is included in basic planning, and the worker knows that the company has set up an inspection process for finding such faulty items. In essence, the work attitude of Western workers has two aspects, unified along a single line of reasoning. On one hand, they will accept the responsibility to perform work processes with clearly defined perimeters; on the other hand, they will not consider doing anything outside those perimeters, regardless of whether or not such action is closely related to the work they are already performing and regardless of how minor the required effort to perform some job may be, even when, viewed from the overall organization, it would clearly be a plus.

The work consciousness of Western workers, then, is demonstrated by these two aspects related to job responsibility. That is why a machine tool operator will not clean his own equipment: the cleaning staff is responsible for cleaning, and the machine tool operator is responsible for running the machine. He will not clean his equipment even if he has time to do so. Based on the same thinking, an office worker will not readily answer the telephone ringing on the next desk for its absent occupant.

Behind such differences in the approach to responsibility taken by Japanese and Western workers, a key difference clearly exists in the relationship between the employee and the company. The basic question is whether an employee is working as an integrated corporate employee or as a worker providing labor under contract. This difference is the underlying reason why Japanese corporations provide their employees with a range of freedom in performing their work that would be unthinkable in Western corporations, for as the voluntary behavior of employees increases, the need for authoritative controls decreases.

These features are clearly evident among clerical workers, but they are also seen clearly among factory workers, even though the latter normally face considerable restrictions in their work processes due to technical conditions related to production.

Western workers work according to manuals that clearly and strictly define their job requirements, and workers are expected to comply faithfully with the contents of the manuals in performing their work. In effect, the manuals organize the work processes.

Manuals are used on production lines in Japan, too, but essentially, they do not have much significance. Japanese workers perform their work in teams. Officially, administration assigns personnel to specific jobs, but in each team there is no rigid indication of a worker's role, only of general job descriptions. If a team member is lacking in some ability, or if a position opens up because a worker is absent, the other members of the team will help and support one another to prevent any drop in the work performance of the team.

Much of the training of employees is done within the team, where expertise is passed on in unique ways from one member to the other. Many of the work teams form closely knit groups, with senior members acting as mentors to inexperienced new members, thereby cultivating close relationships among the team members. These relationships provide the foundation for forming a flexible organization.

The team leader (*shokucho*) in charge of a team is more of a co-worker than a supervisor, usually working on the line with the other team members. His equivalent in the West, the foreman, is a non-union supervisor on the management side, often with a separate office in the factory. He plays a manager's role, giving orders to subordinates. The production work site in Japanese factories, however, is controlled by – or, if 'controlled by' is not an acceptable expression, is moved by – the group of employees in charge of the work site.

In the plants of a certain automaker, for example, each of the work sites on the production line has the authority to stop the conveyor belt. Also, when a new model is being introduced, the production line's speed is kept at a low level. Only after the workers have become accustomed to the new processes is the speed increased in line with the 'learning curve'. Of course, it is the workers themselves who increase the speed. The production line speed is directly proportional to the work load, and an increase in the line speed applies additional pressure on the worker. It is natural in the West for workers to resist such an increase in speed and for management to conduct detailed work analyses to somehow get the workers to accept an appropriate speed increase. But this is not needed in Japan.

Production workers in Japan sometimes try, on their own initiative, to find ways to improve work procedures, and even machinery, at their work site. In the Kyoto Plant of Mitsubishi Motor Co., for example, 2,000 direct workers – 60 percent of the total work force of 3,400 employees – are organized into 220 small groups called 'improvement squads'. These groups meet to discuss everything from the status of minor work site problems to the operation of sophisticated machinery. Recently, the groups began studying electronics on their own and have already designed a machine that uses a minicomputer. As many as 320 new production-related machines – counting only those officially on the company's books – mainly for promoting automation, have been originated by line workers. Among these 'homemade' machines, many came from fine ideas too strange for engineers to have conceived. Only 'amateur' line workers could possibly have thought of them. Some say the principal benefit of using equipment designed by workers is that malfunctions can be quickly repaired.[13]

Japanese workers are aggressive in trying to resolve production control problems through such means as suggestions and QC (quality control) circle activities. Another example from the automobile industry concerns the start-up production of a new passenger car model. Within only one or two months of the initial marketing of the model, the company's production line workers submitted several thousand suggestions for improvements. True, many of the suggestions had little or no value, but some could not possibly have been thought of by the company's engineers with their originality and their potential for realization because they closely fit the actual situation at the work site and were tied to improvements in the production system.

The process of receiving and acting on suggestions from production line workers has been highly systematized by most of Japan's larger corporations. In fact, four-fifths of the suggestions in companies with 1,000 or more employees and two-thirds of the suggestions in companies with 300–999 employees are utilized.[14] Through the suggestion system, a company collects work improvement proposals from workers and rewards those whose ideas are used. Industry widely adopted this system after World War II as a means of promoting worker initiative and improving production control. During the first oil crisis in the early 1970s, use of the suggestion system expanded tremendously and the total number of suggestions grew by geometric progression. The results of a survey of 643 companies by the Japan HR Society and the Japan Suggestion Activity Association show that there were 52,990,000 suggestions submitted during 1988. The members of foreign study missions visiting Japanese plants around that time often found such figures unbelievable, fantasy rather than fact.

Suggestion systems also exist in American companies, of course. As shown in Table 2.1 however, their diffusion rate in industry is quite low and the number of suggestions per worker is only a fraction of the number in Japan. Many American companies have to depend on high monetary rewards to provide workers with an incentive for making suggestions.

Table 2.1 *Comparison of suggestion systems in the United States and Japan*

	US	Japan
Participation (%)	14.0	54.2 (80.0)
Suggestions per Person	0.15	4.73 (31.45)
Adoption Percentage (%)	24.0	60.7 (83.5)
Average Reward per Suggestion (¥)	30,530	852 (379)
Economic Effect per Suggestion (¥)	339,595	15,823
		(5,927)

Source: NASS, *Survey by the Japan Suggestion Activity Society for FY1978* (part of data from 1979 NASS materials; based on ¥230 = $1); figures in ( ) are for 1988 (same source).

Aside from participating in the suggestion system, employees at the same work site also actively form QC circles or other small groups and, on their own initiative, discuss ways to improve product quality. The quality control concept originated in the United States in the 1930s as a way to improve product quality by using statistical methods, but the move to form QC circles based on voluntary participation by all workers was first proposed in the 1960s in Japan, where it flourished. As of December 1988,

280,000 QC circles were registered with the Japan Science and Technology Association. The basic principle governing QC circles is simple, and the nature of the circles is such that they are not necessarily limited to quality control. Besides quality control, today they also cover all other areas of production control as well as clerical and administrative areas.

More than a management technique, the move to promote small group activities is a total work site movement based on voluntary participation by workers. And, indeed, many overall production control improvements have also resulted from QC circle and other small group activities, ideas of which only production workers could have thought.

To illustrate, one of the strong points of the Japanese machinery industry is the flexibility of its production control, which allowed it to provide many variations in product quality and functions in response to increasing diversification in demand without losing any of the efficiency of quantity production. One way this was made possible was by the single-step arrangement. Previously, when producing different items on one line, it was necessary to stop the line for several hours to change production dies, followed afterward by much time for testing. Today, the same process is completed in 10 to 20 minutes. The great time saving has tremendous significance for maintaining efficiency when producing small quantities of diverse items. In the past, because it was highly uneconomical to stamp only a few pieces from a die when performing a variety of production runs, a quantity of pieces was produced and stored. With the single-step arrangement, however, it became possible to substantially reduce the storage levels of processed parts, leading to large savings in operational costs, storage space and transportation equipment.

Strangely enough, there was no radical technical breakthrough behind this remarkable improvement in production control. It derived from a combination of simple ideas, such as grouping a number of pipings into a single one-touch joint plug for a single motion connection, instead of connecting a number of pipes one by one. Another idea was 'parallel production', in which some machines on a line were kept operating while others were stopped to change dies. Important advances were thus made as a result of an accumulation of numerous detailed improvements introduced at the work site, improvements it would hardly be possible to conceive of in the research laboratory.

Judging from these practical examples, it appears as if the field of industrial engineering, normally an area left to graduate engineers, is being taken over more and more in Japanese plants by production line workers. The engineers, meanwhile, are moving toward specialization in research and development.

As these facts indicate, it is clear there are essential differences in the relationship between workers and the company in Japan and in the West. To a degree, Japanese workers have not only assumed the role of production supervisors, they have also assumed the role assigned to engineers in Western companies. And based on that foundation, one can even say that Japanese workers have assumed the role of innovators at the work-site level.

One of the sources of the vitality found in Japanese industry and companies lies in the voluntary and positive participation by production workers toward promoting improvements in production control.

5 Comparison of 'Management Participation'

As described in the preceding pages, Japanese employees play an innovative role in promoting production control and technical improvements. Although the sharing of corporate risk, work systemization and the introduction of innovations are normally considered entrepreneurial functions that are by nature the responsibility of entrepreneurs who own and manage a company, such functions in Japan are distributed widely over a company's entire work force. From this viewpoint, it can be stated that Japanese employees not only assume a part of the role played by engineers in Western countries but also assume, at least partially, the responsibility of the entrepreneur. This development was a necessary eventuality in the Japanese environment, where employees became integrated into the corporation and the corporation became composed of corporate employees.

Already explained is the meaning of total participation in management, frequently mentioned as a special feature of Japanese corporate management. Although the phrase may seem to be a management slogan, to a certain extent it is an actual reflection of the contemporary reality in Japan.

In Europe, especially in Central Europe and the Scandinavian countries, various forms of worker participation in management are being implemented or are undergoing trial runs. In West Germany, for example, joint decision-making legislation enacted in 1976 stipulates that a company's audit board must be composed of equal numbers of members of management and labor.

Because the audit board in West Germany ranks above the board of directors and has the authority to appoint and dismiss the president and other directors, and because management must follow the basic management policies established by the audit board, the fact that labor representatives sit on the audit committee with status equal to that of shareholder representatives means that labor and capital share the authority to decide the most important management policies for the company.[15]

The Scandinavian countries are also taking an energetic stance toward worker participation in management. In Sweden, for example, it is a legal requirement under the Legislation Concerning Participation in Board Meetings by Employees of Corporations and Economic Organizations that all companies with 25 or more employees must have two labor representatives on their board. Furthermore, under the joint decision-making legislation important matters such as those related to personnel, capital investment and changes in business operations are subject to joint decisions by labor and capital.[16]

Such trends in management participation by labor in European corporations changed management into a joint endeavor based on agreement between workers and shareholders, a format introduced to promote the socialization of corporations, and one that effected considerable revisions in the control structure previously found in traditional capitalist organizations.

Labor's participation in management in the forms found in Western corporations is totally different from the participation seen in Japan.

Japanese-style participation in the unique corporate structure seen in Japan is related to the pursuit of management rationalization and is developed spontaneously. In contrast, European-type participation is introduced artificially, through legislation, and cannot be sustained without legal enforcement.

In the European corporate structure, where a bipolar confrontation between capital and labor continues to exist, worker participation in management may be good for workers but is not favorable from the management (or capitalist) point of view. In fact, a West German management organization once filed a suit claiming that the joint decision-making legislation was unconstitutional because it violated property rights, an action which was said to have led to mounting tension between labor and capital.[17]

From the standpoint of rationalizing management, providing equal voting rights to labor and management, two parties with conflicting interests will turn policy decision-making into a matter of negotiating a compromise. In terms of maintaining conformity and integration in management policies, it will be impossible to avoid facing quite severe difficulties.

When there are factions with conflicting interests in a social group, it is quite natural to try to mediate between such interests systematically through a democratic process. But one must remember that corporations and local autonomous bodies are quite different entities. As important elements in a nation's economy, corporations must continually promote innovations and maintain a high level of efficiency while being exposed to fierce competition from other corporations, both foreign and domestic.

Even if there is no doubt that the Euopean type of labor participation in management has made corporations, as social groups, more democratic and socialized by allocating to workers part of the responsibilities for decision-making in management policies, the question remains, however, whether such participation is a rational choice when viewed from the original role of corporations being responsible for economic activities.

The fundamental problem is not the unequal distribution of authority; it goes beyond this problem. As long as the bipolar confrontation between capital and labor remains, the loss of unity and autonomy in management cannot be avoided no matter how equitable a system of decision-making is, since doing anything other than resolving the confrontation merely transfers it to an organized venue.

In the European style of labor participation in management, workers participate as a group in an area of authority traditionally concentrated in top management. Inside the corporation, meanwhile, the autocratic system of control over workers and a corresponding passive work attitude on the part of workers are left completely as is. That type of participation clearly raises the power and position of the labor union as an organization, but it does not immediately lead to freedom in the daily work processes of the individual worker at his work site.

If the European system of participation could generate among workers a genuine subjective interest in management, it is also possible that that might indirectly create the conditions for realizing participation at the work site level, but it is difficult to see how participation in top-level management via a labor union could prompt feelings of responsibility among workers. This is because although workers in Europe are, in fact, already exerting a strong influence on corporations through their labor unions, this move has not led to the development of any sharp awareness among workers about participating in management. Labor unions use their clout to protect the interests of their members. They intentionally avoid any situation in which they might become so involved in management that they would be forced to consider the total corporate picture. Such involvement could make it difficult for them adequately to protect the interests of their members.

Concerning the behavior of English workers and labor unions, Paul Einzig has written the following. He tells us it is possible that workers who have gained power and developed a master complex can direct such power in a totally opposite direction from any intentional participation in management.

> The 'we are the masters now' attitude has led to considerable deterioration in industrial efficiency. The standard of workmanship has declined in many factories, because the workers simply refuse to tolerate any criticism of their work. This is particularly the case with firms which operate the system of piece-work payment, so that attempts to maintain and improve the quality of the manufacture are resented not only because they imply criticism, but even more because they are bound to slow down the output and to reduce earnings. In the past, workers took genuine pride in the quality of the goods they had produced and in the reputation of their firm. In many factories that spirit is almost completely gone. Most workers are now only interested in their pay packets.[18]

In West Germany, it seems that the mental separation from the corporation of workers progressed more quickly after World War

II, when labor's participation in management was legally established as a system. During the prewar period, employees working in major industries had pride in their companies. Workers at Kruppindustrie, for example, called themselves 'Krupplers', and those at AIG, 'AIGlers'. Today, such expressions are almost never used. Many German workers have reached the point where, like their English counterparts, they are now only interested in their pay packets. It is extremely difficult, therefore, to say the joint decision-making system has helped to integrate workers into corporations and develop them to the point at which they have a positive interest in management as members of the corporation. If the joint decision-making system is able to make any contribution at all, it is perhaps only to the extent of convincing workers that because they have joined the shareholders as joint masters of the corporation they should adopt an appropriate attitude.

Although there may be a conceptual connection, however, between the fact that representatives of unions to which individual workers belong are participating in corporate decision-making and the development of a subjective desire among workers to be positively interested in their daily work, there is no assurance that the workers themselves actually make such a connection in their minds.

At any rate, in economic activities, the most routine of everyday behavior, it is hard to believe that appealing to an ethical sense could have a lasting effect. Matters such as self-interest and a sense of responsibility in corporate management are problems of realities, not ethics. A sense of responsibility for a company definitely emerges when employees are placed in responsible positions, whether by desire or not, by taking a share of the corporate risk.

Japanese workers have a sense of responsibility because in their fundamental relationship with their company they stand to lose if they do not have it. Or, rather, although when viewed from the outside they seem to have a sense of responsibility, actually on the inside it is no more than a result of calculations by the workers based on what they feel is in their best interest. It may be merely that one is looking at the behavior that results from those calculations and attributing to Japanese workers a stronger sense of responsibility than Western workers.

Actually, it does not make any difference whether Japanese workers have a real or only a superficial sense of responsibility.

What is important is not the internal psychology but the external behavior. Japanese-style participation by workers in management did not emerge after workers first acquired authority; rather, it came about after workers were made to assume corporate risk which gave them an awareness of voluntary participation. Thus, 'internalized' corporate employees were created, and resulting naturally from that situation was de facto participation in decision-making that befitted an awareness of responsibility.

It seems quite clear that in order to tie the personal behavior of a free individual to a higher level of public good, a system based on harmony of interests will provide a greater guarantee of success than an appeal to a sense of ethics.

Part II: *Comparison with Socialist Corporations*

As has been shown, the Japanese corporate system differs substantially from the conventional capitalist corporate system. One wonders, then, how it compares with corporations in socialist systems. Although some will say there is not much sense in comparing corporations existing under different systems, the fact is that national economies have risen above classifications of systems and have developed in diversified ways, depending on the circumstances in the particular country. Today, then, the demarcation between capitalist and socialist systems is not as clear as is generally thought, and identifying the special features of corporations in socialist countries will help to bring out more sharply the special features of Japanese corporations.

Contemporary socialist economic systems can be divided into two major types: the Soviet collectivism type, based on the principle of planning; and the self-management type, typified by the system in Yugoslavia, where worker-controlled corporations and a market economy are joined together. The economic systems in the majority of socialist countries, including Asian countries such as the People's Republic of China (PRC), North Korea and Vietnam, follow the Soviet system, but in some of the countries in Eastern Europe, such as Hungary and Czechoslovakia, one can see in corporations some elements of self-management by workers, although not to the same degree as in Yugoslavia.

Corporations in the PRC and Yugoslavia, representing the two major socialist systems, are discussed in the following pages. Some readers may feel the Soviet Union would be a better choice for a discussion concerning corporations operating in a planned economic system, but the author selected the PRC for personal reasons. He had the opportunity to observe directly the situation in Chinese enterprises and therefore felt more qualified to comment on the situation there than on the one in the USSR.

1 Corporate System in the PRC

The economic system in the PRC is an example of the Soviet type of planned economy under a centralization of power. During the past few years the PRC has attempted reforms that grant a wider range of autonomy to corporations, an indication that the country recognizes the system's rigidity and inefficiency. The situation is still quite fluid, however, and the corporations are therefore discussed as they existed before the introduction of reforms.

There is no control by capitalists, of course, in the control structure of Chinese corporations. Neither do corporations have much autonomy. Broadly speaking, the State Economic Committee is at the apex of the economic control structure in the PRC, and through ministries for each industry it directly controls corporations and the distribution of funds and commodities.

The corporate director, roughly equivalent to a company president or plant manager in Japan, is a Communist Party member appointed by the Party. It seems that the Party often appoints old military men or Party bureaucrats, men not necessarily knowledgeable about managing corporations. Meanwhile, corporate managers are appointed by the corporate director, subject to the Party's approval.

Viewed from the corporation side, under this type of control system the planning authorities allocate the elements of production, i.e., funds, commodities and labor, to the corporation. In addition, the State controls almost all factors of corporate management, such as product category, production quantity, volume of raw materials and fuel to be used, as well as cost and productivity. Regarding the control of these factors, eight directive indices, or goals, having an effect equal to law, are indicated to corporations. The factory director is responsible to the State for achieving these goals. (The eight directive indices have recently been condensed into four.) In Japan, some 40-odd years ago, not long after World War II, there was a period when raw materials and funds were allocated to important industries; in the PRC, however, controls cover much more than the mere allocation of production factors entering into internal management.[19]

In accordance with authority not being granted to corporations in the PRC, neither are they given responsibility. If negative business figures result, therefore, the State makes up the difference from the national treasury; if profits are realized, the State absorbs almost all of them. Given these circumstances, Chinese corporations, have, in essence, no substance as corporate entities. The corporate director is responsible for achieving a number of separate norms, but has no further responsibility. For example, assume that the director increases productivity through some kind of corporate efforts. As the end of the fiscal year approaches, however, the corporation naturally runs into shortages of raw materials, fuel, etc. Since the labor supply is fixed, in order to adjust the plant's operations, the corporation may have to halt production for about a month for maintenance and repairs.

Under such a system of total control, individual corporations are nothing more than organizations for achieving norms set for them, and from the start one cannot view corporate management as a single integrated body. Although corporations originally are meant to be unified bodies of management, in the PRC it is impossible for the corporate directors to take responsibility for managing them that way.

It becomes exceedingly difficult, under such a system, to organize corporate management in a rational way or to develop an internal driving force for corporate growth. Deputy Executive Director Huan Xiang of the Academy of Social Sciences of China speaks about that situation as follows:

> The lack of management autonomy in corporations under a
> highly concentrated planned economy system is tantamount
> to tying the hands and feet of the corporate management staff,

thereby suppressing their initiative and creativity. On the production side, the corporation must achieve planned production goals the State has set, and the responsibility of the corporate management staff is limited solely to nominally achieving these goals. There is no sense of personal responsibility toward the factory, users or society. It is also of no concern and irrelevant to the corporation whether the items it produces comply with the needs of society or not. Profits are returned to and losses are replenished by the State. Nothing changes whether results are good or bad. Such a system removes all spirit of enterprise from the management staff toward improving the corporation.[20]

Corporations in China are controlled not only externally, but also internally by the State organization. Responsibility for internal controls lies with the Party. Figure 2.2 shows the internal structure of a typical major corporation. A glance shows that such a structure differs considerably from those of corporate organizations in Japan. First of all, the corporate director is ranked below the Party Committee. Also, a political board answering directly to the Party Committee is set up that takes no orders from the corporate director. Its functions cover police duties, propaganda, education and the command of civilian soldiers. The labor union comes under the political board, which means that labor unions in the PRC are under the control of the Party.

The corporate director is also a member of the Party Committee and is responsible for plant operations. The Party Committee, headed by the secretary, controls the corporation from political and ideological standpoints. The power to appoint or replace the corporate director resides in the Party and is implemented through the Party Committee.

The balance of power between the Party Committee, or the secretary, and the corporate director has varied considerably over the years. At times when economic development was emphasized, the power of the corporate director was dominant; when the political stance was under contest, the secretary had more power. During the Cultural Revolution, for example, corporate management functions were totally absorbed by political action factions, and the Revolutionary Committee instituted a system of unified control. Currently, economic development is being stressed, and although the position of the corporate director remains below the

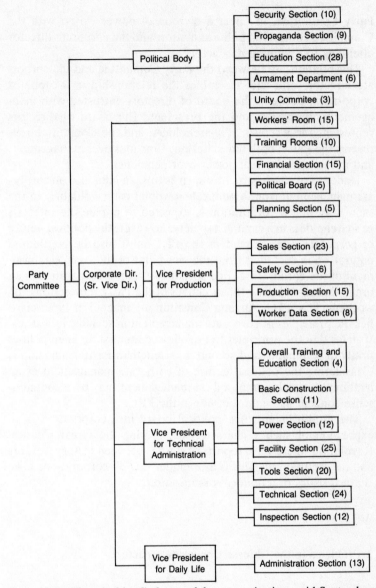

Figure 2.2   Tientsin bicycle factory labor organization: mid-September 1979.

Source: Materials from Japan Productivity Center.
Note: Besides the above, there are also 15 divisions in the production area under a vice president for production; there are a total of 272 persons in the production divisions.

Party Committee, in effect a division of power exists, with the Committee controlling political matters and the corporate director attending to operating the factory.

This relationship between the Party Committee and the corporate director somewhat resembles the relationship in a capitalist corporation between the board of directors entrusted with management supervision and the president. The board of directors represents the interests of shareholders, and the Committee represents the Party; both have checking functions over management, and in fact exercise real power over personnel.

Under a corporate structure such as this, an influence on corporate management from a political viewpoint is unavoidable. In the same way that a corporation is expected to pursue the interests of shareholders in a capitalist society, however, the political nature of corporate management in the PRC must also be considered natural when regarded from the viewpoint of the basic establishment of the corporation. In a socialist system, a corporation is an organ that must follow the directives of the Party representing the working class. (The Angang Constitution, enacted in 1960, clarifies the principles of corporate management in socialist industries. It states that the principles to be followed are first 'to keep politics firmly in command' and second 'to strengthen Party leadership'.) Considering the political nature of corporate management as an irrational distortion imposed on management may be a commonsense concept in Japan, but not in the PRC.

The establishment of a political board in a corporation is an expression of such a characteristic. During the Great Cultural Revolution, there were reports of clashes between factory workers and the Red Guard. This is a reminder that all corporations have characteristics of a political organization.

2 Problems in the Chinese Corporate Structure

The situation in which control of corporations by the State system and Party structure undermines corporate cohesion and unity is similar to the way in which shareholder control brought about a bipolar confrontation between management and labor in capitalist corporations. The corporate director and other managers above section managers in a Chinese corporation are almost all Party members with a separate status from the general masses of workers, who are mostly non-Party members. As mentioned before, the Party has the power to appoint and dismiss the corporate director, and, although the corporate director appoints vice presidents and section managers, these appointments are subject to the Party's approval.

If the collective interests of the general workers are always in agreement with Party policies, there are no problems. And, in principle, that is how it is supposed to be. In the actual practice of corporate operations, however, these two elements should often be at odds with each other. At such times, it is difficult to believe that corporate managers in the situation described above will try to pursue corporate interests against the wishes of the State and the Party.

Huan criticizes the common weaknesses of Chinese corporate managers as follows:

Corporate management staff members are concerned only with the higher level officers and how to impress them. They have no interest in the market situation, pay no attention to the type, specification or quality of the products they produce, do not pursue the interests of the factory, and need only achieve the goals impressed on them by higher authorities. By producing more than the planned goals, they protect their positions, and in extreme cases some resort to lies and deceit.[21]

Within the corporation, a split related to a conflict of interest will appear between the corporate supervisors and the general body of workers, whose interests are centered on wages, the intensity of the workload and other matters pertaining to their working lives. Under such a system it is impossible to avoid the formation of an autocratic top-down control system, and, on the other hand, the appearance of workers with a lethargic attitude who only feel the sense of being controlled.

On this point, Ma Huang, Executive Director of the Industrial Economics Institute of the Academy of Social Sciences of China, states:

Some of our supervisory and management staff have forgotten their worker status, have failed to follow the doctrine of the three equalities (equality of workers, engineers and managers), and in their contact with the masses have even assumed attitudes of being lords and masters.

On the other hand, some of our workers do not recognize their status as protagonists and fail to take the corresponding attitude toward their work and the corporation for which they work. In their contact with corporation leaders, some act as if those people were capitalists.[22]

Ma says such situations arise because the feudalistic tradition in China has not been fully eradicated. And it may not be possible to say that that tradition has not brought about such attitudes, although the real problem probably lies with the system. Workers do not recognize their status as protagonists because they are really not protagonists. In the same way, supervisory and management level staff members fail to behave like workers because in terms of both their position and their interests they are no longer ordinary workers. Under a system like this it is only natural that there are difficulties in uniting the workers within the corporation and concentrating their energies on achieving corporate goals. Huan also recognizes that, compared with the Japanese situation, the participation of workers in management in the PRC is insufficient.[23]

The raising of corporate control standards is recognized as a strategic task for realizing the four 'modernizations', and the PRC is now working energetically on countermeasures for that purpose. Many experts from various Japanese organizations and corporations are engaged in developing specialists and providing consultation to corporations in the PRC. Many Chinese study missions have visited Japan, and many trainees have studied in Japan. Through these exchanges, the problems concerning management control in the PRC are becoming clearer.

The problems can be classified into three major groups. First, there are problems arising from the tardiness of production control, appearing in such areas as an overall weakness in manufacturing technology, inadequate planning in designing layouts, general lack of work standards, tardiness in the standardization of products, existing standards being too lax, poor equipment maintenance, insufficient order in arrangement and other factors in the factory, many uneven places on the floors, many oil stains, and so forth. Just as was done in Japan in the past, these problems can be expected to be gradually improved in the PRC through conscientious efforts.

The second category of problems relates to inefficiencies that accompany a planned economy. There is a lack of severity in overall management, stemming from the fact that the State assumes corporate responsibility, replenishing deficits and absorbing profits. Insufficient marketing efforts result from a lack of contact with the market, owing to the purchase of output in one lot by the State organization in charge of distribution. Many corporations have surplus inventories, and they tend to produce in-house the parts they use, principally because there is little flexibility in a planned economy for procuring materiel and raw materials, making it difficult for corporations to obtain these quickly when needed. (There is a reference in the PRC to what is called the 'three 80 percenters'. It refers to the fact that the actual allocation of material will be only 80 percent of the total planned requirements, materials on order for receipt will be only 80 percent of the actual allocated amount, and the materials received will be only 80 percent of the ordered amount. In other words, the amount of materials actually delivered will be only one-half of the required amount.)[24]

There are also many examples of wasteful investment in plant and equipment, and one can find many facilities with low operational factors. This is probably because a major part of such investment funds was supplied as financial grants (interest-free, non-reimbursable funds), which made it difficult to develop any idea of the cost of capital. Intensive production at the end of the month and production instability are flaws found in planned economies that bind corporations to achieving set targets, such as is also seen in the Soviet Union.

At present, a radical change is under way in the economic control system in the PRC. Directive indices have been simplified into four principles, capital investment funds are becoming loans rather than grants, and certain rights are being granted to corporations, including the right to market production achieved over and above goals, the right to retain part of the profits gained in the corporation and the right to hire workers. The general trend, then, is moving toward the introduction of a market mechanism.

As these changes begin to show results, the existing defects and flaws should gradually decrease.

There is, however, a third category of problems which cannot be attributed to either low standards of management controls or to the absence of the market principle. They mainly concern problems related to human workers.

In November 1980, Mitsuo Ogura, a Japanese management consultant, visited the PRC to provide guidance in management controls. Some of his comments are as follows:

> I saw no workshop discipline at all. Work attendance charts are posted in all workshops, but absenteeism rates are high and, since rest periods are not clearly established, there are workers reading newspapers, eating, engaged in idle talk, and so forth during working hours. The results of work samplings at a certain plant showed operating rates of 60 percent for workers and 50 percent for machinery. Productivity is extremely low.[25]

Poor awareness among workers of the need to improve their work, many shortcomings in work attitude and work manners, a shortage of multi-function workers at the same time that mutual cooperation at and among work sites is not conducted smoothly, poor horizontal communication in the organization, which leads to everything being turned over to supervisory staff to adjust, and the methods necessary for TQC and other company-wide efforts not working out well, are all problems that will not be resolved by introducing market principles. This is because these same problems are also found to a greater or lesser degree in corporations in capitalist countries, and yet market principles have already been developed there to their highest level.

Clearly, the foregoing problems do not derive from the backwardness of management control in the PRC, nor are they due to market principles not being used. This suggests that an entirely different approach is necessary to resolve the problems.

The behavior of workers in regard to the above problems depends on how deeply the workers are integrated into management. In short, only when workers have a self-assertive interest in corporate management, have the disposition as integrated members of the corporation to support the corporation, and a system exists to support that desire, will positive attitudes toward work and mutual and voluntary adjustment activities among workers be realized.

The essence of this problem lies in the pivotal point of how deeply the workers have been integrated into the corporation. At present, workers in the PRC consider the corporation as something external to work. This can be seen from an article that appeared in the March 18, 1980 edition of the *Beijing Journal*, which introduced an episode that took place in a Shanghai factory during the days of the Group of Four.

> The employees were not dependable. Some reported for work at 7.00 a.m. and then wasted more than an hour before starting their jobs. Although the work day ended at 3.30 p.m., some workers started taking baths shortly after 2.00.
>
> Four conscientious female workers assigned to the factory called on the workers to try to exceed the goals set for them. This created quite a furor on the shop floor. One 'kind' worker told one of the female workers, 'You have been here only a short time, and are already thinking of raising the work goals. That could lead to much grief later on.'

Chinese workers, like the above, feel that if they work too hard, the goals will be raised – which is not so different from what workers in a capitalist corporation say if they work too hard: the standard tasks will be raised and they will lose as a result.

In a capitalist corporation, the spirit of fellowship among workers is highly developed, but in a totally different sense from the awareness of being a member of a common corporate body. The workers look upon the corporation as opposed to their common interests and often join together in ways that dampen corporate growth, such as by conducting strikes, preventing a decrease in jobs by not overworking, and being reluctant to introduce work improvement proposals that might raise the standard task.

Such reactions on the part of Chinese workers suggest the possibility that a sense of fellowship resembling that found among workers in capitalist countries is being formed.

Japanese consultants are especially surprised at the lack of interest shown by Chinese workers toward being promoted. According to a survey conducted by the Japan Productivity Center at two plants in Tientsin and one plant in Harbin, the interest of workers in Tientsin Factory A (shown in multiple replies) in personal income was 64 percent, but the interest shown toward promotion was only 2.6 percent. In Tientsin Factory B, the same figures were 32.5 percent and 1.9 percent, respectively. In the Harbin Factory, the figures finally moved closer, with 22.3 percent interest in personal income and a 14.4 percent interest in promotion.

If such a lack of interest in these three factories indicates a common tendency, what is the underlying reason? Is it because higher positions are all occupied by Party members, which makes these positions almost inaccessible? (The actual situation is hard to ascertain because it is also possible for workers to become Party members after promotion.) Or is it perhaps due to the after effects of the Great Cultural Revolution, with workers thinking that moving up to highly visible positions will not lead to anything worthwhile? Or perhaps might it just be that Chinese workers think that promotion is not essentially a matter with which an individual should concern himself in the first place? The reasons are not clear.

Regardless of the reasons, however, the lack of interest in promotion indicates a low level of commitment by Chinese workers to succeed within the corporation. It also shows how workers are integrated just that much less into the enterprise.

In Japan, because employees have been integrated into corporations to the extent that success in the company has come to signify success in life, the reward of promotion is a much stronger incentive than monetary rewards. For many years after entering a company, under the seniority system the difference in wages received from year to year by employees is, as one observer remarks, 'Only enough to buy a couple of packs of cigarettes a day'. Nonetheless, it acts as a strong incentive, because any difference at all expresses the evaluation placed on the employee's work performance and will have an important bearing on his promotion potential in later years.

If, however, the degree of integration by employees into a corporation is low, it will be difficult to expect voluntary contributions to the corporation from them and job promotion incentives will have little effect. Therefore, the only effective methods of motivating employees that remain are money and fear of unemployment. In the PRC, the State has introduced measures that allow for the payment of monetary and other material incentives to workers who perform well and the dismissal of workers who are grossly inefficient.

Such measures, however, will definitely lead to strengthening the egotistic desires of the individual. It will cause workers to relate individual work performance even more directly in their minds to remuneration. And it will strengthen the tendency for them to reduce their relationship to the corporation, and to society-in-general, to the level of a business transaction.

It goes without saying, of course, that such a system does not always lead to negative consequences in terms of labor efficiency.

In Japan, for example, some salesmen – such as auto salesmen – work on a commission basis, and receive an amount of money for each vehicle they sell. Income thus depends largely on sales results. Sales activities are conducted on an individual basis and a salesman's contribution can be clearly determined by the actual amount of sales in money terms. In a work situation of this type, it is possible to realize considerable results solely through simple material incentives.

The factors considered essential for industrial workers in a large organization, however, such as positive attention toward various improvement opportunities within the factory, the spirit of cooperation among workers in helping each other raise their efficiency as a team, and taking the initiative in communication and in making adjustments, are possible only through a spontaneous desire on the part of each worker to make positive contributions to the corporation. The labor format needed to manage many persons working in a large organization to cooperate organically makes it difficult to evaluate objectively, separate from the overall organization, the work contribution of each employee.

Controls enforced on labor through an application of rewards and punishment may affect matters that can be controlled in terms of quantity but the control of quality is difficult. The persons concerned in the PRC are trying to expunge the present system, in which everyone receives the same income, whether he works or not, and where a worker will not be dismissed no matter how indolent he may be. (In the PRC, this is referred to as a 'metal rice bowl', i.e., a bowl that will not break even when dropped.) On this point, however, those persons should note that Japanese workers – who are closer to the metal-rice-bowl situation than Western workers – are showing greater spontaneity and initiative, while Western workers who were taken the furthest away from the metal-rice-bowl situation, do not always display such spontaneity and initiative.

3 The Necessity for Uniting Management and Labor

At present, a situation exists in the PRC in which workers may refuse to work unless there is a material reward in the form of money. This type of situation develops when management and labor are not adequately united. In other words, Chinese workers have not been sufficiently 'internalized', which is a reflection of the fact that there is almost no mechanism for having the workers share corporate risk.

Some changes have been made, but until recently, the Chinese system called for the State to decide on almost all aspects of products to be manufactured by a corporation, from product type to production quantities, pricing, usage of materials and supplies, and so forth. From the viewpoint of workers, because the fate of their corporation is determined by planning authorities they can only feel to be far removed from themselves, it is impossible from the start to cultivate among workers a sense of making efforts themselves to improve their company's future. In addition, because there is no market competition there is no fear of bankruptcy, and since even if there are profits they go to the State and if there are losses the State covers them, there is thus no way for workers to comprehend what constitutes growth for the corporation.

The problem from the start lies in the absence of corporate risk. The guarantee of long-term employment and the fact that little difference exists in the treatment of workers can constitute a powerful tool for integrating workers into the corporation if the two are implemented by a corporation facing fierce competition in the market. The reason that the same system is showing opposite results in Japan and the PRC is that corporate risk exists in the former but not in the latter.

In a fiercely competitive environment, this kind of system will change an individual's self-interest into a group-centered interest, to produce a situation that makes it possible to unite employees and release their energies toward achieving corporate objectives. In the Chinese environment, however, where almost no corporate risk exists, the system only diminishes the will to work founded on personal greed, and provides nothing to replace it.

If corporate risk can be generated with the introduction of a market mechanism in the PRC, long-term employment guarantees and equality in the treatment of employees will produce a mechanism for transferring corporate risk to the workers and make it possible to integrate the workers into the corporation. If the corporation is successful, the results will be divided almost equally among the workers; if it fails, the losses will also be borne almost equally among the workers. If the worst case occurs, and the corporation goes bankrupt, all employees will equally lose their job guarantee and become unemployed. The larger the rewards (which need not necessarily always be material rewards) in good times and the greater the suffering in bad times, and the more fairly both are distributed, the more direct and stronger the ties become between the corporation and the workers.

Long-term job guarantees tie a corporation's development and the life and future of the employees closely together. And equality in treatment produces more direct ties between corporate results and personal interests. In the PRC, because the income disparity between factory workers and farmers is quite large, because there is a disparity between the cultural level of urban and agricultural areas and because there is a huge number of unemployed and semi-unemployed workers, factory workers think that working in a factory is a privilege. That alone is almost sufficient to make it fully possible to unite the corporations and the workers.

The first essential task, therefore, is to create corporate risk, a system whereby the market is provided with a function that rewards successful and punishes unsuccessful corporations. The second task is to create a mechanism, any kind of mechanism, to transfer corporate risk to the workers. When these two conditions are completed, long-term employment guarantees will not only unite the corporation and its employees materially, but also will become a source of feelings of allegiance toward the company. Equality of treatment will become a base for creating a feeling of solidarity and mutual cooperation in work performance. In a word, it will be possible through this method to effect a strong fusion of management and labor.

The PRC is now in the midst of reforms centered on introducing a market mechanism and the principle of competition. The first condition, the creation of corporate risk, can probably be achieved as the reforms progress, but the second condition, the transfer of corporate risk to workers, is by its nature a problem that cannot be resolved by introducing these principles. Rather, it has aspects that will produce directly opposite results. In the PRC today, where some have become firm believers in market principles, the trend concerning the second point is clearly heading in the opposite direction. The further these reforms are carried out, the more that corporations in the PRC will probably approach the situation in Western corporations, but some doubt remains about whether doing so will draw out the maximum capabilities of workers and lead to ways of utilizing them within the corporate organization.

The authorities in the PRC in charge of economic reform do not seem to have a strong awareness of the fundamental importance of integrating management and labor. This lack of awareness results from the belief, as Ma points out, that 'under conditions of socialism, self-awareness by the great mass of workers reaches unprecedented heights'.[26] This belief is supported by their understanding, as Xue Muqiao says, that 'under the socialist system, the means of production have already become the common property of society-in-general or groups and belong commonly to the working masses. Workers are the protagonists in the means of production; they are not separated from the means of production, and do not sell their labor as is done in capitalistic societies but unite to own, control, use the means of production and together perform production.'[27]

Marxist thinking in the PRC says that in a capitalistic society, in which there is confrontation between capitalists and workers, workers must take a stance against management; in a socialist society, however, such a situation cannot exist. If it does, it arises, according to Sun Shangqing, from 'the long period of feudalistic rule that produced traditions and customs of small individual manufacturers that are still exerting a strong force on our ideological culture and influencing our social life in various ways.'[28]

As a means of overcoming this factor, 'continuous efforts must be made by intensifying the whole breadth of ideological education and socialist controls.'[29]

A priori convictions about a system's superiority will reduce the possibility of finding within the system itself the solution to problems.

The dictum in the PRC that workers are the masters of the corporation is justified through a complicated theory which says that the PRC is a nation controlled by the working class; all corporations controlled by the State are consequently under the control of workers, and therefore, each individual worker, as a member of the working class, is master of the corporation.

This theory must be called an ideology, for even if a worker understands it conceptually when someone says to him that he should take the initiative and participate in the activities of the corporation because he is one of the masters in a nation with a population of 1.1 billion, in practice it is impossible for him to feel this keenly in his daily life. In a sense, such a feeling is beyond the imaginative powers of an ordinary human being.

In order to realize an integration of management and labor, it is not enough to get rid of the capitalist class. A systemized structure must also be built that makes it possible for workers to take the initiative in participating in management at their daily work site. And the core of such a structure must be the assumption of corporate risk by the workers. In other words, an artificial situation must be created which brings about a strong and deep convergence of interests between the corporation and the worker, a situation in which unless workers participate in corporate activities as a group they will suffer losses as a group.

During the period from the successful end of the Revolution until 1956, the Chinese economy made great advances. Within the four years from 1953 to 1956, average wages increased by more than 30 percent and total production grew by 50 percent. During this same period, foreign settlements and other remnants of semi-colonialism, as well as the system of absentee landlords, warped capitalism and other irrational systems remaining from old China were swept away, and various political and social organizations were established to form the framework of the new society. It is obvious that what supported this period of emergence and construction was the assertive spirit that was intensified by the Revolution and that spread among all levels of the Chinese people.

Revolutionary fervor is a motive force for carrying out great reforms throughout an entire society, reforms that are unthinkable in times of peace. The problem, however, is that the fervor does not last long. In particular, among the various human activities, especially highly routine ones, such as economic activities, it is impossible to rely on such fervor over an extended period of time.

The corporate system in the PRC does not contain an internal factor capable of generating initiative among workers. Revolutionary fervor will eventually cool down and various forces within the corporate system will gradually erode the work ethic and initiative of the workers, causing corporations to lose their vital driving force. This loss of drive is unavoidable, for although the system requires a powerful moral awareness among the workers to function effectively, it is actually demolishing the morality which is its sustaining element. Chinese factories are consuming the work ethic of the workers, in much the same way as they consume raw materials.

At least as far as economic activities are concerned, even the moral upsurge related to the Revolution was not as effective as the continuous influences enforced on the minds of people through various systems incorporated into their daily work sites. In that sense, then, it can be said that most of the growth of the Chinese economy and much of the success or failure of the four 'modernizations' depends on whether a system can be created inside the economic structure that can mobilize worker initiative. This is because the PRC, like Japan, is a country that basically has no choice but to rely on its human resources as the motive force for its economic progress.

4 The Corporate System in Yugoslavia

Another way of shedding some light on the Japanese corporate structure from a different angle is to compare it with corporations in Yugoslavia. This is because Yugoslavia has a market economy system, and, in terms of there being no corporate control by capitalists or shareholders, one can view Yugoslavia as having bolstered even further some of the characteristics of large corporations in Japan.

In Yugoslavia, controls exist over foreign trade and some industries, but there is also market competition and, as a result, bankruptcies and unemployment. There are also strikes. As far as its control structure is concerned, however, the Yugoslavian corporate system is the complete opposite of corporations existing under typical capitalist economic systems. In the Yugoslavian economy there are no corporate shares and, naturally, corporate control by shareholders or capitalists does not exist. The special feature of the Yugoslavian corporate system is a system of self-management by the workers, which can be explained as follows.

Each production unit forming one technical work group in a corporation comprises anywhere from several dozen to several hundred workers. The unit is called a Basic Organization of United Workers (OOUR). In turn, a number of OOURs are organized into worker associations (RO) that provide specific finished products or services to the outside. An RO can be considered equivalent to a corporation under a capitalist system, but the difference is the high level of autonomy given the OOUR work-site units.

The OOUR is a management unit having its own balance sheet and capable of operating as an independent profit center. It establishes its own production goals, it has the authority in matters related to personnel, wages and the distribution of profits, and it is the principal unit for making contracts and has the authority to decide on joining or quitting an RO. When compared to a Japanese corporation, it is similar to an independent operating division, but is endowed with vastly greater authority and autonomy.

The foundation of the self-management system lies in the Workers' Council which is established in each OOUR, RO and Compound Organization of United Workers (SOUR), a higher ranking federation composed of OOURs and ROs. The Workers' Council of the OOUR is composed of representative members elected from each of the OOUR workshops (supervisors are not qualified to be elected). The RO Workers' Council is composed of representative members from the OOURs belonging to the RO. The SOUR Workers' Council is also formed from the members elected from the OOURs.

The basic controlling power of this series of organizations reverts back to the total assembly of employees, but powers are mainly implemented by the Workers' Councils. In the corporation (RO), the Workers' Council appoints the general director, approves annual corporate plans and annual business reports, and decides on the disposal of profits as well as corporate rules and regulations. The general director is publicly recruited through newspapers and in other ways.

For the most part, self-management by workers is performed indirectly through the election of representatives to the Workers' Council. Depending on the problem, however, the will of the workers can be exercised directly on management through OOUR workers' meetings or through a general vote. The general director is responsible to the workers controlling the corporation, or, more directly, to the Workers' Council, the equivalent of a board of directors in a capitalist system. In reverse, viewed from the workers' eyes, the Workers' Council is the organ for controlling corporate management from the standpoint of the workers.[30]

In this manner, the corporate control structure in Yugoslavia has turned the structure found in capitalist countries a full 180 degrees. When viewed as a system for having labor participate in management, and in terms of it eliminating the control of capitalists and realizing independent corporate control by workers, it has progressed a step further than the joint decision-making system by workers and shareholders found in West Germany and the Scandinavian countries and is the most thoroughgoing system.

5 The Actual Status of Self-Management

Take a look at how this system is functioning in actual practice. From the standpoint of management effectiveness, the self-management system has aspects that must be described as very inefficient. The following report describes what the results would be if the self-management system were implemented in strict compliance with the rules.

A certain wool fabric manufacturing company wanted to produce a mixed wool and synthetic fiber fabric. Before reaching a final decision on producing the new fabric, a number of formal and informal discussions were necessary.

First, in-company indoctrination was necessary to explain what synthetic fabrics were and the fact that they had started becoming popular, as well as to explain the need to raise productivity, thus making the workers aware of the need for reforms. Next, several plans had to be prepared for comparison to convince the workers that the wool-synthetic fiber fabric was the most promising plan. This required obtaining the agreement of supervisors in charge of production, marketing, finance and other areas. It was also necessary to hold an expanded supervisory council meeting with the participation of factory foremen, department heads and labor union officers.

Finally, it was necessary to hold an assembly meeting of party activists to receive approval. It was centered on the Workers' Council members and included the expanded supervisory council members, the factory workers council members, management committee members, labor union officers and the party chief secretary assigned to the corporation. If approval could be obtained in the meeting, it would then be drafted into a proposal and submitted to the Workers' Council for a decision.

If approval could not be obtained because of a conflict of opinions, and if the general director and others who drafted the original plan still wanted to carry out the program, they would either have to call for a general meeting of workers or place the plan before a general vote of all employees to receive a decision.[31]

If the foregoing accurately describes the general situation in Yugoslavia, one can see that the self-management system and management efficiency clearly cannot be achieved together.

Masayuki Iwata introduces the following case that occurred in a Yugoslavian company. The case demonstrates that if the self-management system were to be strictly implemented, it would have the potential to cause workers to become lax and confused in their discipline, which could, at times, endanger the existence of the corporation itself.

In trying to fully defend the principles of democracy, both the Federation of Communist Party Members and the local chapter of the labor union failed to take any steps to assure the selection of the most appropriate persons for the self-management organ. This resulted in the selection of a warehouse worker to be chairman of the management committee. The worker was completely ignorant of the many problems of production, but on becoming head of the assembly of workers, he believed he had become master of the corporation. He abandoned his job at the warehouse and spent all of his time visiting one office after another, shouting at the office staff and ordering them to provide him with service.

A rift subsequently occurred between the Management Committee and the Workers' Council, resulting in the creation of several factions. It became impossible for the members of the Management Committee and the Workers' Council to carry out constructive activities. For example, the Workers' Council consumed a total of 107 person-days discussing how much to pay a legal expert. Sick leave and other types of absenteeism began to increase. Financial procedures and accounting ledgers became inaccurate and delayed, thereby failing to present a true picture of the actual situation.[32]

Because of such problems, the result in Yugoslavian corporations seems to be a situation where self-management has become a mere empty shell and where the stronger the actual corporate control by general directors the better the corporation's results seem to have become.[33]

Table 2.2 clarifies the power of various groups to influence management decision-making. It shows that the real influence

Table 2.2 *Comparison of influence exerted by various groups in Yugoslavia*

Group	Average Order
Top management	1.0
Workers' council	3.8
Management committee	3.8
Professional senior staff	2.2
The Party	6.0
Middle management	3.1
Supervisors	4.7
Highly-skilled & skilled workers	6.4
Semi-skilled & unskilled workers	7.3

Source: International Institute for Labor Studies, *Bulletin* No. 9 (1972): p. 164
Note: 1 = Maximum Influencing Power

exerted by the self-management organ (the Workers' Council and Management Committee) is ranked below that of top management, staff and middle management, indicating that self-management by workers in Yugoslavia is already de facto superficial, and something quite close to technocratic control has been realized.

Nonetheless, Yugoslavia has not yet been able to achieve the goal of responsible management control by worker groups as envisioned by the drafters of the system. According to Iwata, however, it cannot be denied that when one views the total picture, the situation appears to be leaning toward the two extremes of worker tyranny and control by top managers and technocrats.[34]

6 Problems with the Self-Management System

When seen from the viewpoint of economic rationality, the first problem in self-management socialism is the enormous amount of administrative processing necessary for the implementation of self-management. This problem was amplified by the introduction of the social planning system in 1976. Under this system, the unit of self-management by workers must establish more than 50 categories of self-management contracts on its activities. To establish these contracts, time and money are consumed, many important decisions are delayed, and because the workers do not have the ability to process various types of information, they tend to become passive.[35]

The second problem lies in the fact that the self-management system recognizes large autonomous powers not in the corporation but in the OOUR. The OOUR not only plays the central role in a wide range of contract matters (even in joint venture projects with foreign corporations, the contracting party for the Yugoslavian side is the OOUR, not the corporation), but it also has its own balance sheet, accumulates and distributes profits, and even has the right to hire workers. Therefore, even within the same corporation, a worker's compensation will vary according to the OOUR to which he belongs.

A system like this can only undermine autonomy in corporate management. This is because each OOUR is often apt to give priority to its own profits rather than considering the overall corporation's profits or what is most economically rational for the corporation's management.

In Japan there are companies like Maekawa Seisakusho, the world's largest maker of refrigeration equipment, which give a wide range of autonomous powers to their individual manufacturing divisions while maintaining almost no centralized control.[36] Such systems were adopted because they were judged to be the most efficient from the standpoint of the special features of the refrigeration equipment industry. They are not forced on the corporation as is the practice in Yugoslavia.

A system providing a wide latitude of autonomy to worker groups at the work site does not always invite inefficiency. In contrast to earlier periods of capitalism, however, when capitalists were directly managing the workers, one sees that today, regardless of the economic system, the existence of indirect operations such as R&D and sales promotion have become essential. Under these circumstances, there is no assurance that the most efficient system for corporations is providing autonomy to groups of hands-on workers.

The third problem concerns restrictions placed on the free development of management because the system does not allow the issuing of shares. Since workers share in the profits of their own OOUR, if the profits accumulated within an OOUR are used for investment in the same OOUR there is no problem, but there is also no incentive to invest in an OOUR in a separate production technology group. Although interest may be paid from such investments, there is no way for workers who are responsible for the original profits to participate in profits by receiving dividends. Because workers in a newly established OOUR will receive the profits realized, it is difficult to expect existing OOURs to cooperate with them in terms of investment, and support thus must be obtained from the State, the autonomous provinces, the commune federation, or the commune itself. But because of their very nature these organizations will introduce political and social factors into their deliberations for decision-making which will warp the economic rationality of such investments.[37]

The factors undermining autonomy in corporate management are essential factors to self-management socialism: the autonomy at the work site is an expression of self-management, and the removal of shares is proof of socialism.

Another problem in the self-management system of Yugoslavia is the inadequacy of the mechanism to integrate workers into management. There are no career employment nor seniority systems in Yugoslavia. Naturally, no matter how strong the authority wielded by the general director, the Workers' Council has a strong voice in matters concerning the dismissal of workers and often overrides management decisions. In this sense, workers can be said, in effect, to have job guarantees.[38]

A systematic mechanism to retain workers in the corporation, however, is not always adequate. The current unemployment rate of more than 10 percent (excluding those workers, as everyone knows, who work in other countries) is an incentive for workers to remain with their present companies. But in the future, if that rate draws close to the full employment level, there will likely be greater labor mobility between companies. It goes without saying, of course, that this is because even the Workers' Council cannot prevent a worker from leaving a corporation if he wants to. Since workers in Yugoslavia receive profit allocations, it cannot be denied that to that extent the self-management system has some influence in integrating labor into management, but that influence is not sufficient to cause workers to stay. Rather, the principal factor keeping workers from leaving is supported largely by the coincidental factor of the current high unemployment rate.

Because of these circumstances, there is a tendency for corporations to be influenced strongly by worker-related factors when making profit allocations. Concerning this point, it is exactly the same as in the type of corporation controlled by technocrats. This is because no matter how strong the leadership shown by general directors is in carrying out their everyday managerial duties, it is necessary for them to receive a vote of confidence every four years in a Workers' Council election. Such a requirement inevitably causes the income of workers to be raised beyond the limits placed by increases in productivity.[39] To make such wage increases possible, every effort is made to increase prices. Just as workers in a capitalist system will unite to obtain increases in wages. Yugoslavian workers will also unite to raise product prices.

Under these conditions, the depreciation of corporate capital will be delayed, the renovation of facilities will become difficult and, finally, the inflation rate will be accelerated (in December 1988, retail prices were up 251 percent versus a year earlier). In recent years, this has led to a chronically unfavorable trade balance and either stagnation in, or a shrinking of, the economy.

Despite the high expectations placed on self-management in various countries, the spiritual base supporting such a system is clearly diminishing in Yugoslavia. The self-management system in Yugoslavia is said to have reached the stage in which it has become recognized that a fighting spirit is no longer a beneficial attitude, and self-management organizations are finding it more difficult to find workers willing to assume such responsibilities.[40]

Strikes are on the increase in Yugoslavia, caused, according to the Zagreb newspaper *Vjesnik*, by the 'wide gap existing between philosophy and reality'.[41]

Iwata had the following to say regarding why Yugoslavian self-management is facing difficulties:

> It was apparent in the early stages of self-management that workers did not have an adequate sense of responsibility and strong ethics, and even today, 20 years after its adoption, this remains a serious social problem.
>
> When this fact is studied closely, it must be quite obvious that workers, who throughout the pages of history have always been the exploited, the abused, the ruled, the managed and the controlled, have not developed within themselves the sense of responsibility and ethics founded on basic qualities of self-management, free management and free control required in a controller, a decision-maker and a manager. The present system, however, can be called self-management by workers exactly because it reflects as is the low level of awareness held by workers. By realizing their low level of ethics and shallow sense of responsibility – as exposed by the self-management system – workers will reflect on their behavior and, through serious self-criticism and group criticism, will establish a social consciousness and a sense of responsibility as workers on their own.[42]

Although such aspects definitely may exist, the true nature of the Yugoslavian problem lies not in ethics, but in the faults of the system itself.

While the system grants authority to workers, there is no close relationship between their interests and their corporation's rises and falls. Work groups in Yugoslavia have much authority concerning the allocation of profits and thus there exists a limited degree of mutual benefit in the short term, in the sense that workers participate in the profits if the corporation shows good results. But if the corporation goes bankrupt, workers suffer almost no unfavorable effects at all, although the general directors are restricted from holding similar positions in other corporations for a certain period.

Social welfare is guaranteed through local autonomous units peculiar to Yugoslavia called communes, and if a corporation bankrupts they can find another job. The ties of common interests are very weak between the corporation and employee in Yugoslavia, and it is impossible for Yugoslavian workers to be strongly interested the way Japanese workers are in the ups and downs of their corporation.

Medium-sized and larger corporations in Japan and the self-managed corporations in Yugoslavia are similar in terms of the limited extent or the total absence of capitalist control, but there is a difference concerning the position of the worker. In Japan, workers have been turned into corporate employees, but in Yugoslavia, as Albert Meister points out, corporations are lacking elements where employees bear corporate risk:

> The problem exists in the absence of group punishment, similar to individual punishment, that emerged naturally in capitalistic models. Labor groups have authority, but when failures occur they are never punished in the sense of taking blame for group failure. There is no collective responsibility in a socialist corporate group corresponding to bankruptcy in a private corporation.[43]

Mainly in accordance with their employment customs, Japanese employees are firmly tied to the corporation and will suffer as a group for the failures of their corporation. Bankruptcies not only cause unemployment, but also – regardless of any personal responsibility – nullify any accumulation of intangible worth, such as future promotion possibilities and pay increases for the individual worker, the accomplishments of the worker, and the corporation's evaluation of those accomplishments. The foregoing are the source of the employee's self-assertive interest in corporate management and the root of his fierce, competitive energy.

Yugoslavian workers are freed of punishment in almost all situations. In that context, it is only natural that competition in the market does not intensify and that the tendency is to consider corporations as targets for 'milking'. In short, the difference between Japan and Yugoslavia lies in the fact that Japanese employees control corporations as corporate employees whereas Yugoslavian employees control corporations while remaining as workers. The capitalists in the early stages of capitalism invested their own funds to buy facilities and employ workers, and they managed their companies with a sense of responsibility. The source of that sense of responsibility was not tied to their control of the corporation but to the fact that they invested their own money, forcing them to bear the corporate risk as individuals. They paid close attention to details and enthusiastically managed their company knowing that they would suffer losses if they did not. On the other hand, Yugoslavia's self-management system first granted control and then waited in vain for a sense of responsibility to develop. It is pure fantasy to believe that control by management alone can develop a corresponding level of responsibility.

In Japan, employees were forced to develop a sense of responsibility by their assumption of a share of corporate risk. They learned to exercise authority due to self-assertive participation in corporate operations. One can say of this situation that responsibility gave birth to authority. Yugoslavia is trying to achieve the opposite.

It is clear that the Yugoslavian system is directly contrary to the capitalist system. Yugoslavian legislators probably reasoned that since capitalists controlled corporations in a capitalist system and Yugoslavia was a country of workers, it was essential for workers to control corporations. Thus, a system completely antithetical to capitalism came into being.

Nonetheless, between these two seemingly opposing systems, there is a common basic point. Both capitalism and Yugoslavia's brand of socialism consider the corporation as an object to control and not as an arena of participation. The two systems exist in the same dimension. Likened to a clock, they share the same face, but the hands of the two systems are 180 degrees apart. The Japanese system, meanwhile, has a different clock face altogether; it exists in a different dimension.

Notes

1 Kazushi Suzuki and Heizo Takenaka, 'Nihon Kigyo wa Chokiteki Shiya de Toshi – Eiberu Riron ni Yoru Nichibei Hikaku' (Japanese Corporations Invest with Long-Term Perspective – Japan–US Comparison Using Abelian Theory). *Nihon Keizai Shimbun*, (Tokyo), February 2, 1982.

2 Akihiro Okumura, *Nihon no Toppu Manejimento* (Top Management in Japan). Tokyo: Daiyamondosha, 1982, p. 33.

3 G. F. Mechlin and D. Berg, 'Evaluating Research – ROI Is Not Enough', *Harvard Business Review*, 10–11 (1980), p. 94.

4 Yukio Sato, 'Tsuyosa wa Ikashi Sarani Atarashii Seisan Gijutsu no Kaihatsu e' (Utilize Strengths and Further Develop New Production Technology), *IE*, 10 (1980), p. 18.

5 Moriaki Tsuchiya, 'Gendai Kigyo no Jirenma' (Dilemma of Contemporary Corporations), *Hogaku Semina Zokan, Sogo Tokushu Series 14, Gendai no Kigyo*, Nihon Hyoronsha, 1980, pp. 29–30.

6 Robert H. Hayes and William J. Abernathy, 'Managing Our Way to Economic Decline', *Harvard Business Review*, July-August (1980), p. 75.

7 *Washington Post*, March 29, 1981. Also, external directors account for 85 percent of all directors on the Board of General Electric, a high percentage among American corporations. See: Shiro Ishiyama, ed., *Nichibei Keiesha no Hasso* (Ways of Thinking of American and Japanese Managers). Tokyo, PHP Research Center, 1980, p. 253.

8 Regarding this point, see: Sumner Marcus and Kenneth D. Walters, 'Assault on Managerial Autonomy', *Harvard Business Review*, Vol. 56, No. 1, January-February (1978), pp. 57–66.

9 'Amerika no Shagai Juyaku to Juyaku Kennin Seido' (American System of External Directors and Concurrent Directors). *Shoji Homu,* November 25 (1979), p. 36.

10 Shiro Ishiyama, ed., Konosuke Matsushita and Louis Lundborg in *Nichibei Keiesha no Hasso* (Ways of Thinking of American and Japanese Managers). Tokyo, PHP Research Center, 1980, pp. 257–65.

11 Ningen Noryoku Kaihatsu Senta, ed., 'Rodosha o Toshite Mita Eiko-kubyo' (The British 'Sickness' Seen through Workers). *Ningen Noryoku Kaihatsu Shiriizu*, 51 (1978), pp. 12–13.

12 Koji Tatsuoka, 'Gogome Gijutsu' ni Tsuyoi ga 'Hachigome Gijutsu' ni Mada Yowasa' (Strong in Terms of Mid-Range Technology but Still Weak Concerning Higher Range Technology). *IE*, 10 (1980), p. 21.

13 Yoshiro Ikari, 'Nihon no Jidosha Kojo – Seisan Gijutsu Reberu wa

Tashika ni Takai; da ga Jakuten mo' (Japanese Automobile Plants: Indeed, the Level of Manufacturing Technology Is High, yet There Are Shortcomings). *IE*, 10 (1980), p. 25.

14 Policy Planning and Research Department, Ministry of Labor, *Roshi Komyunikeishon Chosa Hokoku* (Report on Survey of Communication Between Labor and Management), 1984.

15 Concerning the joint decision system in West Germany, see: Kyoichi Futagami, *Nishi Doitsu Kigyoron* (Discussion of West German Corporations). Tokyo, Toyo Keizai Shimposha, 1971.

16 Concerning the system of management participation in Sweden, see: Ningen Noryoku Kaihatsu Senta, ed., 'Sei Hokuo Yonkakoku no Rodosha Keieisanka Hikaku' (Comparison of Worker Participation in Management in Four Countries of Western and Northern Europe). *Ningen Noryoku Kaihatsu Shiriizu*, 35 (1978), p. 20.

17 Yoshitoshi Mabuchi, *Hadaka no Nishi Doitsu Keizai* (West Germany's Economy without Adornment). Tokyo, Nihon Shoseki, 1979, pp. 195-8.

18 Paul Einzig, *Decline and Fall? Britain's Crisis in the Sixties*. New York, Macmillan/St Martin's Press, 1969, p. 134.

19 Concerning the system of corporate management in the PRC before introducing reforms, see: Kazuo Asakai, *Chugoku no Kigyo Keiei* (Corporate Management in China). Tokyo, Japan Productivity Center, 1972, pp. 65–76.

20 Huan Xiang 'Chong Guanliao dao Jingli' (From the Bureaucracy to Company Presidents). *Jingji Guangli*, Jingji Guanli Zazhishe 11 (1980), XI-6.

21 Huan, XI-5.

22 Ma Hong, Guanyu Gongyie Jingji Guanli Wenti (Concerning Problems of Managing an Industrial Economy) Tigao Qìyie Jìanli Shuiping (Let's Raise the Level of Corporate Management). Beijing: Zhongguo Shehui Kexue Chubanshe, 1979, p. 12. This book was compiled from reports of an enterprise administration research group under the aegis of the State Economic Commission.

Japanese experts who visited Chinese plants reported that an atmosphere exists in which workers and their supervisors cannot talk frankly to one other. For example, see: Mitsuo Ogura, 'Shakaishugi Keizai Kensetsu to Chugoku Kigyo no Jittai' (Establishment of Socialistic Economy and Actual Situation in Chinese Enterprises). *Sekai Keizai Hyoron*, Sekai Keizai Kenkyu Kyokai, April (1981), p.9.

23 Huan, XI-7. 'In Western nations, according to the article, much importance is placed on labor's right to speak out in corporations. For example, in Sweden, West Germany and Japan, where the economy has developed comparatively strongly, labor is participating in management and workers speak out in a wide area of issues.

Meanwhile, although a slogan offered by followers of Mao Tse Tung has urged Chinese companies to 'let supervisors and workers participate in management and let both parties work closely with members of the political works committee', these processes are not being carried out well. Japan is doing a much better job in this area.'

24 Ma, p. 23.
25 Ogura, p. 6.
26 Ma, p. 12.
27 Xue Moqiao, *Zhongguo Shehuizhuyi Jingji Wenti Yianjiu* (Research of Problems in China's Socialist Economy). Beijing, Waiwen Chubanshe, 1980, p. 109.
28 Sun Shangqing, *Guanyu Qiyile Guanli Wenti* (Concerning Problems in Enterprise Administration) Tigao Qiyie Jianli Shuiping (Let's Raise the Level of Enterprise Administration). Zhongguo Shehui Kexue Chubanshe, 1979, p. 12.
29 Ma, p. 12.
30 Regarding the system of self-management in Yugoslavia, see: ILO, ed., *Yugosurabia no Kigyo ni Okeru Rodosha Jishukanri Seido* (Labor's Self-Management System in Yugoslavian Enterprises). Tokyo, Shiseido, 1974, Part II.

    The summary of the self-management system as related in this book is owed in great part to the following two sources: Masayuki Iwata, *Jishukanri Rengo Rodo Shisutemu no Rinenzo* (Ideal Image of Self-Management Federated Labor System), pp. 157–166; and Japan–Yugoslavia Economic Committee, *Nihon to Yugosurabia* (Japan and Yugoslavia). 1981.
31 JETRO, ed., *Yugosurabia no Shijo Keizai to Kigyo Keiei* (Yugoslavia's Market Economy and Enterprise Management), 1977, pp. 59–60.
32 Masayuki Iwata, *Rodosha Jishu Kanri* (Self-Management by Workers). Tokyo, Kinokuniya Shoten, 1978, pp. 200–201.
33 Veljko Rus, *Sangyo Minshushugi to Jishukanri: Yugosurabia no Keiken* (Industrial Democracy and Self-Management Experience of Yugoslavia), jointly translated by Akihiro Ishikawa, Sen Inuzuka and Takashi Suzuki. Tokyo, Godo Shuppan, 1980, p. 136.

    A number of studies indicate that the more centralized the power of an enterprise, the more successful the economic performance of that enterprise. Generally, the successful managers to date have been 'benevolent dictators'. Though the 'benevolent dictators' do not cooperate with the self-management organization (as the situation has been unstable in Yugoslavia), they have won the support of the workers.
34 Iwata, p. 209.
35 Nozomu Abe, 'Jishukanrigata Shakaishugi ni Okeru Keikakuka no

Genjitsu' (The Actual Situation Regarding Planning under the Self-Management Type of Socialism), *Keizai Hyoron*, 5 (1980), pp. 144–5.

36 Masaru Kamata, *Ikigai Keiei no Gaika* (Victory of Management That Shows Employees' Work Is Meaningful). Tokyo, Nihon Keiei Shuppankai, 1976, pp. 31–52.

37 Much was learned from Nozomu Abe about problems related to the self-management system.

38 Albert Meister, *Jishukanri no Rinen to Genjitsu* (Ideals and Reality of Self-Management). Tokyo, Shinyosha, 1979, pp. 225–6.

39 Meister, p. 56.

40 Meister, p. 247.

41 'Keizai Seicho o Habamu Mujun to Masatsu mo Yugo Jishukanri Shakaishugi no Jittai' (Contradictions and Frictions Hampering Economic Growth Are Also Part of the Actual Situation in Yugoslavia's Self-Management Socialism). *Sekai Shuho*, 11–10 (1981), p. 32.

42 Iwata, p. 202.

43 Meister, pp. 218–9.

3 The Progressive Nature of the Japanese Corporate System

In terms of solving various economic issues, how does the Japanese corporate system fare when compared to those of other countries? There are three pieces of circumstantial evidence suggesting that that found in Japan is superior to systems in other countries and that at the very least it has proven to be the most suitable corporate system for meeting the conditions of our twentieth century industrial society.

If one looks at the overall period from the end of the Second World War to the present, it is possible to see that even without discussing economic systems, Japan's economy has greatly outclassed that of every other nation.

Many reasons have been put forward to explain this. These include the advantages enjoyed by Japan owing to its having developed later than other countries; the fact that the destruction of old plants and equipment made it easier to introduce new equipment; totally coincidental external developments, such as the Korean War, boosting the Japanese economy, and so on. The problem here, however, is that these explanations lose their validity when one recognizes that Japan's economic growth has had remarkable staying power and that even today Japan's economy demonstrates outstanding vitality among the nations of the world.

Japan does not have an abundance of land or natural resources; neither can the qualities of the Japanese people be considered particularly outstanding. The frequently mentioned diligence of Japanese workers, for example, as will be shown later, is an extremely doubtful argument. One cannot say either that the Japanese are blessed with a superior intelligence, especially if one notes that even today most of the basic creative achievements in science and technology still come from North America and Europe. Rather than creating advances, it can only be said that the Japanese have generally been better at applying and improving on them. In short, there are no convincing explanations for the

109

tremendous development of Japanese industry to be found in either the land or natural resources, or the diligence or intelligence of the Japanese people.

On the other hand, the Japanese corporate system is unique to Japan. Except for affiliated companies overseas, the only examples of this system are found in the partial introduction of Japanese-style management by some companies in the West. Japan is the only country where this system is established as the social norm.

Regarding this, Toshio Shishido of the Nikko Research Center made the following observations:

> When comparing management in different nations, we become aware of something quite important. Although the management cultures of the United States and Europe, Central and South America, Southeast Asia, and Africa and the Middle East have distinctive characteristics, essentially they all accord with one another. In contrast, the Japanese management culture comprises something quite different and separate. Even the management cultures of the countries of East Asia that are closest to Japan – Korea and Taiwan – belong essentially to the Euro-American stream, and have little affinity with Japan. In somewhat extreme terms, one could say there are two types of management in the world, Japanese and non-Japanese.[1]

These comments suggest that quite a strong argument exists for linking Japan's economic development to its unique corporate system.

The second piece of circumstantial evidence is environmental. In short, the Japanese corporate system evolved in an environment to which it did not always conform and was sometimes opposed, both systematically and ideologically. In this respect, the Japanese system is directly antithetical to the Yugoslavian system. Yugoslavia created its system of self-management when it seceded from the Soviet Bloc, moved away from the Soviet model, and introduced liberal economic elements, while still asserting the ideological need of a socialist state for the 'proletariat' to maintain complete control over companies. This system, therefore, evolved from a political rather than an economical standpoint, and its cornerstone is Yugoslavia's basic concept of 'the State', as defined in its constitution. In fact, whenever Yugoslavia's system of self-management is referred to, the discussion almost always centers on the system's legal structure rather than on how it actually functions.

Meister says, 'Self-management is a creation of jurists rather than of people'. And if one considers the process through which the system was established and the nature of the system, one can find ample reason to question whether self-management is really rooted in the internal necessities of Yugoslavia's economy, i.e., whether it has true relevance as an economic system.

In Japan, on the other hand, the situation is exactly the opposite. Even today, almost all the systems in Japan – comprised of corporate, labor and other laws – are capitalist, but the reality that is developing cannot strictly be called capitalist. However, as long as the systems are capitalist, their influence on Japanese reality works contrary to the formation of a Japanese-style corporate structure.

Concerning postwar Japan as well, one can say the influence of the dominant thinking and ideology also ran contrary to the existing reality. Based on the generally accepted idea of what capitalism should be, Japanese management has been and continues to be criticized as a distorted system which ignores the rights of shareholders.

Marxism, which gained a considerable measure of influence in postwar Japan, continually tried to introduce the class struggle ideology into Japanese corporations that were essentially organized as communal bodies of corporate employees.

Thus, neither the economic system nor the ideology in Japan have encouraged the development of a unique corporate system. Yet in contrast to the Yugoslavian model, the Japanese system has defied the retrogressive and obstructive forces generated by the various systems at work, and gradually became a reality. A close review of the development process provides sufficient reason to suspect that the Japanese system embodies a rationality and practicability firmly rooted in the deepest recesses of the economy.

The third piece of evidence is as follows. Most medium-sized and smaller companies in Japan do not have a strong Japanese quality about them. In short, compared to large corporations, they are much more capitalistic. The capitalist control of those companies is strong, or, rather, one could go as far as to say that in many of those companies the capitalists are also the top managers and employees are not as integrated as in large corporations. But it is interesting to note that when a medium-sized or smaller company becomes outstanding, it tends gradually to resemble a large corporation, at least in terms of how it manages labor.

Shizuo Matsushima documented this phenomenon in a survey he conducted in 1963. In it, he compared 'model' medium-sized and smaller companies with ordinary companies. The 'model' companies were designated by the Small and Medium Enterprise Agency as outstanding companies to be used as references by other companies in evaluating themselves. In his survey, Matsushima said the model companies are 'highly Japanese' and in no way inferior to large corporations in terms of labor management.[2]

This conclusion suggests one of two possibilities – either that companies with a Japanese-style corporate system have an advantage in competitive growth, or that medium-sized and smaller companies are trying to make the transition to a Japanese-type corporate system if they can remove the various restrictions they face because of their small scale. (Compared to large corporations, for example, medium-sized and smaller companies provide a lower-level of welfare benefits and less social status to their employees, with the result that the company risk borne by employees is also lower.) This can also be used as proof when determining that the Japanese-type corporate system is superior to the original capitalist system.

The above facts are all circumstantial evidence. Although some may say that even though they are circumstantial they are quite convincing, others will say no matter how convincing they are, they are still only circumstantial. Concerning the second and third points, in particular, one might also say it is not because the Japanese-style corporate system has universal advantages over orthodox capitalism, but merely that as a result of existing in the special Japanese sociocultural context, the system has demonstrated the potential for being advantageous. That is why the outstanding qualities of this system must be clarified in more specific terms.

1 Changes in Management Structure

In Western corporations, investors and shareholders force heavy demands on management to increase short-term profits. Labor unions, too, force various restrictive practices onto corporations, and the corporation has become the setting for disputes and confrontations between the different interests of labor and management.

In fact, both sides waste much energy on such disputes which hamper the development of rationalized management policies and a labor configuration appropriate for realizing corporate goals. As well, the decision-making process relating to management policy often ends up being a political compromise between the two groups.

The strengths of the Japanese corporation are not easily understood if one looks only at Japan. The nature of those strengths is such that they quickly become apparent when comparing Japanese corporations to those in other countries.

In terms of the degree of freedom they have to pursue policies considered to be desirable for further development, Japanese corporations easily surpass those of other countries. Japanese corporations also excel in terms of the extent to which they can channel the energies of their employees toward achieving corporate objectives. In short, one of the fundamental strengths of the Japanese corporate system is the high degree of autonomy held by management.

The integration of labor and management

A degree of tension exists in labor–management relations in Western countries that many Japanese would have trouble imagining. In those relations, both parties approach each other believing it is to their advantage to draw as many concessions from the other as possible. Both have a certain degree of power, but neither is powerful enough to force the other into complete submission; thus, it is possible to see the development of a sort of political game between labor and management.

Looking at relations with the trade unions, i.e., relations

between labor and management, we see a situation where neither is able to get on with the other, and each is continuously watching the actions of the other. To cite a somewhat extreme example, the following is taken from a record of negotiations between steel workers and their management. Two sets of toilets were customarily built on work sites – one for staff use, and one for worker use. A staff member, however, once caught a worker using the staff toilet. This incident was brought to the negotiating table and management said it could not allow such violations of the rules, and the complaint was duly recorded in the minutes of the negotiations. A bit further on in the same set of minutes, however, a separate complaint was lodged, this time by the workers about the staff using the workers' toilet, which, they claimed, was exactly the opposite of what the staff had just been complaining about, thereby playing tit for tat.

Certainly, as long as the nature of labor–management relations remains one in which both are continually watching each other, it is highly unlikely that they will achieve any degree of getting used to each other.[3]

Few strikes and apparently peaceful labor relations hide the fact that even in West Germany there is no difference in terms of a tense relationship between labor and management. There are few strikes because both sides have a forum giving them equal opportunities for discussion, and workers can have their opinions heard and reflected in management policies. Tough negotiations are held between both sides inside the company.[4] They still face each other with a fundamental conflict of interests. The only difference between West Germany and, say, England is that the latter does not have a systematic framework in which labor and management can talk to each other.

Workers in the West often block the introduction of new technology or facilities. They do so because the size of the labor force is generally calculated on the basis of the total amount of work divided by the number of standard work units. If the introduction of new technology or equipment increases productivity, the number of standard work units increases and there is a definite reduction in employment. That is how the worker thinks. New technology also often renders the old skilled labor redundant. There is no doubt that new technology has a great impact on

Japan's skilled workers as well, but they still have the essential asset of belonging to a specific company. On the other hand, it is natural for workers in the West, who have almost no other asset to depend upon except their own skill, to see new technology as nothing more than a recipe for disaster.

Christopher Herman, one of the spokesmen for the New Left movement in the United Kingdom, advocates, in *How to Battle with New Technologies*, that the following strategies be adopted by trade unions. He says that employees should not lodge voluntary resignations, agree to 'natural reduction', allow the boundaries of previously existing jobs to become unclear, and increase shift work, but should insist on a written guarantee from management that no new technology will be introduced without the prior consent of the workers. Moreover, he comments on labor relations as follows:

> Whenever management says new technology will make the lives of the workers easier, it's up to us to show our fellow workers they're lying. We tell management to prove what they're saying. We say guarantee us in advance there'll be no reduction in the overall labor force and that there'll be an improvement in labor conditions because of fewer working hours per week. We say give us something in writing saying there'll be no increase in our individual work load. Until management responds, we will not work with any new technology.[5]

Even if management somehow finds a way to convince the workers to accept the introduction of new machinery, the workers will resist any shift in labor to other divisions within the company and insist that operations continue in exactly the same manner as before, which often places management in the predicament of having no choice but to accept the double investment this represents.

Einzig made the following comment on this attitude which is so often displayed by workers:

> The way in which British trade unions endeavour to create artificial scarcity of manpower is nothing if not flagrantly antisocial. Millions of men and women are underworked

because of restrictive practices on their individual output and especially on the activities of their mates.[6]

The problem, however, does not essentially lie in the ethics of workers, but in the systematic environment which has led them to fail to link their common interests with the public interest.

Thus, as well as having systematic practices which have clearly lost any semblance of economy, the Western corporate system also carries losses arising from its inability to get workers to show initiative, i.e., invisible losses.

One such problem is reflected in the fact that as workers are trained in the use of new production processes, technology and facilities, many difficulties are encountered in trying to link the effect of this experience, which ordinarily results in an improvement in work efficiency, to an overall improvement in corporate productivity. In the West, the standard task is negotiated and fixed between labor and management – together with attendant wage rates – as a single package. Just as in the discussion of wage rates both labor and management are inevitably confronted with a sharp conflict of interest when it comes to making decisions about the standard task. Thus, it is necessary for management to collect data about standard tasks to support its case for a decision. But when management actually goes out to measure the standard task workers deliberately slack off and slow down the pace of production.[7]

In West Germany, management cannot record task levels without prior notice. In short, they are obligated by law to inform the labor union before carrying out any such recordings to ensure that workers do not suffer any loss as a result. This practice indicates just how closely the conflicting interests of labor and management are focused on this issue.

In the West, the level of the standard task reflects the power balance and other relations between labor and management. That level is decided through a process of dispute and compromise. There is no guarantee that the level finally decided on will be suitable in terms of being sufficiently economic; once the level is set, moreover, it is not easily altered, since an increase in a standard task at the same wage rate is the same as lowering the wage rate, thus resulting in a deterioration of working conditions.

In general, Japanese employees will faithfully attempt to ensure that the effect of experience will be reflected in improvements in work efficiency; also, employee suggestions and innovations at the work site are not individual, coincidental phenomena, but rather, are regulated in the form of a suggestion system and small group activities that are indispensable elements for management. In the West, however, no such systematized initiative can be expected from workers.

Some Western companies have adopted a system similar to the one used in Japan, but it is not easy for them to make it viable in the same way a Japanese company could. The following example from West Germany illustrates this point.

> The suggestion system is not as popular in West Germany as in Japan, but some companies have adopted it and reward good suggestions. But even if work methods may be improved, workers realize that if they propose all the ideas they have for improvements, they will be tying a noose around their own necks. As a consequence, very few workers make suggestions. The reason for the lack of suggestions is that the workers receive piecework wages at an hourly wage rate. The basis for calculating the piecework wages, then, is time and work units, and a work study expert measures the standard work units. If the method of performing work operations changes because of an improvement suggestion, and if, as a result, the number of standard work units increases, real wages are thus, in effect, decreased.[8]

This clearly indicates that the lack of initiative and creativity is not caused by a human resource problem. Rather, the overall environment surrounding the workers is the root cause, and the problem is obviously a structural one.

The company itself does not demand worker initiative as a prerequisite, nor does it expect it. In fact, the management system is devised so that operations are still possible without these elements.

In the area of QC as well, there are severe limitations in a system that is unable to rely on worker initiative.

The formula used to date for guaranteeing quality is referred to as the Acceptable Quality Level (AQL) guarantee. The figure signifies the maximum level of defects per item which would still be acceptable to the buyer in the average production lot. The supplier conducts a sampling inspection at the time the order is dispatched to guarantee the delivery of products at the AQL level demanded by the buyer. If the level of defective items arrived at using this formula was expressed as a percentage quality control level, i.e., one defective item in 100 is acceptable but two or three are not, this system would be sufficiently workable.

Japanese corporations, however, are heading toward PPM (parts per million) control. As the name implies, the PPM control system attempts to reduce the defect rate to a level where it can be measured in units of about one per one million. As a consequence, the previous practice of performing quality checks as part of the inspection process is no longer possible. Also, this system necessitates that all imperfections be removed, as much as possible, at the design stage for the production process and equipment, and that impurities also be removed from the raw materials selected for use. It may be possible, of course, for Western companies to achieve this degree of control, but of the three principal elements affecting the quality of a product – equipment, technology and work level – the main problem is work level. A system unable to rely on worker initiative cannot compete in the area of PPM control.

The traditional QC formula used in the West can basically be summed up as a system under which workers perform tasks that are described in a work procedures manual and inspectors remove defective items during an inspection check. The responsibility for QC lies with the technicians who manage the inspection process; the line workers are only directly obligated to follow the instructions in the work procedures manual. They have no responsibility for QC. For PPM control, however, it is impossible to achieve QC simply by carrying out sampling inspections since the level of defective items must be kept to only a few per million. If one tried to achieve this level of control via inspections, it would be necessary to closely inspect almost every item, which, needless to say, is not an economically practical proposition. What is required for PPM control is an improvement in the work level, which can only be achieved by relying on the initiative of the workers to maintain and improve quality.

If, by chance, some new form of production technology is developed in the future which will effectively remove any possibility that the work level may affect the quality of a product, this point would no longer be relevant. Unless something like this occurs, however, it will not be any easy task, at least for the time being, to attempt to achieve a high level of QC under an operational system in which workers cannot be expected to show initiative.[9]

In any consideration of the issues surrounding the improvement of productivity and QC, therefore, it is impossible to ignore the fundamental differences that are evident between the corporate systems of Japan and the West, i.e., the differences between a system in which management and the workers are united, and one in which capital and labor are forced under the same corporate umbrella while still in opposing camps. Against the background of all the superficial differences in management styles and the structure of labor in Japanese and Western corporations, this fundamental reality remains at the heart of the matter.

The need to internalize labor

It is still a universal truth that agriculture is the so-called Achilles heel of the socialist state. It is well known that, whereas agricultural communes have achieved poor results, highly productive results are seen when approval or tacit consent is given for private management of land. Many reasons can explain this phenomenon, but the truth is that farming simply does not adapt well to the authoritative control which inevitably accompanies communal production systems. Farming is, by its very nature, an occupation in which it is extremely difficult to objectify labor; neither is it easy to measure the value of the labor provided by those engaged in farming, nor to observe their work. It is therefore also very difficult to create an appropriate labor structure through higher level controls. In the final analysis, a system which claims to be controlling agricultural labor really only effectively controls its volume – it is virtually impossible to control its quality.

A Chinese youth from a farming village recalled the situation in his village as follows:

> Farmers earned their living depending on how many work
> points they earned. Those who didn't work, didn't eat.
> Anyway, if you didn't build up enough points, you couldn't
> survive. The people were just like bees buzzing around a hive;
> they all looked quite busy. Very few of them thought about
> such things as work efficiency or receiving a level of

remuneration consistent with their labor because there was nothing they could do to change the situation anyway.

Farmers were rewarded according to the work they did. If they took a day off, they lost a day's quota of labor points, and the day was not counted when accounts were settled at the end of the year. A day's worth of allocated points was reduced. This is why any mechanization or rationalization of farming that can be done manually is not welcomed.[10]

Given the technical conditions of production, on the other hand, industrial labor has little diversification and is highly repetitious, and thus is comparatively easy to objectify and standardize. In relative terms, it is certainly much simpler to observe the work performed by individual laborers according to objective criteria, assess results, punish laziness or mistakes with a reduction in wages or other measures and reward diligence and efficiency with higher compensation, i.e., to use the 'carrot and stick' method of control, with industrial labor than it is with agricultural labor.

Regardless of whether the country in question is capitalist or socialist, both adopt a system of authoritative control from above in industry. In socialist states such as the Soviet Union, for example, a typical Taylor system of management has been adopted.[11] The technical nature of industrial labor has been a significant contributing factor that has somehow allowed these countries to come as far as they have.

Progress in industrial technology today, however, is gradually changing the conditions relating to industry. Not all of the changes being witnessed at present are all encompassing, but the direction in which developments are heading is becoming clear.

Simple repetitive labor is now being increasingly replaced by machinery, industrial labor is becoming more diversified and complex, and quality rather than quantity of labor has now assumed crucial importance. As a result, it has become increasingly difficult for companies to control and regulate industrial labor from above. A situation is now arising whereby management is being forced to rely on the initiative of individual workers, whether it likes it or not.

A more systematized form of basic knowledge and judgment based on that knowledge is now being demanded even within the labor structure of the chemical and other processing industries, which illustrates the kind of labor that monitors control panels in its most typical form.[12] Depending on the circumstances relating to a given work site, the workers themselves, in the interests of accident prevention, may halt either all or part of the production process on the basis of an impromptu examination of machinery. Thus, if a worker makes an incorrect assessment, his judgment may lead to huge losses for the company. In the past, the halting of production had to wait for a decision from management. Today, however, because of changes in the technical conditions of production, it has become necessary for important decisions, such as the one mentioned above, to be left to workers at the work site.

In the machinery industries today, numerically controlled industrial machinery and robots are rapidly replacing not only unskilled labor, but even skilled labor to a certain extent. At this stage, it would probably be better to refrain from making any positive assertions about the effects of this trend on the labor structure, particularly as far as the introduction of robot technology is concerned. Robots are fundamentally man-machine systems that give rise to a demand for a complex and highly skilled type of labor required to carry out the functions of program teaching and 'application engineering', which resolves the questions of the number of robots to be used, the factory layout and the scope of the robots' work according to the needs of each factory.

In companies that have introduced robots, moreover, one can see the emergence of multi-functional workers, i.e., workers whose scope of operations has expanded horizontally so that they operate several different types of machines. Workers have also become vertically multi-functional, such as, for example, when surplus workers at one level of operation undertake tasks at a higher level. The vertical levels upward, for example, could be direct operations, parts programming, design and market research.[13] Expansion of the tasks of workers in either a horizontal or a vertical direction results in making labor more complicated and more sophisticated.

There is a theory which states that automation increases the need for unskilled labor, but it is not generally regarded as a theory founded on sound economics. Although one may say that unskilled labor is simple manual labor, it is at times quite complicated in a mechanical engineering sense. Still, it is certainly much easier to replace unskilled labor with machinery than it is to replace complicated, more sophisticated labor that includes human mental functions. It is essentially economic constraints that are preventing many companies from replacing unskilled labor with automated machinery or robots. This is clearly attested to, it is said, by the fact that companies in the West have not introduced robots to the extent that Japanese companies have because the former have had access to cheap labor in the form of migrant workers and minority groups from lower social strata.

If the capital equipment ratio for an entire national economy were to increase, wages would also increase, giving rise to an even stronger incentive to replace human unskilled labor with machinery.

As this trend continues, the proportion of the labor force accounted for by complex, sophisticated types of labor will grow, and attempts to regulate labor through a system of authoritative controls administered from above will become less and less workable. In that sense, as far as the labor structure is concerned, industry will gradually move closer to agriculture in nature.

In these circumstances, it will obviously become increasingly difficult for any industry's management system to operate smoothly if it is unable to evoke a sufficient degree of initiative from those who work under it, in the same way that agriculture is proving to be a problem for socialist states. It is highly likely that the direction of future developments will inevitably demonstrate even more clearly the rationality of a management system in which labor is internalized and labor and management are integrated.

2 Labor

In abstract terms, one of the fundamental characteristics of the free economic system relates to the way in which individuals, motivated by a desire for private gain, amass all the factors of production and join in the field of a corporation by means of a process of market choice.

Under this type of system, the individual is basically responsible for resolving issues relating to the development and maintenance of his motivation, the cultivation of his skills and the choosing of his jobs.

In Japan, however, reality does not always conform to this model. Responsibility for many of these issues has in fact been shifted to the corporation. The Japanese corporation, in addition to allocating labor, is itself somewhat like an educational institution as far as issues relating to ethics and skills are concerned.

Cultivating labor ethics

In the West, the motivation of workers is one given element in the social environment over which the corporation can exercise very little control. As long as the primary forces supporting the individual's motivation for working – religion and traditional values – prevail, the corporation can reap the benefits. But if those forces weaken, the result would be an extremely undesirable environment for industrial activity. In any case, the corporation has no choice but to accept any given situation. In contemporary industrial society, however, it seems that the social environment has given rise to a clear trend toward a lower level of worker motivation.

This phenomenon can in part be attributed to the weakening influence of religion and traditional values, but it relates also to the fact that the greater the development of advanced industrialized nations, the more affluent their societies become, which results in the emergence of a variety of welfare systems. In this sort of society, unemployment no longer represents the dire threat to the individual that it once did. If conditions of full employment exist, it is still a relatively simple matter for a worker to find a job, and if for some reason no job is available, the worker can still manage to exist on social welfare benefits. It is inevitable that the reduction in individual risk brought about by the transition to a welfare state in effect also greatly diminishes the will to work, which is based on a desire for personal gain as an individual determines his own future. Under the Western corporate system, this sort of decline in worker motivation immediately creates disadvantageous operating conditions for corporations.

Japanese corporations, on the other hand, are equipped with a series of built-in mechanisms for sustaining worker motivation, and a situation like that described above would not constitute a deadly blow to the company. One of those mechanisms stems from the very nature of the corporate system, which places the burden of corporate risk on the individual. For workers employed under a system whereby an individual's position within the company, and, accordingly, his social status, are gradually elevated according to how long he has worked for a company – accompanied by a corresponding increase in remuneration – even if a situation of full employment exists, and no matter how complete the system of social guarantees is, nothing can compensate for the sudden loss in social status carefully built up over the years that would immediately be suffered by an individual if his company were to go bankrupt.

For Japanese workers, then, bankruptcy does not simply represent unemployment. Because the seniority system has also become a social system, re-employment means starting one's career anew from a low rank in another company. If a worker is unwilling to pursue this option, he has no choice but to join a medium-sized or smaller company, or some other organization that places less importance on the seniority system. In either case, he will not be spared the pain of a significant drop in both his economic and, particularly, his social status.

These unique conditions pertaining to Japanese corporations, whereby individuals are compelled to bear the burden of corporate risk as a group – whether they like it or not – operate inside the corporation to cultivate worker motivation.

There is also evidence in contemporary Japan of a decline in worker motivation arising from the influence exerted by society on the individual, in much the same way that a similar decline has occurred in the West.

A survey conducted in 1972, for example, based on interviews with youths from 11 countries around the world, revealed that a relatively higher proportion of Japanese compared to other respondents[14] said they felt it was 'important in society today to have time to take things easy instead of working all the time', indicating that they held ideals opposed to the work ethic. Moreover, the proportion of people who have adopted these values today is steadily increasing.

In particular, one of the distinguishing features of postwar education in Japan is that, while emphasis has been given in schools to encouraging individual personality development and the reinforcement of human rights, it seems that very little attention has been focused on respect for hard work and the individual's responsibilities toward society.

The younger generation, especially, is often criticized for having become increasingly egoistic and appearing to have fallen into a rut of disinterest, lethargy and irresponsibility. Nevertheless, this type of social phenomenon is not necessarily related to a weakening of the work ethic within the corporation.

It is not always easy to measure such trends in quantifiable terms, but the worker absentee rate in Japan compared with other countries (Table 3.1) and the results of a questionnaire asking people about their perceptions of Japanese work habits conducted by NHK (Table 3.2) provide a certain amount of supporting evidence. In fact, it is often said of young Japanese that they undergo a complete transformation once they enter a corporation and become adult members of society.

Table 3.1   *Absenteeism in selected countries (non-agricultural sectors)*

Country	Year	Absenteeism (%)
Japan	1981	1.5
US	1979	3.4
West Germany	1979	7.7
UK	1981	9.9
France	1976	8.7
Sweden	1978	13.8

Source: Ministry of Labor, *Labor in the Year 2000*, March 1986.
Note: Figures for manufacturing industries include absence for sickness or other employee-related reasons. The percentage is derived by dividing the total number of days absent by the number of official working days for the year.

Table 3.2   *The Japanese view of labor (%)*

Statement	Think so	Sometimes think so	Have never thought so
Should always be thinking of improving work	81	13	4
Should have pride in one's work	80	13	6
Should take responsibility to end of one's task	95	3	1

Source: *Nihonjin no Shokugyokan* (Japanese View of Work), ed. NHK Broadcasting Public Opinion Survey Institute (1979), p. 52.

President Johannes Hirschmeier of Nanzan University commented on this point as follows:

Recent public opinion surveys show that among West German and Japanese youth, more young people attach importance to the home and the pursuit of leisure as opposed to those intent on seeking a successful career. In West Germany, however, youth who think this way do not easily change their thinking after they get jobs. In fact, they come to demand more and more from the government and the focus of their interest tends to shift more to leisure than to work. Even if Japanese youth, on the other hand, thought that way as university students, they are re-educated once they join a corporation and are instilled with a great enthusiasm for work, transforming them into proper corporate employees.[15]

Because workers stay with the same company for many years in Japan, the interests and destiny of the company are closely connected with the worker's interests and destiny, and the company evaluates a worker's performance according to his long-term contribution. Mutual self-interest is the basis of that relationship, and because matters are assessed from a long-term perspective, the employee eventually stops looking at his own day-to-day actions in terms of immediate gain and gradually finds that he cannot help but be keenly interested in the future of the company as well.

Once this realization penetrates an individual's thinking at the work site, it naturally gives rise to a set of values which complement this attitude, thereby creating a certain type of disposition. The question of whether the Japanese, despite their seemingly self-motivated work habits, are indeed motivated from within, or whether they are working because the work site atmosphere effectively forces them to do so, is often discussed. In fact, however, this disposition – which has developed naturally – almost exactly matches the individual's inner consciousness, and it is both self-motivated and coercive; it is thus a moot question.

When a Japanese corporation faces some serious difficulty, all of its employees feel threatened, and they often utilize the problem as a driving force to achieve something which they had hitherto considered impossible, banding together in an effort to mobilize their collective determination and energies in a concentrated form in order to overcome the difficulty. This process was certainly a major contributing factor to Japan's success in surviving trade liberalization, capital liberalization and, more recently, the oil crisis, without any serious mishap.

The sheer magnitude of the human energy mobilized in this sort of competition is one of the unique features relating to the capabilities of Japanese corporations, and it is something which should be attributed directly to the structure of the Japanese corporate system itself.

In addition, the seniority system also makes it possible to sustain the morale of a large number of workers over an extended period of time. Western-style competition is suitable for raising the work morale of talented individuals, but the numerous less talented employees are either forced out of the competition from the start, or, alternatively, drop out of the race in the early stages. Under a seniority advancement system, workers are not separated and selected in the early stages. They are observed over an extended period of time, and their performance is evaluated little by little until, finally, a significant distinction is made between those who are promoted and those who are not. Under this system, therefore, a large number of workers are left to work under competitive conditions for quite a long time, thereby enabling the company to extract from them a maximum level of energy on a continuous basis.[16]

Furthermore, besides the fact that the management structure itself has this ability thus to stimulate worker motivation, the corporation itself must also pay close attention to the level of work morale of its employees. This scrutiny is required for a Japanese corporation since the work morale of its employees is a corporate, rather than a social, problem. Because a Japanese corporation has that special quality of being no more than the total sum of its employees, i.e., because a Japanese corporation cannot, in principle, fire all workers who do not demonstrate sufficient motivation and ability and hire superior ones from the market, these special conditions under which the company must operate necessitate that it take great care to see that the work morale and ability of the employees it already has are sustained and improved. When it comes to withstanding competition from other companies, the task of creating an organizational structure which will allow the company to sustain and improve the work morale and ability of its employees is just as important a consideration as matters relating to investment in plant and equipment, technical development and procuring capital. Companies which have built superior structures therefore equip themselves well to overcome competition and develop, but those companies which do not have such a structure will inevitably find themselves disadvantaged in the face of competition.

Japanese companies are particularly enthusiastic in sustaining worker motivation and morale more by compulsory measures than by policy. Actually, they have no other choice. The small group activities, suggestion system and other schemes Japanese companies developed to increase worker participation in the labor process must also be considered in the context of the special conditions that apply to Japanese companies.

The great concern Japanese corporations have for the well-being and welfare of their employees stems from the same circumstances. One distinctive feature of Japan's social welfare system is the great size of the expenses the companies bear. This is particularly true of the expenses borne voluntarily, rather than legal, obligatory expenses.

Some in the West mistake this policy for paternalism on the part of the Japanese company, but the welfare system in Japanese corporations is a highly systematized, structured phenomenon which leaves little room for arbitrary judgment on the part of the corporation,[17] nor is it a reward given depending on how faithful the employees are. As long as an employee stays in the company, he naturally will receive the benefits as his due, and it is thus incorrect to view the social welfare system as an act of benevolence by an autocratic power, as paternalism. Rather than treating employees warmly, there is a type of cold calculation at work. In other words, companies adopt this approach because they believe that although 'oiling a machine will not make it work harder, improving the treatment of human beings does encourage them to work that much harder'.[18] In effect, the welfare benefits represent an investment by the company in maintaining the work ethic of its employees. Still, this type of 'investment' can only be considered as an investment in the context of the special circumstances which dictate that, as a rule, a Japanese company must keep its employees on the payroll for an average of 30 to 40 years.

These circumstances create conditions which do not exist in the West. For example, in an environment such as that in the United States, where workers are constantly changing jobs (the average monthly job separation rate for the United States in 1978 was 3.9 percent; this is a 47 percent annual rate, indicating that almost half of all employees changed jobs within a year),[19] there is no doubt that companies would think twice about whether it is worthwhile to invest in supporting worker morale, and would probably conclude that they would be better off simply trying to attract more motivated labor on the open market.

Thus, against the social background of these changing times, one finds in the West a weakening of values that encourage hard work, a remarkable diminishing of the threat posed by unemployment – which had once stimulated people to work – under the auspices of the welfare state and the weakening of outside influences, i.e. social, upon the individual, resulting in a debilitated desire to work. In this situation, the Japanese corporation has exhibited great strength with its built-in mechanisms for developing and maintaining the work ethic.

In reverse, in fact, it could be said that in this contemporary age, a system assigning such a critically important task as the work ethic's maintenance – a simple task, but one influencing the overall success of industrial society – to society-at-large is bound to reveal its debilitated vitality.

The development of labor's capabilities

Today, besides performing their primary function as vehicles for direct economic activities, companies everywhere also fulfill the role of a kind of educational body. Just how important this role is can be appreciated by envisioning what sort of situation would result if, for example, Japanese industry had to be operated using only knowledge gained from formal education. The Japanese economy would immediately slump to the level of a developing nation, or perhaps fall still further. The very fact that a country has at its disposal an abundant supply of skilled labor in the broad sense of the word, of the high-quality human labor required to oversee and operate an industrial society, is what effectively explains much of the reason for its existence as an advanced nation.

A decade or so ago, for example, the advanced nations were regarded as wealthy while developing nations were regarded as poor. In short, the poverty of the developing nations was attributed to a lack of capital, and as long as this was true it was thought then that simply transferring capital from the advanced to the developing nations would ensure that the latter proceeded steadily along the road to modernization. Later experience, however, has clearly shown that matters are not always as simple as they may appear to be. For example, the oil-producing countries with small populations are undoubtedly more affluent than South Korea and Taiwan, but they are not generally regarded as being more advanced.

It becomes very obvious just how important the store of 'human capabilities' — in the broadest sense — available to a nation really is when viewed in terms of its ability to determine the economic level of the nation. Furthermore, it is vital to create a system designed to develop and efficiently support that human capacity within the company, which is primarily responsible for creating it, not only for the sake of the company itself, but for the sake of the whole economy. In this respect, Japan has devised an excellent system. One of the keys to its success lies in the fact that, under the Japanese system, the corporation and its workers are bound together in a lifelong relationship. Over the years, therefore, the company can reap most of the benefits resulting from the training and education it invested in its employees.

Western-style companies cannot always be assured that they will be able to profit from investments made to develop the human skills and capacity of their employees. The reason for this uncertainty is that employees who have undergone some form of training are subsequently in a position to offer a higher quality of labor to another employer, and may indeed change jobs for better remuneration. When an employee pursues this option, the company loses its investment in his education and training. Moreover, even if a worker chooses to remain at the same company, as long as he has the option of leaving at any time, the company will be forced to raise the level of his remuneration to the level available on the labor market commensurate with his skills to ensure that he stays.

In either case, the benefits of the training and education effectively belong to the worker. Under such conditions, it is inevitable that the company's incentive for developing human resources will be greatly diminished.

In Japan, however, even though a worker may be given training and education, since as a rule there is no possibility that he will leave one company to join another, there is therefore no need to raise his salary, and almost all the benefits of the worker's educational training belong to the company. When investing in the development of specialized skills that can only be used within the corporation, of course, even in the Western corporate system the cost of the training can be fully recovered. In reality, however, any kind of training will always contain some element that can be applied in a general sense, and there are very few instances in which the skills are so specialized as to be of absolutely no value elsewhere.

Thus, the special conditions under which Japanese corporations operate remove the restrictions which constrain companies in the West when it comes to developing human resources, and result in one of the unique features of the personnel system in Japanese corporations.

Many Japanese companies undertake regular personnel reshuffling in the spring of each year. This is a uniquely Japanese practice. In the West, to replace experienced workers who are accustomed to a particular job on a regular basis with novices would be regarded as a totally inconceivable, even absurd, idea.[20] As has already been pointed out, companies in the West adopt a stopgap strategy whereby, apart from when there is a significant problem relating to the ability of the worker who already holds the position, positions within a company are only changed when a gap appears and needs to be filled.

In terms of short-term efficiency, one would have to say that Japan's system is totally inefficient. The reason for the system's use, however, is that a rotation of positions represents a significant investment on behalf of the company in long-term education. When a worker assumes a new position, his general contribution to the company during the initial period that follows will normally be less than that of his predecessor. The extent to which it is less will, at that point, represent a loss for the company. In the case of Western companies, this loss ultimately remains a loss. In Japanese companies, on the other hand, this loss could eventually become a gain since there is a possibility for long-term recovery of the investment.

Given that the rate at which an employee acquires knowledge and experience while carrying out tasks associated with a certain position decreases over time, it is more beneficial for the company in terms of that person's long-term development to rotate him to another position before too much time elapses. Conversely, the direct contribution to the company made by an employee in a certain position will at first be small and, with the passage of time and the gradual leveling off of the rate at which his job performance improves, the contribution will be greater. When faced with the question of whether an employee should be left in the same position for a number of years, it is therefore important to strike a balance between these two functions to calculate the optimum length of time.

In Western-style corporations, however, since a company usually cannot expect to reap the benefits of education and training, it is unable to reach this optimum length of time. This inability clearly demonstrates one of the strengths of the Japanese corporate system: its ability to develop human resources effectively. Moreover, this type of personnel policy, which embodies an educational viewpoint, is applied at all levels of the company, all the way to the ordinary line workers.

The fact that Japanese factory workers initiate improvements and display ingenuity of their own accord must be attributed in part to the broad vision and flexible thinking which results from having been required to work in a number of different positions.

Given the relative absence of educational and training activities in Western companies, particularly when compared to the efforts of Japanese companies, one finds that it is more common in the West for industry education and vocational training to be undertaken at the individual's own expense. American businessmen will often attend business school between jobs in order to build up their skills and knowledge with the objective of going out into the market to obtain even better working conditions. (There are very few business schools in Japan,[21] and almost all who attend are salaried workers whose companies pay them to undertake the course.)

In contemporary industrial society the role of R&D has become crucially important and it is now possible to witness an intermittent stream of innovations from corporations. Furthermore, companies which formerly operated under almost identical production systems based on the same technology are today developing their own production systems to respond to original R&D and innovations. As a consequence, the type of skills that individual employees need now differ markedly from one company to the next. In addition, one can now see a trend toward a shorter life span for skills which, although valuable at one time, become outdated by the continuous introduction of new technological reforms within a relatively short time.

Under these circumstances, if skills are cultivated primarily outside of the company, this system makes it very difficult for a company to ensure that the wide variety of skills it requires are properly catered for; moreover, it is even more difficult for such a system to produce the kind and level of skills that the company will require in the future and which generally follow in the wake of a company's innovations. The only organization capable of accurately determining what sort of human skills will be required for a particular project is the company itself, as it plans its innovations and moves toward implementing them.

The decline of the position of the *meister* in West Germany in recent years is another symptom of this phenomenon. Under such conditions, therefore, there is no escaping the fact that the system of delegating initiative for the development of skills to individual companies is more rational, and that this 'internalization' of human resources has left the Japanese corporations in a superior position.

3 Job Rotation Inside the Company

Japanese companies carry out internal labor shifts extremely smoothly. They are able to do so for several reasons. First, employees of Japanese corporations are not workers but corporate employees, and, unlike workers in the West, they are not strongly tied to a particular job. As long as they remain in the same company, neither their wages nor any other conditions of employment are likely to change as a result of a shift to a different type of work.

Second, the re-education which accompanies a shift to a new type of work is generally undergone at the company's expense, and no economic burden is placed upon the individual employee.

Third, the personnel system revolves around the concept of having workers regularly experience many more jobs than workers in the West.

In Japan, when the organizational structure of a company

changes as a result of an expansion in the volume of work or the introduction of new technology, or, alternatively, when an imbalance arises in the extent of the operations carried out by different departments due to depressed business conditions, a massive reshuffling will often take place, which might even include turning production workers into salesmen. For example, concerning personnel adjustments carried out during Japan's serious recession following the first oil crisis, seconding and changing job location were moves used as widely as moves such as reducing or halting off-season hiring and placing limits on overtime. (*Report on Movements of Labor Force: 1974–76* survey commissioned by MITI, 1976.)

Looking at a breakdown of labor shifts in terms of types of work as indicated in Table 3.3, it is obvious that the greatest shifts took place within the manufacturing sector, and that significant reshuffling also took place between the widely divergent areas of administration, clerical work and sales. The large-scale reshuffling of workers undertaken by Toyo Kogyo (Mazda) is one example of a number of measures that were adopted in an attempt to break out of the management slump, which had been continuing since 1974 in the wake of the oil crisis, and the depressed demand for rotary engine passenger cars. In order to recover from the slump in sales of rotary engine cars, the company decided to take workers off its production lines, give them a week-long sales training course, and send them out for eight months to the dealers as salesmen. Between 1974 and 1980 a staggering 13,000, or roughly half of the company's entire labor force, underwent this sort of training.[22]

Matsushita Electric Co. also experienced difficulties at almost exactly the same time due to a slump in the sales of color television sets. The company consequently adopted a 'half-half' system whereby it stopped production on the factory floor at midday and sent workers out to sell excess inventory in the afternoon.[23]

It would be difficult to conceive of a similar situation occurring anywhere outside Japan.

The fact that labor reshuffling takes place so freely within Japanese companies not only allows the company to display great strength in periods of recession, but allows the smooth implementation of readjustments to the job structure and the contents of work which accompany the adoption of new technology and pro-

Table 3.3 Rotation between different jobs in 1 1976 (1977 survey) (units: persons; %)

Item	Clerical to Mfg.	Clerical to Sales	Mfg. to Mfg.	Mfg. to Sales	Sales to Mfg.	Design/Tech. to Sales	Design/Tech. to Design/Tech.	Total
Av. per/co.	1.7	4.4	47.5	4.9	1.0	1.9	14.1	75.4
Reason for rotation	(2.3%)	(5.8%)	(63.0%)	(6.5%)	(1.3%)	(2.5%)	(18.7%)	(100%)
Increased demand	16.0%	35.1%	12.1%	33.0%	17.3%	37.1%	12.9%	
Decreased demand	1.4%	9.1%	14.1%	12.3%	8.2%	10.1%	6.8%	
Revise % of direct workers	33.3%	11.2%	2.5%	4.0%	13.3%	5.1%	0.4%	
Revise age makeup	4.2%	3.7%	4.5%	1.8%	5.1%	1.1%	3.2%	
Simplify organization.	13.2%	4.5%	6.3%	3.1%	8.2%	5.6%	10.0%	
Changes in prod. mfd.	5.6%	2.9%	14.3%	6.2%	7.1%	5.6%	15.8%	
Intro. of labor-saving machines	1.4%	2.1%	10.9%	8.4%	1.0%	2.2%	39.4%	
Integrate/close work sites/offices	5.6%	3.3%	11.8%	7.5%	8.2%	6.7%	9.0%	
Expand/open work sites/offices	6.3%	9.9%	13.6%	13.2%	5.1%	12.4%	13.6%	
Link in educ./training	13.2%	18.2%	10.0%	10.6%	26.5%	14.0%	24.7%	

Source: Nihonteki Koyo Kanko no Yukue (Trends in Japanese Hiring Practices), ed. Business Behavior Division, Industrial Policy Bureau, MITI (Noritsu University Press, 1981)

duction methods and makes it possible for Japanese companies quickly to follow rapid advances in technology.

Advances in technology continually change the nature of the demand for labor in different job categories. In Japan, these changes are dealt with smoothly within the corporation, but in the West, where workers belonging to a particular job category join together to form a type of 'labor cartel' aimed at protecting their common interests, such changes are met with a strong resistance which is not easily overcome. In the West, a dual conflicting structure exists between labor and management, thus necessitating an intersecting labor union to protect the common interests of the workers. There is no denying the reason for its existence. There is no guarantee, however, that labor unions will use their influence only for the idealistic purpose for which they were originally created, i.e., to protect workers from 'capitalist exploitation'. Once people have been given power, regardless of the purpose for which it was initially granted, it is only to be expected that, in accordance with human nature, they will attempt to use that power to gain the maximum possible profit for themselves. Thus, one finds that in the West a system has developed which does not readily coexist with the rapid injection of new technological advances. Under these circumstances, it is inevitable that in this respect, the Japanese system will show itself to be far superior.

4 The Organizational Structure

Companies in the West must structure their organizations around the worker as the basic unit, whereas companies in Japan can create their organizations using corporate employees as the basic unit. What this means, first of all, is that because a worker does not have a subjective interest in the company's management, he cannot be expected to participate voluntarily in organizational activities, and, second, because there is always the possibility that a worker will leave the company, the company must always be prepared for that eventuality by objectifying and standardizing labor. In contrast to Western companies being forced to create their corporate organization under these restrictive conditions,

Japanese companies do not have to consider such constraints. This results in a fundamental difference in the nature of corporate organizations in Japan and in the West.

Features of the corporate organization in the West

One of the fundamental features of corporate organization in the West is that it is created as a collection of functions. In Western terms, a company's organization is regarded as a structure incorporating a number of functions which are necessary to achieve the management objectives of that company. (The word 'function' is used here to signify the different types and amounts of work which should be carried out using standardized methods and skills.)

A collection of a number of these functions constitutes a set of jobs, and positions are established when people are given the authority and responsibility to do those jobs; a systematic structure is created to link every position without any redundancy or deficiency. The schematic arrangement of these positions is what is known as the corporate organization.[24] People are allocated to positions after the fact, so to speak. Based on the responsibility and authority with which they are charged, they set out to perform their jobs, and in doing so preserve the schematic order of the organization as a whole, allowing it to move as precisely as a machine.

In reality, the corporate organizations of companies in the West do not always match this idealized formula in every respect, and in recent years some companies have attempted to create a different type of organization in view of the inflexibility of more traditional structures. In general, however, the above formula still accurately describes the most essential features of the corporate organization in the West. It is clear that the formation of this organization is inextricably linked to the nature of the Western-style corporate system.

First, this type of organization closely reflects the fact that employees are tied to a particular job rather than to the company itself. As long as workers remain tied to a job, a company must employ them on the basis of their ability to perform that job. That is why the company organization must be created in the form of a systematic linking of jobs.

137

Second, because employees may quit at any time, the organization must inevitably be structured around objectified jobs as units. If the greater part of all jobs effectively consists of the personal capabilities of the individual people who perform them, then it will not be possible immediately to know what sort of vacuum will be created if an employee decides to quit. Moreover, if that person is the only one in the company with any knowledge of that job, then that knowledge may disappear completely, locked as it is inside the head of the former employee. For the organization to continue functioning smoothly even with an influx and outflow of personnel, it is therefore necessary to objectify – in the form of a manual – the knowledge that is locked inside the head of each employee and the know-how which he has instinctively picked up while 'on the job'. For exactly the same reason, a machine part that needs to be changed must always be standardized before it can be replaced.

Third, as this type of organization functions in a systematic way, there is no necessity whatsoever to rely on individual initiative. This is because the organization itself was established as a complete body of jobs which do not contradict one another, and was in place before any employees joined the company. After employees are attached to the jobs, all they have to do is follow the manual and obey orders from above, functioning as individual units. There is no need for employees to think about the significance that their actions will have for the company. As long as they immerse themselves in the performance of their duties, the system linking the jobs will ensure that the activities of all employees as a whole will be conducted in an organized manner. The fact that jobs are objectified also makes it possible to check whether a given employee is performing properly, and therefore whether his responsibility is being duly carried out.[25]

In this sense, this type of organization is closely linked with the capitalist corporate system. In simple terms, as long as the basic units of the organization are individuals who act freely in accordance with their own desire for private gain, the organization cannot be constructed in any other way. Under such circumstances, in fact, it is probably the most rational form of organization. Nevertheless, if this prerequisite were to be removed, this form of organization would not necessarily stand up to the test of rationality. The great advantage of this type of organization is that it is created to run like a machine, with no waste, and in the most rational manner possible. Yet, on the other hand, the organization's 'machine-like' quality places limitations on it.

The nature of this type of organization is essentially fixed and stationary. When the organization is formed, the activities required for the corporation to operate are determined in advance, and are subsequently divided into jobs. This particular aspect may not be seen as a serious drawback under conditions such as those which existed for factory workers in the nineteenth century, when most workers simply had to repeat the same tasks over and over again. Today, however, the environment in which companies must operate is extremely complicated and constant efforts to improve production methods on the factory floor are required, not to mention forward-looking research and development and a quick and accurate grasp of subtle changes in market trends. It is virtually impossible for any company, finding itself in such a volatile environment to which it is forced to respond in a creative manner, to anticipate what activities will be required of it in the future and to incorporate those activities into a manual.

Masaru Ibuka, Honorary Chairman of Sony Corporation, made the following observations on this point:

The mainstream thinking about the transistor changed seven or eight times over a 20-year period, and since the introduction of integrated circuits, there have been about three different development flows. Viewed in this light, the fundamental thinking for producing things has changed about once every two or three years. That's why it was no longer possible to instruct workers to do their work a certain way, such as was done with mass production and assembly lines. Since we were unable to give workers a standard set of procedures for performing their jobs, they used a process of trial and error to increase production yields and took the initiative in creating new work methods.

Under those circumstances, operators were given a considerable degree of freedom in the manufacture of transistors. They displayed great interest in trying to think of ways in which the final production yield of transistors could be improved, and regarded the task as a challenge. This process allowed for a significant degree of freedom and gave the workers scope to use their own ideas to make improvements.[26]

As Ibuka's comments indicate, if a company wishes to pursue accurate production control with respect to rapidly changing technical conditions, then it is left with no option but to give workers the freedom to use their own initiative.

Also, because people are treated just like parts of a machine under this type of organization, the system is inferior in that only a small part of the multifaceted human capabilities of each person can be utilized. The human work force is different from raw materials, fuel, land and other production factors: it is a much more complicated and diverse resource. And yet, because this type of organizational structure treats human labor as a fixed element, it produces a situation in which human activity is confined and fixed within standardized job boundaries, and the company is unable to utilize fully the capabilities of the entire work force. People who have been employed to perform a specific job certainly are constantly presented with opportunities outside their normal area of work where they can contribute to the company. The Western type of organization, however, cannot, as an organization, take advantage of such opportunities.

To start with, it is impossible not to harbor doubts about the suitability of this manual type of control on the rapidly advancing contemporary industrial society. This system may certainly have been suited to simple, repetitive labor, but the nature of labor has become more sophisticated and workers are becoming more highly educated. Today, many factory workers have a high school or even better education, and a control system which constrains the functions and responsibilities of workers within the predetermined confines of simple tasks is extremely wasteful in terms of achieving maximum utilization of the human capabilities available. And one wonders if it might not result in a lowering of morale.

Also, as further progress is achieved in automation and robotization, and simple labor tasks are increasingly performed by machines, the quality of labor itself has become much more complicated and sophisticated, just as the areas in which a single worker performs various duties have become more diverse. Because the Western-style corporate organization confines the activities of the greater part of the workers within the organization to the fixed boundaries of a manual, the responsibility for almost all forms of creative activity must be shouldered by top management. It is a fallacy, however, to believe that top management is always in the best position to assess what is really most suitable for the company. Although this would not be so if top management had all the essential information required for the company's activities at its fingertips, it remains true that in a Western-style corporate system, where information inevitably tends to be concentrated at the top management level, there are aspects of conditions on the factory floor that the floor workers themselves know best, just as those who know sales best are the salesmen.

This type of organization effectively excludes the possibility that workers may quickly grasp the countless opportunities which continuously present themselves at the work site for improvements in sales methods, machinery and production methods and for dealing with unforeseen circumstances. As a result, the organization as a whole finds it inherently difficult to adapt to changes quickly and to face the new problems which are born of change and to deal with them creatively.

As a result of the rise in the capital/labor ratio which has accompanied capital accumulation, the value of labor has become much greater than before. Many years ago, when capital was scarce and labor abundant, it may have been economically viable to waste human 'machines' who had elaborate and almost infinitely diverse capabilities and flexibility by giving them simple, repetitive tasks, but it is no longer economically feasible to do so today. Also, the economic system demanding that people be used in this way is no longer capable of effectively solving present-day economic problems. Today, the results realized from a nation's economic system are almost certainly determined to a considerable degree by the extent to which corporate organizations are capable of making the best use of precious human resources and harnessing them to achieve corporate objectives. Despite this fact, the company organization as it exists under the traditional capitalist corporate system is incapable of performing this function. At the very least, it is incapable of performing it sufficiently well. In conforming with the labor structure itself, under this system workers can at best be termed as little more than mere robots. Their job descriptions are just like the programs that are built into robots, and they follow the descriptions to the letter. It is natural that, unlike their Japanese counterparts, Western workers oppose the introduction of robots since workers can be replaced by robots, but corporate employees cannot.

Features of the corporate organization in Japan

In form, most companies in Japan also have a corporate organization designed to act as a controlling mechanism. This is merely a front, however, and the real workings of the organization take place in a way that is often totally unrelated to the official organization. This does not simply mean that a few Japanese modifications have been made to what is still essentially a Western-style controlling mechanism. The organization of Japanese corporations stems from a fundamentally different set of principles. None of the features so commonly attributed to the Japanese corporate organization – so-called bottom-up or consensus-style decision-making; emphasis on 'harmony'; unclear boundaries for responsibility and authority; an organization revolving around people – could possibly exist under the organizational principles of a Western-style controlling mechanism.

A controlling mechanism organization is structured so that no contradiction and no duplication exist between the boundaries of authority and responsibility relating to each job position. Given that one of the features of the Japanese-type corporate organization is the relatively vague nature of boundaries relating to authority and responsibility, as a matter of course an organization of this nature should have difficulty functioning in an organized and coordinated manner. In addition, it is inconceivable that the organization would be able to find jobs to suit people. It is only possible for an organization to function in an organized and coordinated manner when particular tasks are assigned to each job position and those tasks are carried out as stipulated. If the nature of the jobs and tasks involved is changed to suit the capabilities and personalities of the people performing them, it is obvious that the organization will fall into chaos. As long as the consensus system is also based on the control mechanism organization principle, it will never be achievable. The organization itself constitutes an independent linking of decision-making carried out within the framework of separate jobs. Consensus-style decision-making must effectively be perceived as something which introduces the participation of unrelated parties into a decision-making process which should really be carried out within predetermined boundaries of authority and responsibility, and would surely lead to a complete breakdown in the order of the organization.

The concept of bottom up, also, is at the very least a form of decision-making that could not be completely contained within the framework of this type of organization.

As long as they are evaluated in terms of the organizational principles on which the capitalist corporate system operates, all of the features of the Japanese-style corporate organization must be considered as obviously rendering the organization ineffective, causing confusion and being extremely dubious in terms of their capacity even to support or maintain the organizational structure. In reality, however, it cannot be denied that Japanese companies, far from being reduced to a state of confusion, are functioning quite well. This clearly demonstrates that Japanese companies are in fact operating under a system that is based on totally different organizational principles from those which exist in the West.

Japanese companies do not organize workers; they organize corporate employees. The corporate employees behave as an extension of the company itself, and their relationship with the company does not take the form of a commercial agreement, but rather a lifelong affiliation. At an individual level, some employees may not conform to this general pattern, but in principle, this is the way in which the two are connected and Japanese companies use this structure as the basis for building their corporate organization.

Because a fundamental commonality of interests exists between the company and the corporate employee, the company can rely on the corporate employees to demonstrate initiative, and the more initiative shown, the less the need to use authoritative means to control them. Also, because management can assume that corporate employees will continue to work at the company, there is no need to have all the jobs objectified in the form of a manual at all times. Not only is this unnecessary, it is also detrimental to the company itself. Corporate employees who approach their work in a subjective manner with initiative and enthusiasm produce and sell 'better'. If people with this sort of work attitude are subjected to a manual form of standardized control from above, not only will they lose their flexibility, resilience and worker morale, but they will be rendered inefficient. This naturally leads one to the conclusion that, rather than adopting this approach, it is far better for a company to place wholehearted trust in the initiative of its employees and to leave matters in the experienced hands of those actually working in particular situations.

Corporate employees judge for themselves what is best for the company, and, within the framework of their designated area of responsibility, take initiative to contact related divisions and sections to discuss issues. In the course of doing so, they act in an organized manner.

The organized activities of these corporate employees can be described as a process whereby the individual determines his or her own position and role within the organization and carries out activities of his or her own accord that are in keeping with the objectives of the corporation. Such actions form a part of the process of harmonizing which takes place between corporate employees. In other words, teamwork is at the core of the Japanese corporate organization.[27]

In Japan, members of a corporate organization are not individuals who have been attached to positions which designate that they must perform certain duties: they are expected to behave as corporate employees and extensions of the company. As a result, although an individual's field of responsibility does have set limitations, his or her vision and thinking should be just as broad as that of top management, which must encompass the entire corporate structure. Although it may not be realistically possible to expect this from every person in the company, employees in Japan who have the ability to do this are evaluated very highly, for such behavior conforms with the principles of Japanese corporate activity.

Adjustments in work procedures are made voluntarily between parties with concerns at relatively low levels of the organization, and corporate employees are required to ensure that, among their suggestions for adjustment, anything which needs to be considered in terms of the total corporate framework be balanced and well thought out. This principle applies equally both to those in the office and to those in the factory. In short, the behavior of workers itself is of an organized nature and does not depend on rules and directives. Yoshiro Hoshino had an interesting experience relating to this point.

Hoshino took a short trip aboard a British LNG tanker, sailing from Uraga, south of Yokohama, to LNG bases of Tokyo Gas and Tokyo Electric Power at Sodegaura, across Tokyo Bay. The ship's officers were British, and the seamen were mainly Chinese. The workers for Tokyo Gas were Japanese. The following are some of the comments related to the working styles of the two groups. Hoshino was impressed by the quite obvious differences between them.

Hoshino: All the Japanese were helping. No one gave any orders at all. There were supervisors there, but they didn't say a word. The workers just set about taking care of the task at hand. It didn't seem to make any difference who did it. They just fastened wires to a crane. On the ship's side, however, only the officer with final responsibility was allowed to perform this task. The ordinary seamen did nothing at all.

Miyazaki: That's probably because a manual clearly outlined all the work procedures, and the ordinary seamen weren't permitted to do that work.

Hoshino: It seemed as if there were no clear division of duties, and that the Japanese were moving around as they pleased. In effect, though, there was an ordered discipline, and everyone's role was set. On the other hand, the seamen and officers did not appear to have clear roles. They worked almost haltingly. The Japanese worked diligently without needing commands from anyone, but effectively there was order and real dynamism in their movements – each and every one was done in a professional manner.

Miyazaki: In Singapore, a supervisor at the Jurong Ship Yard told me how he viewed Japanese and other workers. Other workers seemed to build spaces between each other that could only be filled by a supervisor giving a number of orders to pull the workers together. Japanese workers, on the other hand, were already closely united. And when there seemed to be gaps between them, they closed the gaps without being ordered to do so. There was no need to give orders to each worker. They seemed naturally willing to rely on and help each other. Your experience with the LNG ship seems to indicate the same thing.[28]

Teamwork is the essence of Japanese organizational activity. Teamwork is not, however, a peculiarly Japanese phenomenon. Even the phrase itself is an English expression, and no Japanese expression exists which can be used to describe the same phenomenon in exactly the same way. Teamwork is something which emerges from almost any group of people as long as the following two conditions are fulfilled. First, all members of a team must be voluntarily working together to achieve a set objective. This condition is satisfied within Japanese corporations because all employees are corporate employees rather than simply employees. Second, each member of the team must have enough information to be able to determine his own role and position within the team, and that information must be used so that all team members have a unified perception of the circumstances in which the team is placed.

For teamwork undertaken by small groups, this information can be gathered naturally, without any systematized framework, as long as each member of the team uses his 'eyes and ears'. For a company or other large organization, however, it is not possible to conceive of such a function occurring naturally. Some special measures are therefore required to ensure that information-gathering takes place.

Japanese companies have certain practices related to decision-making. In the *ringi* system, for example, written proposals are passed around to relevant people for their comments and acceptance. By the time the proposal reaches the person with the authority to accept or reject it, it has thus already been seen by a number of other people. There is also *nemawashi*, where those concerned unofficially discuss a matter to pave the way for its later approval at an official meeting. Meetings are frequently held that do not always seem to be tied directly to decision-making, but which nonetheless serve an important purpose. In such ways, voluntary adjustments are made among corporate employees in Japanese companies in an organized way. Information is exchanged, and viewpoints are integrated.

Toshio Doko, past president of Toshiba Corp. and former chairman of the Japan Federation of Economic Organizations, commented on this point as follows:

There is one school of thought which claims that a person's position is determined by the volume of information he has. The people at the top of the pyramid must handle large amounts of information, and those at the bottom can get by with handling much less. Using that reasoning, if the job system can be represented by an upright pyramid, the distribution of information is represented as an upside down triangle. Management to date has certainly displayed this characteristic. If work can be achieved by relying on orders and instructions, then this is sufficient.

Under a system which allows each individual to set objectives for himself, however, to act on his own accord with authority, and to freely exercise creativity, the nature and form of information must be different. From the point of view of those in charge, since responsibility and authority have already been delegated, they cannot subsequently take interfering action or issue instructions. The only thing they can do is provide information. They have a responsibility to provide those under them with greater volumes of crucial information, and they must ensure that the amount of information their subordinates have is effectively equivalent to the amount of information they themselves have. An ideal degree of communication would mean that every level within the company, regardless of its location, had access to an identical amount of information.[29]

In this type of organization, it is necessary for each individual to have an extensive and balanced understanding of the order of priorities relating to the policies of the company and the environment surrounding it. A person cannot successfully perform his work duties with only information on his own area of responsibility and specialized knowledge. Information should flow down not only through the layers of the organization as it does in a pyramid-style structure, but also from all related departments and bureaus as well.

In a Western-style company, therefore, as long as the manual method of organization is firmly established, even if the individuals occupying each of the different jobs have no information about the overall company situation, and consequently no idea of the significance of their own job within the company, it is sufficient for them simply to perform the tasks assigned to them. In a Japanese company organization, on the other hand, if the flow of information is blocked, the result would be a lethal functional breakdown. In this sense, it is not the manual, but rather the information itself, which renders possible the organizational activity that exists within the Japanese corporate structure. The teamwork which is made possible by the joint possession of information actually forms the substance of an organization which replaces the systematic linking of jobs.

It would be closer to the truth to consider that a person's vertical position in a Japanese company does not refer to the amount of authority vested in an individual or how powerful the authority is that he wields, but rather to the scope of his field of responsibility. A section chief can assert his opinion relating to any field for which that section has responsibility, whereas a president has the right to give his opinion on any issue affecting the company. This is the extent of the difference between the two. Members in subordinate positions have a much greater and more specialized knowledge of their own field of responsibility. The more senior the position, the less detailed the knowledge a person has in relation to any one subject, but, on the other hand, the more extensive the field of responsibility. Although those in less senior positions are asked for opinions based on specialized knowledge of a subject, those above them are required to make balanced judgments based on the consideration of a number of factors which are presented to them.

In Japanese companies, the president's instructions often represent little more than a vague indication of the general direction in which the company is heading. Directives are sent down from the president's office to the lower levels of the company, the results of a detailed examination are reported to the top, and decisions are eventually arrived at through a repetition of this feedback process. The president's instructions are often effectively rejected at lower levels in the company, one more manifestation of the fact that the corporate organization of Japanese companies is not a hierarchy of authority, but rather a mechanism for information exchange.

Also, because the organizational activity of the company is dependent on teamwork, the accurate dissemination of information throughout all levels of the company is a crucially important condition for the organization, one created by the nature of the Japanese corporate organization itself.

As a consequence, decision-making takes place in a manner which is quite divergent from the methods employed in the West. Western corporate decisions can generally be broken down and identified as decisions made by individuals assigned to certain jobs, and for that reason individual responsibility can be questioned. In Japanese companies, however, decisions are made on the basis of opinions and information emanating from each of the responsible parties, which are subsequently collated and used to create what is considered to be the best possible proposal for adoption. In the process of Japanese decision-making, opinions are formed within the network of information exchange, and a number of different pieces of information, judgments and opinions are then added to or subtracted from these as part of a process which could aptly be described as self-refining. Rather than saying 'someone decides', therefore, it is probably more fitting to say 'decisions are gradually formed'. If the specialized knowledge of an employee at the bottom of the organization is such that it has an important bearing upon a particular issue, his opinion has the potential to become the basis for the entire company policy. It is therefore hardly surprising that the staff system and system of specialized jobs have failed to take root in Japanese companies which practice this type of decision-making.

In the West, those occupying the top positions in a company have the most authority, but this does not necessarily guarantee that the proper quantity of information required to make decisions will be at their disposal. They may not have the required information because the organization is based on the principle of ensuring that employees work through a system of orders, and since the system is not necessarily replete with the characteristics necessary to ensure the smooth exchange of information, it requires a staff system in order to fill the gaps. Japanese corporate organizations, however, represent in themselves a huge information exchange mechanism, and staff members and specialists therefore cannot easily find their places within the organizational structure.

In fact, management in Japan is even popularly referred to as *o-mikoshi* (free reins) management. The term actually refers to the portable shrines carried on people's shoulders during festivals. The moniker emphasizes how unrealistic it is to think of management in Japan as a situation where managers are the rulers and all others are the ruled.

As described above, organizational activity within Japanese companies is carried out by virtue of a process of the regulation of activities undertaken voluntarily by individual corporate employees who have been supplied with enough information to allow them to independently determine their role and position within the company as they act in keeping with the organizational character itself. In other words, the Japanese corporate organization is not something which is first designed and then established around a network of fixed jobs, but rather something which exists within the very process of the mutual harmonizing of corporate employees acting on the basis of broad perceptions of the overall situation. Unlike Western companies, Japanese companies do not determine the complete body of activity needed for the company in advance, and subsequently proceed to break those functions down into jobs to which they can assign individuals. In fact, exactly the reverse is true. It is what might be called the after-the-fact accumulation of the results of activities undertaken by large numbers of corporate employees who decide for themselves what the company requires that effectively constitutes the sum total of corporate activity.

If the traditional corporate organization is considered as one which has a static structure, it can be said that, in contrast, this type of organization is essentially rooted not in its structure but rather in a process of dynamic, organized activity, and, as a consequence, instead of the repetition of fixed job tasks, it is far more suited to 'seizing a particular set of objective circumstances or facts in the course of continuing corporate activities, and from them, producing new objectives and policies'.[30]

In other words, this type of organization is one which, overall, has a marked bias toward moving forward in search of reform. In the eyes of those who are used to a traditional corporate organization, which is just like an inflexible machine, the Japanese corporate organization appears as something which gives the impression of an organism with a life of its own, largely dependent on its inherent flexibility.

Since this type of organization does not constrain multifaceted human capabilities within the confines of a predetermined system of jobs, it creates conditions which allow people to fully realize their human abilities and potential.

In this respect, when considered in terms of its actual organizational activity rather than in terms of its superficial structure, the Japanese corporate organization can be described as being completely at odds with the controlling mechanism type of organization prevalent in the West.

A new type of corporate organization known as the matrix organization was introduced to companies involved in the space development industry in the United States in the 1960s, and many other companies in other industries adopted it in the 1970s.

With the emergence of a rapidly changing environment, the increasing difficulty of predicting future developments, the unexpected changes in market demands, sudden shifts in the strategies employed by competing enterprises and the increasing frequency with which companies began to find difficulties in anticipating technological advances, plans became extremely difficult to sustain and companies were faced with a need to collect and process large volumes of information. One of the aims of the matrix style of organization was to respond to these circumstances and enhance the information processing capabilities of the company by initiating a mutual exchange of information covering many different fields.[31]

The fundamental characteristics of the matrix organization follow.

1 Separate organizations are created for functions and products (or markets) in the form of a matrix, so that an individual manager no longer reports to one supervisor, but follows the directives of two senior managers

2 Whereas the traditional corporate organization assigns jobs to individuals and the senior manager has the responsibility for coordinating the work of a number of individuals, the matrix organization is characterized by the way in which it formulates teams which are assigned to particular projects and accomplishes tasks through teamwork.

Stanley M. Davis and Paul R. Lawrence, who formulated the principles of the matrix organization, have asserted that Japanese-style management has many features in common with the matrix organization. This commonality is especially true, according to their theory, insofar as Japanese culture is characterized by:

1 Effective harmonizing among groups

2 A greater degree of emphasis on commitment and orientation toward the organization rather than on individual areas of speciality

3 A tendency to follow group decision-making rather than individual authority that has been transferred

4 Mutual cooperation even when one individual must exceed the boundaries of his field of responsibility in order to help another

5 A greater emphasis on the process of the organization itself rather than on the structure of the organization

6 The time taken to make decisions – and, once made, the surprisingly quick implementation time.

Davis and Lawrence go even further and claim that, to begin with, the Japanese corporate organization is essentially a matrix organization.

> If the Japanese culture is so receptive to the tenets of the matrix, why haven't more of their corporations used it? In part, many have, such as in project teams and task forces. But more to the point, the Japanese don't have to create a formal matrix structure and name for "it" the way we do, because matrix structure and behavior is an intrinsic part of their way of being.[32]

The author would like to reserve judgment on their claim that 'the structure and functions associated with the matrix' are 'already naturally incorporated into the commonplace corporate organization' because of the influence of Japanese 'culture' rather than the influence of the Japanese corporate system. Nevertheless, it cannot be denied that the nature of the matrix organization outlined by Davis and Lawrence is remarkably similar in many respects to the way in which Japanese corporations actually undertake their activities.

The theoretical design of the organizational model which represents the matrix organization was based on experience gained in the high-technology industry of space development, and the fact that many of the elements which characterize this model are reflected in and are ultimately common to the activities of the Japanese corporate organization indirectly exposes the essence of many of the special features of the Japanese corporate system.

As stated above, not only is it possible under the Japanese corporate system to create an organization which is different from the traditional style, but creating such an organization is more natural and rational.

For example, as in many other industries, the rationalization of the production control system of the postwar steel industry began with the introduction of American management thinking, which was, at that time, considered to be the most rational. A Taylor system approach was firmly implanted whereby standardized work procedures were created after analyzing the laborers' skills, and all the workers had to do afterward was follow procedures.

After the start of the period of rapid economic growth beginning about mid-1950, however, this system was gradually abandoned. This abandonment did not occur because of an emerging awareness of defects inherent in the system, but simply because companies began to run out of people. The American style of operation required process workers and interim inspectors, but because of the boom in the construction of blast furnaces, it was not possible to find enough workers for such jobs. As a consequence, companies were forced to have factory workers perform those jobs as well, which produced surprisingly good results.

Thus, the abandonment of the Taylor system became the opportunity for spreading the idea that workers were responsible for quality and for giving workers widespread real authority and autonomy in the production control process.

There can be no doubt that a similar series of events took place in many other industries. And the fact that, almost without exception, they took exactly the same direction demonstrates that the progression of the corporate organization along this path was inevitable under the conditions created by the new Japanese corporate system.

Hence, behind the system and facade of a control mechanism type of organization similar to that found in the West, Japanese companies are actually operating under a totally different form of organization. Thus, although companies will have formal regulations outlining duties, most employees will probably never have seen them.

This is yet another example of the estrangement between system and reality, between appearance and actuality, which characterizes the Japanese corporate organization, and, in fact, the entire Japanese corporate system. Efforts to close this gap have only recently begun to be initiated. In recent times, many companies which refused to be constrained by convention, such as Honda Motor, Sony, Shinichiden, Maekawa Seisakusho and Kyoto Ceramics, have been experimenting with creating an organizational form which differs markedly from the previously accepted concept of the corporate organization, embodying an extraordinary degree of creativity. Not all of these new forms of organization will become lasting institutions, and there will probably also be some among them which will never leave the confines of the company in which they were created. Nevertheless, the 1970s will almost certainly be remembered as a time when Japanese companies initiated many rather radical experiments as they tried to create a new form of corporate organization suited to the Japanese corporate system.

This movement represents a process of breaking away from Western principles of organization, and, at the same time, an attempt to realize the latent potential of the Japanese corporate system to the greatest extent possible.

5 The Humanization of Labor

As discussed thus far in this chapter, under the conditions which exist in contemporary industrial society, the Japanese economic system can certainly be described as superior in terms of its effectiveness. Nevertheless, the final evaluation of an economic system does not depend on effectiveness alone. If the nature of the system were such that it oppressed the people working within it, and the high degree of efficiency was obtained as a result of the oppression of humanity, such a system would not necessarily be considered desirable.

Japanese companies, particularly, are typified by a corporate organization which is self-inclusive to a large degree and, like a nation, quite cohesive. If one were to reflect on the fact that once a person joins a Japanese company there are, in effect, severe constraints on that person quitting, this might make some people feel there is a strong possibility that although the Japanese economic system is highly efficient, that is being paid for with the oppression of humanity. In fact, however, this is not true.

Although it is true that, in effect, market constraints exist on labor in Japan, Japanese corporate employees have a significant degree of freedom when it comes to working within the corporate organizational structure, what might be called organizational freedom. Moreover, not only are these two conditions compatible, a positive link actually exists between them. In other words, constraints on market freedom work to produce organizational freedom.

Japanese companies are not organized through reliance on a system of fixed jobs; they are organized through teamwork.

Another way of expressing this would be to say that they are organized around units of people rather than jobs.

As previously stated, the organizational principles of Japanese companies require that an individual put himself in the company's position, decide for himself what the company needs, and with an awareness of the role that he plays as one part of the entire whole, initiate action accordingly.

Regardless of whether an individual has the ability to properly fulfill this role, autonomy in making judgments and freedom to display initiative are granted to him. This means that an individual does not simply work as instructed, but is expected to behave autonomously as a corporate employee. In other words, compared with workers in the West, corporate employees in Japan are provided with a volume of information and a degree of freedom in their activities that are more than sufficient for letting them appreciate the significance of what they are doing. The alienation of labor is often ascribed to 'lack of authority' and 'meaningless work', but compared with companies in the West, Japanese companies have a relatively low incidence of these elements.

The corporate organization in the West is structured around jobs as the basic unit, and an individual must fit himself into his job. Since in the West it is considered that an individual should perform the job tasks assigned to him, there is no expectation — with few exceptions — that he will actively do something for the organization, and the environment is not conducive to facilitating the manifestation of such sentiments.

The following comment was made on this point by an American businessman who resided in Japan for many years:

In Japan's case, however, in the formulation of various activity plans for the company, many corporate employees are actually involved in the process of producing those plans, and real 'participation', so to speak, is taking place. In terms of both internal company communication and improving worker motivation this is a tremendous weapon. America operates under a so-called top-down system where decisions are made at the top, and those not at the top simply follow orders and have no feeling of participating in anything. It is unrealistic to expect such devotion to following orders.[33]

Insufficient information also contributes to the self-alienation of labor. Western-style organizations are structured in such a way that information is seldom provided to individuals. Routine work is performed by following the manual, and all other matters are dealt with by following the orders issued by superiors and reporting on the results. The normal daily flow of information within an organization of this type is in a vertical direction, and it flows primarily from top to bottom. Orders cannot be completely excluded as one form of information, but they certainly do not provide the individual with any direct information about the environment surrounding the company and its activities. It is a common practice in Japanese companies for superiors to explain to their subordinates the background and the reasoning behind a particular directive from above in order to obtain their understanding and support, but in the West, this sort of action is the exception rather than the rule. Regardless of whether or not subordinate workers understand the reasoning behind an order, as long as it is issued with the authority of the superior concerned, it is automatically assumed that it will be obeyed.

A person's 'will to work' stems to a large degree from a real awareness of the significance of his own job. That is why meaningless forced labor, whereby people are made to dig holes and simply fill them in again, has been used as a cruel form of punishment. In the type of organization that exists in the West, a small number of people at the management level are given the total responsibility for steering the company in the right direction and they therefore have jobs which stimulate and encourage them to work. The mass of workers, on the other hand, see labor as a necessary but painful evil which cannot be avoided if they are to earn a living. Thus, under this system, the two inevitably become polarized.

A concentration of authority not only brings with it a concentration of freedom, but also gives rise to a concentration of information, which, in turn, leads to a concentration of 'work significance' and 'will to work'. This is another inevitable result of this type of corporate organization, and as long as this organizational structure remains inextricably linked to the corporate system, it must be recognized that it is ultimately a product of that same corporate system.

The 'revolt' of the workers

The oppressive effect the Western-style corporate organization has on the people who work inside it is firmly rooted in the controlling mechanism essence of the organization. In accordance with its own inherent reasoning, the more this type of organization is rationalized, the more obvious its defects become. Especially since the 1960s, with the advent of technological innovations and expansion in the scale of companies, as a result of the widespread introduction of 'labor fractionalization' and pyramid-style organization in an attempt to rationalize management, the mass production factories of the West began to be seriously affected from the latter half of the 1960s by lethargy, sabotage and an increase in the rates of absenteeism and resignations on the part of workers.

The strike which occurred in 1972 at a General Motors plant in Ohio is typical of this era, and in one sense embodied an epoch-making significance. Given that strikes until then generally had been used by workers as a weapon to obtain higher wages from the company, the strike at Rosetown was of a clearly different nature.

In reporting this incident, the *New York Times* called this strike 'the robots' revolt'.[34] The workers were not using this strike as a bargaining tool, but as a declaration of their 'abhorrence of labor itself'. The unauthorized absenteeism rate at General Motors' plants during the 1970s was 5 percent each day on average; at Fiat this rate had reached almost 10 percent in 1971. It is well-known that at one point the Swedish automobile manufacturer Volvo was faced with a situation where almost half the workers in its factories displayed frequent absenteeism, and the company was eventually forced to embark upon a program of discontinuing conveyor belt activity in some of their factories in order to create work sites that would incite a 'will to work' in employees.[35]

The fundamental cause of this problem is that rationalization based on Taylorism had gone as far as it could. In the past, decisions relating, for example, to the tools and methods that should be used to perform the work had been left up to the workers in many areas, and production control was also largely a voluntary function and a responsibility of the workers. After the adoption of this system, however, the workers lost almost all of their rights to control production and their right of choice relating to the production process. Instead, their existence was reduced to the level of being like mere machines passively operating at a uniform pace. This system represented the embodiment of the ideal form of the controlling mechanism type of organization. Despite the advantage it had to offer of a resultant increase in productivity accompanied by higher wages for workers, it cannot be denied that, at the same time, it dehumanized the labor process to an extreme degree.

Today, companies in the West are still groping for an answer as they continue their efforts to discover a technique that will make it possible to combine more humanized forms of labor with high rates of efficiency.

Only time will tell whether their efforts will bear fruit, but it is difficult to be optimistic. One only needs to look back at the way in which the situation developed in the past, with the dehumanization of labor being accompanied by the progressive rationalization of production methods. If the labor process in the West is 'humanized', it is highly likely that this will inevitably lead to inefficiency in the corporate organization. Taylorism is in itself essentially something which was conceived of when the workers, who effectively controlled the production work sites, began to employ systematic soldiering to prevent the company from reducing their wages rates.

If management abandoned any direct control it had over the production process itself, and left it up to the workers to use their initiative to make decisions, this would result in a return to the conditions which originally existed before the introduction of Taylorism. That is, the situation would inevitably return to 'organized sabotage' on the part of the workers. In terms of their relationship with the company, as long as the workers continue simply to sell their labor to the company, the most rational behavior for the workers will always be to attempt to obtain the greatest amount of compensation for the least work possible.

The company has no choice but to use this type of authoritative control in order to mold the workers, who essentially have a conflict of interests with the company, into some form of organization. If nothing can be done to change the fundamental roots of this system, companies in the West will ultimately find themselves unable to escape the basic confines of this traditional form of organization.

This is yet another of the problems confronting companies in the West. Much of the industrial stagnation, weakened competitiveness and declining vitality experienced by these companies stems from their use and control of humans as they would machines, and the blame should rest with the system which has oppressed the freedom of those who work within it. This problem has occurred because, under this system, production efficiency and human freedom in the labor process are linked antinomically, and the more entrenched the mechanical control of human beings becomes, i.e., the greater the degree of human oppression, the more efficient the production process.

To date, attempts at encouraging worker participation in management, and efforts to humanize labor – such as efforts made by Volvo and Saab – have ultimately been blocked by the same barriers and ended time and time again in frustration. As long as this antinomy remains a product of the Western corporate system, and as long as nothing can be done about its root cause, the introduction of a few pieces of legislation or adoption of new techniques will be ineffectual in breaking through the barrier.

Economic advancement is the foundation of the welfare of a nation. It may be an exaggeration to claim that an immediate improvement in welfare results from any economic development, but, without it, it would not be possible to achieve sustained improvements in the lifestyle of the people. Under the system which exists in the West, however, economic development is accompanied by the devastation of labor and the destruction of a healthy social psyche. This system must therefore certainly be described as clearly abnormal.

The core of the problem lies with the initiative of the workers. The greater the initiative demonstrated by the workers, the less the necessity to rely on authority. Such initiative can be consciously produced through a deepening and strengthening of the communion of interests between the company and the workers. As the initiative grows stronger, the driving force of the company will not rest with the authority of top management, but will result instead from true mass participation by the workers themselves in the labor process. Organizational activities will also be achieved through the voluntary coordinating actions of the workers themselves, i.e., those actions will result from teamwork.

This does not mean that there is no oppression of humanity in Japanese industry. But the Japanese corporate system is structured so that it allows for the coexistence of organizational efficiency and the freedom of those working within it to a far greater degree than the Western system. Alternatively, it has the flexibility to ensure that the efforts made toward achieving this actually bear fruit. Of course, just as there can never be an organization which is wholly dependent on authority, neither can there be an organization which is wholly dependent on initiative. Japanese companies, however, by creating a consensus of interests between the company and the individual, have been able to achieve true worker participation, something which has been totally unattainable with Western methods.

Attempts to humanize labor

Shigeru Kobayashi, former director of Sony Corporation, has greatly influenced other companies in contemporary Japan with his experiments and subsequent success in creating a new organization at the Sony Plant in Atsugi. He attributes the success of Japanese industry in the postwar era to the following:

> . . . after Japan lost the war it had nothing left but human
> resources, so it used those human resources to the maximum
> possible extent within modern industry and developed a new
> management philosophy and management techniques to
> harness them. This was an epoch-making phenomenon and
> completely different from the old style of management
> created in the West, which controls people in a mechanical
> fashion and breaks their spirit.[36]

The Japanese corporate system gives as much freedom as possible to workers, which makes it possible to create an organization that ties their total human potential to the corporation's growth.

Under the conditions that existed in Japan, there was no compelling reason for creating an organization to control workers. Thus, although Japan was under the strong influence of American-style management, Japanese companies gradually moved away from it. Today, the old traditional controlling mechanism type of organization and control system have been deliberately replaced by new methods. And as far as the nature of the corporate organization is concerned, a wide variety of trial variations are now being tested which are far removed from the previous pyramid-style organizational model.

Small group activities, too, which have become popular in recent years, are a reflection of a conscious move to apply Japanese organizational principles at production work sites. They are based on individual initiative and willingness, and promoting these human qualities makes it possible to create an organization that enables many people to discover a will to work within themselves. It is also a system that makes it possible for various innovations to emerge from within the organization (Table 3.4).

Table 3.4 *Specific results of small group activities (%)*

	Overall	Managers	Supervisors	Work site leaders
Communications improved	55.9	69.7	55.9	52.2
Work site atmosphere improved	49.2	49.5	47.3	50.1
Became more positive toward work	47.0	56.9	46.4	44.1
Fewer mistakes in work	43.5	44.0	38.7	46.4
Work efficiency improved	43.1	40.4	40.1	45.8
Useful for self-development	37.7	30.3	46.4	35.7
Improvement suggestions increased	33.9	26.6	40.5	33.1
Fewer mishaps and accidents	27.0	22.0	30.2	26.2
Work site structure bolstered	26.5	27.5	27.5	26.2
Good on-the-job training results	23.8	50.5	17.1	20.2
Good cost-cutting results	22.4	11.0	32.0	19.0
Work became more pleasant	16.8	15.6	14.9	17.9
Learned methods and acquired knowledge	16.6	5.5	21.6	17.0
Improved product quality	15.5	9.2	22.1	14.4
Increased sales volume and value	14.4	33.9	2.3	16.1
Improved production technology	12.8	26.6	40.5	33.1
Improved attendance	12.4	6.4	14.4	12.7
Don't know	2.5	2.8	3.2	1.7

Source: *Wagakuni Kigyo ni okeru Keieisanka no Shorai Bijon ni Kansuru Chosa – Wagakuni ni okeru Shokuba Reberu no Sanka no Rironteki Kaimei* (Survey on Future of Participation in Management in Japanese Corporations – A Theoretical Clarification of Participation at Work Site Level in Japan), survey by Shakai Keizai Kokumin Kaigi for Sangyo Kenkyujo, 1981, p. 109.

If Taylorism is thus the ideal behind control-type organizations, then small group activities must surely be the most faithful concrete reflection of Japanese organizational principles.

The ideals behind small group activities are described as follows in a QC circle outline prepared by a group in Japan that has contributed much to the spread of small group activities.

The theory that it is sufficient for a worker simply to perform his duties as prescribed is widely supported, especially in countries other than Japan, and there is also broad acknowledgement of the effectiveness of the rationalization achieved as a result of this method. Nevertheless, in reality, those who actually perform the work on a day-to-day basis are the ones who know those tasks best, and in many cases, they are the only ones who know about them at all. Also, Japanese workers, who are generally well-educated, would interpret instructions to simply do the job as they are told to do as a suppression of their initiative and humanity.

If workers were encouraged to do more than just fulfill their duties according to the plan in the work site, if they were encouraged to question and probe problems, undertake improvements that can be executed in the work site and present opinions and information without hesitation relating to improvements that cannot be undertaken in the work site alone, this would amount to a tremendous strength within the company. It is possible for workers to do this in Japan. It is the aim of QC circles to achieve this effect.

The objective of QC circle activity is . . . to develop respect for humanity. A work site which does not respect humanity is a work site in which people are alienated, personality is ignored, human strengths are undervalued; it is a work site in which people are treated like machines and discriminated against. This situation is virtually tantamount to telling workers, 'You will not be treated like human beings in the work site; here your humanity will be ignored. The work site should be seen as a place where labor is provided in exchange for money, so look for somewhere else to fulfill your own humanity.'

But the work site is the place where workers spend a considerable amount of their lifetime. Just imagine how wonderful it would be if it were to become a lively place, full of vitality, a place where humanity is respected.[37]

This synopsis will almost certainly leave its readers with many and varied impressions. Some people will readily identify with the efforts being made by Japanese companies to turn the work site into a more human environment, whereas others may interpret it as a cunning technique used to manipulate workers to obtain greater profits for the company. Regardless of the company's real intention, however, or even given that its actions are based on an ulterior motive, if it results in a more human labor structure, that should be good enough.

Concerning the intentions behind small group activities, moreover, if the fact that the company introduced these activities with the aim of increasing corporate profits is judged to be bad, then the expression 'ulterior motive' is also not entirely inappropriate. But such a judgment relates to how admirable the motivation is of Japanese managers showing respect for the humanity of workers and of the purity of their intentions, and, as such, it is not tied to a criticism of this system. Rather, it should be regarded as the highest form of praise that can be given to the system.

In the Japanese corporate structure, the company is made to depend on the initiative of its employees and, in return, the company makes efforts to satisfy their human wants. A company faced with fierce competition has no choice but to do so; if it does not, it will lose out in competition. Actually, however, such a criticism serves to highlight the fact that the Japanese system provides an agreement of interests, in which resides the firmest guarantee in human society of respect for humanity in the work process.

The peculiarities of the Japanese concept of labor

Some would argue that people in the West generally view labor as a hardship which has to be suffered in order to make a living, a necessary evil which is best kept to the barest minimum possible. In contrast, the Japanese are said to view work as a pleasure.

The problem with this sort of theory, however, is that the Japanese who are actually working find it difficult to take such an argument seriously. For the Japanese, work is often accompanied by many painful trials, tribulations and stresses, just as it is for people in other countries. Work is hardly a pleasure. On the other hand, neither is it simply a hardship.

For the Japanese, working is equated with living, and just like any other area of an individual's life, it is accompanied by all the joys and sorrows, hardships and satisfactions that go with it – at times portrayed in the most condensed form. Because the company is not organized around jobs as units, but rather, around the people themselves in the same way that other groups in society are organized, the individual automatically brings with him to the company the behavior and values that he adheres to in society-at-large.

Thus, for the Japanese, there is generally no radical discontinuity between an individual's home life, work site life (there is no phenomenon in the West which accurately corresponds to this expression) and the other areas of his life. Private life and work life become merged into a unified whole.

According to a survey conducted by Shinichi Takezawa and Arthur M. Whitehill among workers from both the United States and Japan, 73 percent of respondents in Japan replied that they considered their company to be either a part of or the central focus of their lives. In the United States, on the other hand, the corresponding figure was a mere 21 percent, and most respondents replied that the company is 'a place where they attempt to work together with management to achieve common objectives during working hours only.' Another common response was that the company is 'simply a place to work and has no connection whatsoever with the private lives of workers.'[38]

In the light of these circumstances, then, it is not strange at all to find Japanese characteristics strongly reflected in the work site lives of the Japanese. But there would not be much meaning in comparing the work site lives of the Japanese with those of workers in other countries, such as in, say, the United States, France or the PRC, because the work sites that would be the objects of the comparison are not American, French or Chinese but have something 'singular' about them. What would be found is something common to all of them in their singularity, no matter what the economic system and no matter what the social customs or practices. That singularity exists totally apart from society-at-large in any of the countries compared, representing a different dimension of living space.

Where can freedom, equality and democracy be found in the work sites of the United States or France? If the French or the Americans considered the work site to be a part of their life in the way that the Japanese do, there would be no place for their philosophies and lifestyles to coexist within the same life dimension. The reason for the coexistence of these elements can only be interpreted as stemming from the fact that workers in those countries do not consider their working hours, which account for a significant proportion of their lifetimes, as a part of living. In order that they can live like humans on weekends and vacations, they adopt the attitude of 'closing their eyes and letting it pass' at all other times. Labor is a required and necessary evil as a means of obtaining a civilized living.

Following this train of thought makes it possible to explain why those in the West criticize the long working hours of the Japanese so persistently, and why they continue to refer to themselves as civilized each time they do so.

The criticism of long working hours is itself off target, for working hours do not have the same significance for the Japanese that they do for workers in the West. In Japan, first of all, there is not as clear a distinction between work and private life. Also, the Japanese include an appropriate amount of fun in their work, and they continue to think about work and discuss it with their colleagues even after working hours. The concept of a wage rate, too, essentially does not exist in Japan. And since labor itself is not regarded as a hardship or as a necessary evil, there is no need for accurately determining the relative value of work as a drawn-out hardship or evil.

The real core of the differences between Japan and the West in relation to labor does not lie simply in the volume of labor, i.e., the length of working hours, but, rather, in the quality of that labor. In other words, it lies in the difference between the forms of labor.

When the West German Minister for Economic Affairs, Otto Lambsdorff, visited Japan in 1980 to attend the funeral of former Prime Minister Ohira, he made great efforts to visit Japanese companies. After returning to West Germany, he said that 'West German laborers should work harder', pointing to Japanese workers as an example. This pronouncement was met with a violent wave of resistance from labor circles, and Eugen Loderer, president of the Metal Trade Union, was quoted as saying, 'This is absolute nonsense. Telling us to work like the Japanese is like returning working conditions and social practices back to the Stone Age.'[39]

Lambsdorff's comment was also mistaken. The Japanese do not work harder than the Germans; they work differently from the Germans.

Concerning Loderer's remarks, rather than saying he misunderstands the real situation in Japan, I think his words accurately reflect European circumstances. In short, contemporary Europeans believe that 'labor is not a part of civilized life'.

Are the Europeans abnormal for believing that labor is something distinctly separate from life and civilization, or are the Japanese abnormal for believing that labor is just one aspect of life? The only country which has actually adopted a Japanese-style labor system is Japan. Comparatively speaking, therefore, in terms of numbers, Europe would appear to be the norm and Japan the exception. But normality and abnormality can hardly be determined on the basis of numbers alone.

Looking back at past societies, it is well-known that within traditional societies in any country, labor was generally accepted as a part of life. There can be no doubt that, compared with present times, the lives led by people in ancient days were filled with much more hardship. Despite this, however, labor was regarded as an indispensable element in living by both farmers and artisans alike. When looked at from a historical perspective, the current situation which prevails in Europe clearly belongs to the minority stream, and would actually be determined as abnormal in the results of an historical majority ruling.

Labor itself is not inherently a hardship. Europeans, for example, from politicians to artists, certainly do not regard their work as all hardship.

Neither would artisans who create items by hand agree that their work is all hardship. And yet, no matter how creative a particular task may be, as soon as it is carried out by a group, Europeans think of it as becoming a hardship.

Thus, rather than saying that labor itself constitutes hardship, it would be more correct to say that hardship emerges from within the formation of organized group labor. This should lead one to wonder whether there is anything within that organized group labor which transforms labor into hardship. Westerners, however, regard their organization of labor as being universal, and they do not stop to think that there might be a totally different form of labor organization.

The author cannot believe that a social organization which forces workers to perceive labor simply as a hardship could be the norm. Every society is dependent on labor. A society which encourages its members to think of one of the most fundamental aspects of its existence as a hardship is effectively practicing a form of self-denial.

Notes

1 Toshio Shishido, *Nihon Kigyo in USA* (Japanese Companies in the US). Tokyo, Toyo Keizai Shimposha, 1980, p. 150.
2 Shizuo Matsushima, *Chusho Kigyo to Romu Kanri* (Labor Management at Medium-sized and Smaller Companies). Tokyo, University of Tokyo Press, 1979, pp. 293–359.
3 Ningen Noryoku Kaihatsu Senta, p. 25.
4 Mabuchi, pp. 173–4.
5 Christopher Herman, 'Shin Gijutsu to Tatakau Hoho' (How to Battle with New Technologies), *Gekkan Rodo Mondai*, 4 (1981), pp. 56–9.
6 Einzig, p. 161.
7 Ningen Noryoku Kaihatsu Senta, ed., 'Nishi Doitsu no Shokuba to Maisutaa Seido' (The Work Site and the 'Meister' System in West Germany), *Ningen Noryoku Kaihatsu Shiriizu*, 56 (1979), p. 21
8 Ningen Noryoku, 'Work Site', p. 21.
9 For reference on the features of PPM control, see: Shin Miura, 'Nihon-ryu Hinshitsu Kanri no Tenkai' (Development of Japanese-Style Quality Control), *Hyojunka to Hinshitsu Kanri* 135 (March 1982), 7; and Katsukichi Ishihara, 'PPM Kanri no Kangaekata to Susumekata' (Thinking about and Approaching PPM Control), *Hinshitsu Kanri* 31–9 (Sept. 1980), pp. 8–9.
10 Dai Ito, *Chugoku no Ushinawareta Sedai* (The Lost Generation in China). Tokyo, PHP Kenkyujo, 1982, pp. 161–3.
11 Makoto Kumazawa, *Romu Kanri no Kusa no Ne* (Grassroots of Labor Management). Tokyo, Nihon Hyoronsha, 1976, pp. 118–21.
12 Shizuo Matsushima, *Rodosha Kanri no Tokushitsu to Hensen* (Characteristics and Development in Labor Management). Tokyo, Daiyamondosha, 1962, pp. 445–6.
13 Ningen Noryoku Kaihatsu Senta, ed., 'Kodo Jidoka Kojo no Genjo to Mondai' (Present State and Problems of Highly Automated Plants), *Ningen Noryoku Kaihatsu Shriizu*, 78 (1981), p. 215.
14 Tamotsu Sengoku and Atsuko Toyama, *Hikaku Nihonjin Ron* (Comparative Study of the Japanese). Tokyo, Shogakukan, 1973, p. 23.
15 Ken Tsuji, *Nihonjin wa Hatarakisugi ka* (Do the Japanese Work Too Hard?). Tokyo, Asahi Sonorama, 1981, p. 150.
16 Ryushi Iwata, *Nihonteki Keiei no Hensei Genri* (Structural Principles of Japanese-Style Management). Tokyo, Bunshindo, 1977, pp. 152–3.
17 Dore, p. 15.
18 'Tokushu: Kigyo Fukushi Shin Jidai' (Special Feature: New Age in Corporate Welfare), *Nikkei Bijinesu*, 11 (1980), p. 44.
19 Shishido, p. 87.

20 On this point, see Hirohide Tanaka, *Gendai Koyoron* (Modern Theory of Employment). Tokyo, Nihon Rodo Kyokai, 1980, p. 347.

21 In Japan, where in-house training is common, educational institutions with curricula for business schools include SANNO College, Keio University, Waseda University and Nomura Management School. One example where companies pay tuition fees for students they send for study is the School of Management at SANNO College.

22 Kiyoaki Takata, *Matsuda Hakusho* (Mazda White Paper). Tokyo, Recruit Shinsho, 1980, pp. 82–3.

23 Asahi Shimbun Keizaibu, ed., *K.K. Nippon Shindan* (Diagnosis of Japan Inc.). Tokyo: Asahi Shimbunsha, 1981, p. 118.

24 Yasuo Okamoto, *Gendai no Keiei Soshiki* (Contemporary Management Organization). Tokyo, Nihon Keizai Shimbunsha, 1980, pp. 25–8.

25 On the characteristics of decision-making in Western companies, see Tashiro.

26 Ningen Noryoku Kaihatsu Senta, ed., 'Nihon ni Okeru Keiei no Ichirei – Soni Kabushikigaisha ni Miru' (A Case in Japanese Management – Sony Corporation), *Ningen Noryoku Kaihatsu Shiriizu*, 6, (1974), p. 13.

27 Concerning the point that the organized teamwork activity characteristic of Japanese companies is linked to the presence of internalized workers, see Yamada, pp. 48–59.

28 Summary of comments by Makoto Kumazawa, Yoshiro Hoshino and Yoshikazu Miyazaki in the roundtable discussions 'Kanrishakai to Rodo' (Managed Society and Labor) and 'Kigyo to Rodo' (Business and Labor), *Jurist*, Special Issue (1979), p. 269.

29 Toshio Doko, *Keiei no Kodo Shishin* (Action Guidelines in Management). Tokyo, Sangyo Noritsu Daigaku Shuppanbu, 1970, pp. 46–7.

30 Shigeru Kobayashi, *Soni wa Hito o Ikasu* (Sony Makes the Best Use of Personnel). Tokyo, Nihon Keiei Shuppankai, 1965, pp. 5–7.

31 Stanley M. Davis and Paul R. Lawrence, *Matrix Management*. Addison-Wesley, 1977, pp. 14–7.

32 Davis and Lawrence, p 55.

33 Robert B. Klaverkamp [phonetic] 'Kinben o Umu Shakai no Shikumi' (Mechanisms of a Society That Encourages Diligence), *Manejimento*, 11 (1980), p. 85.

34 Concerning evaluation of this incident, see Makoto Kumazawa, from p. 83.

35 Takashi Uchiyama, 'Rodosha no Chosen ni Yuragu Beikokugata Shohin Seisan' (American-Style Product Manufacturing Rocked by the Labor Challenge), *Ekonomisuto*, 6–10 (1980), pp. 10–12.

36 Shigeru Kobayashi, *Soni wa Hito o Ikasu* (Sony Makes Use of People). Tokyo, Nihon Keiei Shuppankai, 1981, Preface.

37 Zaidan Hojin Nihon Kagaku Gijutsu Renmei, ed., *QC Saakuru Koryo* (Principles of the QC Circle). Tokyo, Nihon Kagaku Gijutsu Renmei, 1970, pp. 17–18.
38 Shinichi Takezawa and Arthur M. Whitehill, *Work Ways: Japan & America*. Tokyo, The Japan Institute of Labor, 1981.
39 Tsuji, pp. 40–41.

4   Kigyoism as an Economic System

 There has been increased worldwide interest in Japanese corporate management in recent years, and many foreign delegations and observers have visited Japan to view the situation in person. The following is a close approximation of what they usually experience.

> Businessmen, technicians and even line workers have all rushed to visit Japan from the West, filled with a great deal of curiosity and interest, and a strong desire to unlock the secrets and unravel the paradox of Japan. What they invariably hear and learn at the places they visit relates to the total company quality control system (TQC) and the activities of QC circles which are widely utilized at the actual shop floor level. These types of systems are not particularly novel to them, since, when you think about it, these phenomena originated in the West – Japan actually imported them. When the visitors remember this, they feel a certain sense of relief for a time.
>
> They consequently proceed to attempt to convince themselves that Japan is not hiding any special secrets or tricks; the Japanese are doing nothing out of the ordinary from which high quality products result.
>
> Nevertheless, on returning to their respective countries, these people suddenly find themselves faced with a dilemma. It is not particularly difficult to revive and implement the various systems that they saw being used in Japan in their own companies. However, when they actually reach the implementation stage they become aware of a significant problem which they had hitherto overlooked. That is, they suddenly realize that they did not adequately investigate the matter to properly understand what actually makes it possible to operate the total company participation system so widely used in Japan.[1]

Generally speaking, in other words, the management techniques of Japanese companies, by their very nature, are not easily conveyed in the form of systematized knowledge. And even if they can be so conveyed, knowledge alone is insufficient, and the techniques can only be implemented and absorbed into the work site with great difficulty. Therefore, regardless of the number of lectures foreigners attend in Japan, or how many work sites they observe, they never quite feel that they have grasped the essence of that for which they are searching. In short, something always escapes them. That's very understandable, of course, because the management techniques are linked essentially to the basic nature of Japanese companies, and they flow directly from that well-spring. In order to truly understand the management techniques, then, one must first gain an understanding of the nature of the Japanese corporation.

Many economists – like Masaru Ibuka of Sony Corporation[2] – who understand the management practices of Japan and other countries feel that what is called Japanese-style management cannot be broken into a mass of separate, fragmented techniques, but rather, that it has a fundamentally different aspect which lies between the two styles of management and differentiates it from them.

The problem is: what is that something?

Much has been said about this subject. And even if each person's opinion does not always clearly lean toward one side or the other, one can divide the overall opinions into two general categories. One set of beliefs holds that what gives Japanese-style management its characteristics, so different from Western management, exists only in Japan, and is tied to the unique historical background, tradition and psychology of Japanese society and people. The other category of opinions holds that although for the present the objective, systematized structure of Japanese corporations is found only in Japan, it has a universal quality that makes it possible to use it in any country.

In short, it comes down to whether Japan's management techniques comprise a way of culture or a system.

1 On Japan's 'Uniqueness'

At present, most people hold the former category of opinions, not only in Japan but even more so in other countries. It is typified by the following comment made by Philip Caldwell, former president of the Ford Motor Company.

> *Editor*: Do you mean it's all because of the Japanese?
> *Caldwell*: The harmony in the basic conditions for competition remains in a broken-down condition. Wages are far too low. This is because Japanese workers obviously have different wants and ideas than American workers.[3]

Although digressing slightly from the main focus of the arguments outlined thus far in this book, it is important, before proceeding any further, to examine the validity of several elements which comprise the first category of opinions which was mentioned above.

The 'diligent Japanese' theory

One of the elements is the theory that Japanese corporate management works well because Japanese workers are naturally diligent. The concept of diligence, however, is ambiguous. If one tries to measure it quantitatively, one could use the number of hours worked as a yardstick for comparing Japanese with others. But even if it could be said that the Japanese work somewhat longer hours than their Western counterparts, it is not a significant difference. The available statistics for making an international comparison are based on real working hours per week, and even at that level, the hours Japanese work are not notably long. Also, those statistics do not include such phenomena as moonlighting or *Schwartz arbeit*, which are common in the West. If they did, the gap between Japan and the West might be reduced even further. As well, a number of other countries clearly have longer working hours than Japan, which makes long working hours difficult to use as an explanation for the vitality of Japanese companies or the way they improve their productivity. It cannot be denied that the five-day work week is not as widespread in Japan; neither is the length of vacation time taken by Japanese workers, compared to vacation time to which they are entitled, as high as in the West. But if that is used as a yardstick, then the newly industrialized countries and the developing nations, where the five-day work week and the annual vacation system are even less frequently used, should have a great advantage over Japan.

It is certainly true that many Japanese work beyond their set working hours, but a comparison of how they work shows a tendency for them to concentrate less than Western workers. The following observations were made by an American executive posted in Japan.

> The Japanese are often referred to as people who are diligent and work hard, but if this is meant to signify, for instance, that they never digress from their work but continue single-mindedly and completely attentive to the task at hand in a highly efficient manner, I would not always agree with such a statement.
>
> The adjectives hardworking and diligent may evoke an image of someone who always works at top speed, devoting himself to his work without rest, but this certainly does not describe the Japanese. It is quite common to see office workers gossiping among themselves, smoking cigarettes or doing nothing in particular for 15 or even 30 minutes at a time.
>
> In many cases what are referred to as 'meetings' or 'negotiations' amount to nothing more than co-workers sitting down to have a cup of tea. In one sense, I think this is a manifestation of a great deal of flexibility within the company, and in that respect it is important . . .
>
> It is the same in the factories. The nature of the labor unions is also a mitigating factor, but in the United States a single worker usually works with one machine, whereas in Japan, one worker will be responsible for four or five machines. This is certainly better in terms of representing greater efficiency in terms of manpower, but this does not necessarily mean that employees are always working without ever digressing from the task at hand. By looking only at the actual factory production line, no evidence to suggest that Americans are slow workers while the Japanese are fast can be found.[4]

Every Japanese who has ever worked alongside an American in an American company expresses great surprise at the extent to which Americans display a high degree of concentration on the job at hand. Once the working day is over, of course, American workers leave immediately, and in that respect they are certainly different from Japanese, who tend to stay around to chat after working hours or go off to a bar for a few drinks to discuss work-related activities.

To explain the Japanese attitude toward work in a positive light, one could say it is freer and more relaxed. But Japanese do not concentrate on their work to the same degree as their Western counterparts. Japanese do not tend to make a clear distinction between working and non-working time as workers in the West do, and thus certain aspects of the situation do not lend themselves to the explanation that the success of Japanese corporations is simply a result of Japanese diligence. Such characteristics of Japanese workers are a consequence of the fact that overall, they have no clear sense of selling or providing their labor to the company. Rather, they view work as something to be tackled positively, and this attitude has nothing to do with racial characteristics.

Executives in the West really work quite hard, whereas, in contrast, the so-called 'windowside'[5] Japanese employees do very little. The reason Western executives work so hard is that they have a real sense of being movers in the company, and know that if they succeed they will also profit personally. The so-called 'windowside' class in Japan do not work because they have lost faith in the belief that if they contribute to the company they will eventually be rewarded. It is also difficult to explain this phenomenon in terms of racial characteristics.

The homogeneous race theory

The premise of the next theory is that Japanese corporate management results from the homogeneity of the Japanese race. In particular, the fact that teamwork functions so well, that companies do not rely on manuals, that employees naturally work in unison through tacit understandings to achieve corporate goals and that greater emphasis is placed on trusting relationships between people rather than written contracts in business dealings, are all characteristics attributed to racial homogeneity. On this point, there is no denying that Japanese are a much more homogeneous race than Americans. As such, in contrast to a nation in which people from a variety of racial backgrounds and cultures must operate together at the same work site, a country with a homogeneous population will, generally speaking, certainly have less trouble achieving effective communication within the corporate organization; furthermore, it should be much easier to develop good trusting relationships both within and between companies.

Particularly in recent times, groups of minorities who are not necessarily fluent in English have come to account for a large proportion of the factory labor force in certain parts of the United States. As a result, it has been pointed out that some plants are often faced with communication problems between workers. Certainly this sort of problem hinders the operation of the corporate organization.

Of course, to immediately assume that the operational method in the United States, centered around manuals and not always reliant on teamwork, along with the emphasis on written contracts, stems from American racial diversity would be jumping to conclusions. Although the United States is a racially diverse nation, it is not, like the Soviet Union, a confederation of racially different republics. Americans are basically fused by a common language and lifestyle. Despite the fact that some differences stemming from racial origin exist in the United States, the overall cohesiveness of the people as Americans is generally far stronger.

The same is true to an even greater extent for European nations. Britain, France or Germany certainly cannot be described as racially diverse nations. Britain, of course, includes Scotland, Wales and Northern Ireland with their independent local traditions. And Germany, which has a long tradition as a *territorial-staat* is still a federated nation today, and there are significant historical and traditional differences between member states of that federation. But can these factors be tied to the features of corporate management? Although there are some differences between the English and the Scots, and between the Bavarians and the North Germans, they all still have a far sharper awareness of their cohesive identity as being 'British' or 'German'. And it is far too conceptual a discussion to suggest that a European style of management was created in order to overcome the multiracial aspects of the region.

The fact that companies in the West adhere to a system which focuses on the doctrine of written contracts, for instance, can be easily explained without having to resort to citing cultural or psychological causes. In the West, the company is nothing more than an abstract mechanism, i.e., it is not organized as a cohesive body of people, like companies in Japan. The person with whom an individual is doing business today may quit his company tomorrow and join a company with which the first individual's company has a conflict of interest. Under such circumstances, it is not possible to deal with separate individuals, and there is no method available for guaranteeing the reliability of promises other than using a written contract to clarify the relationship between the two parties in terms of rights and responsibilities.

In Japan, regardless of an employee's position or job in a company, and even though there may be exceptions, one can basically trust that the individuals with whom one is negotiating are corporate employees representing the wishes of their company and acting accordingly. It is from such a context that Japanese contractual practices have emerged.

For exactly the same reason, the concept of the 'right of representation' has lost almost all its significance in Japan. There is no reason whatsoever, in a corporation with corporate employees, to restrict the number of persons qualified to represent the company to a select few. It depends on the particular matter, but as long as a corporate employee has sufficient information to allow him or her to deal with a problem, in practical terms that person can represent the wishes of the company. This type of problem, in short, is rooted in the company structure.

If this argument still remains unconvincing, let us look at Korea. The Koreans are an even more homogeneous race than the Japanese. Historically, Korea has consistently been united under a centralized system of power, and it never had a decentralized feudalistic governmental organization as did Japan.[6] As a result, there is a marked lack of regional differentiation in Korea. For example, in Japan, people in the Kanto region understand almost nothing of the dialects heard in Kagoshima or the Tohoku region. In Korea, excluding certain areas such as Cheju Island, there are no comparable regional differences.

Also, although the Koreans are a homogeneous race like the Japanese, the Korean corporate management style resembles the American rather than the Japanese in form. Some exceptions are managerial control by owner families, which is fairly common, and the move for management to have strong blood ties.

If the fact that the Japanese are a homogeneous race is really a valid explanation for the many features which characterize Japanese companies, including the communal nature of the organization, its equality, bottom-up or 'free reins' management, the close nature of human relationships in the company, and the performing of jobs by teamwork, then one would naturally expect the Koreans, who are an even more homogeneous race than the Japanese, to demonstrate these characteristics to at least the same degree.

In reality, however, this is not so.

As Table 4.1 suggests, the president of a Korean company has much more authority than his Japanese counterpart, and so-called top-down management is practiced. As far as hiring is concerned, much weight is attached to occasional or temporary hiring to meet demand, just as it is in the West. There are very few companies with a system of regular hiring each year (Table 4.2). Moreover, while the percentage of regular employees leaving the company each year is between 3 and 5 percent in Japan, comparable figures in Korea are as high as 10.9 percent in large corporations and 16.8 percent in medium-sized and smaller enterprises.[7] If the statistics for female employees who leave their jobs are not included,

Table 4.1 *Extent of top management (%)*

Position	Japan			Position	South Korea		
	a	b	c		a	b	c
Managing director and above	58.5	57.9	50.0	President	63.5	56.8	79.9
Board of directors	21.1	21.1	20.0	Chairman	17.3	21.6	6.7
President	13.5	12.7	20.0	Senior managing director and above	9.6	10.8	6.7
Other	5.2	6.1	–	Director	9.6	10.8	6.7
Chairman	3.7	2.6	10.0				

Table 4.2 *Method of hiring (South Korea) (%)*

Method	a	b	c
Regular hiring only	8.2	11.8	0.0
Irregular hiring only	65.3	55.9	86.7
Both regular and irregular hiring	26.5	32.3	13.3

the gap between the percentages for the two countries would probably be even greater.

Scouting is also commonly practiced in Korea, and it happens most frequently in companies in the same industry. In Japan, however, scouting rarely occurs, and when it does, it seldom involves shifts between companies in the same industry. Thus there is a sharp contrast between the two countries (Table 4.3).

Table 4.3   *Type of organization targeted for scouting (%)*

Organization	Japan			Organization	South Korea		
	a	b	c		a	b	c
Other corporations	34.8	33.8	50.0	Other companies in same industry	36.4	29.2	55.6
Government agencies	16.1	16.9	12.5	Other corporations	33.2	29.2	44.4
Other companies In same industry	15.5	15.4	18.7	Financial institutions	9.1	12.5	0.0
Financial institutions	10.6	10.5	12.5	Military	6.1	8.3	0.0
Universities, research institutes	10.6	12.0	0.0	Universities, research institutes	6.1	8.3	0.0

Source: *Research Concerning Comparison of Overall Productivity in Japan and South Korea*: 59, 71,76; *Report by Committee Comparing Productivity in Japan and South Korea*, Japan Productivity Center, (March 1981).
Note: Figures are %; a = all companies; b = large corporations; c = medium-sized and smaller companies

In line with the mobility of employees in Korea, as outlined above, Korean labor unions are organized on an industry-by-industry basis. (However, the present Korean government is attempting to restructure this system by promoting legislative measures aimed at introducing company rather than industry labor unions.)

Systems for urging employees to remain with a company are also not particularly advanced.

In the strictest sense of the seniority system as seen in Japan, no such phenomenon exists in Korea. There is almost a taboo, however, in placing a younger person in a post above someone older, unless the younger person comes from the bureaucracy or has some fundamentally different background. An employee's salary increases with his age, but this has no direct connection to the number of years of service to a particular company.

Hence, there is no strong connection between the employee and the company in Korea, and because 'owner management' is so widespread among all companies, whether large, medium-sized or small, there are very few elements which comprise the Japanese type of communal corporate body.

The following remarks were contained in the results of a survey made by the Japan Productivity Center about the differences in the relationship that exists between the individual and the company in Japan and Korea.

> Japan is a society in which the group to which an individual belongs forms the basis for his social status, and his life is determined in terms of working toward common goals as a member of that group. As a result, not only does he obtain a guarantee of support for living, but at the same time discovers from within that process a meaning in life. On the other hand, Korean society provides a stark contrast to this: it is generally considered that, rather than belonging to a single, closed group and devoting oneself to that group, it is preferable to develop and maintain individual relationships with a large number of different people. This is seen to result in mobility and freedom of choice for the individual, rather than restricting him to the confines of a group.[8]

Hence it can be seen that the corporate structure in Korea, and the social relationships which are formed within that structure, are very 'un-Japanese'.

Korea is a particularly important nation which must be included in any consideration of Japanese problems, since Korea is not only a highly developed industrial nation, but also has many sociocultural elements in common with Japan. Thus it is extremely difficult for both the homogeneous race and the sociocultural elements arguments to be given any validity, given that the same elements can also be found there.

Many countries around the world are already attempting to develop their own original forms of corporate management, tailored to suit the particular needs of their national situation. The time has long passed when it was sufficient simply to use the West as a comparative criterion for analyzing the Japanese situation. It is only natural, even apart from the homogeneous race theory, that a large number of other theories, which initially seemed to be cogent, will lose their validity when compared with many other countries, the way our contemporary era demands.

179

The groupism theory

This theory says that the Japanese system can only be realized within the psychological structure created by the groupism peculiar to the Japanese. This theory, however, gives no clear indication of exactly to what the term groupism refers. Besides, if one asserts that a relationship exists between groupism and the Japanese system, but is unable to produce any proof substantiating the claim that the Japanese are in fact group-oriented, then, as Yoshio Sugimoto so aptly phrased it,[9] the argument amounts to nothing more than mere impressions, the fragmented experiences of foreigners or an arbitrary collection of proverbs.

Does groupism mean that the leader of a group issues orders and the members of the group submissively obey them, or does it mean that members of the group use their initiative and act positively to achieve what they consider will benefit the group as a whole? These two approaches are poles apart. Which type of groupism do commentators in this field attribute to the Japanese? It cannot be a manifestation of both, as it is impossible for the two to coexist. In one, the leader takes the initiative and leads the group's behavior; in the other, it is the group members themselves who show initiative.

Given that the nature of the groupism theory is thus rather nebulous, it is very difficult to criticize. Also, there are many strange aspects to the arguments given to support it. For example, some plants in Japan have a practice of assembling workers each morning before the start of the working day to sing the company song. This scene is often seized on by foreign media and used when introducing the working conditions in Japanese companies. In reality, however, this type of practice is more the exception than the rule in large corporations in Japan. Nevertheless, the foreign television crews that come to Japan ignore the real situation, capture a scene showing factory workers lined up singing on film and consequently produce it as proof of the group-orientation of the Japanese.

Depicting this situation as typical seems quite strange to the Japanese, but foreigners probably like to use such scenes because they are consistent with the vague image of Japanese groupism held by many Westerners. This type of action can be cited as an example in which the media succeed only in reinforcing existing stereotypes, rather than reporting the real situation. Given that employees singing the company song may be atypical, and because that kind of behavior certainly would not be found in any Western company, one cannot deny that it might be interpreted as an extreme manifestation of Japanese groupism. But if one claims that singing the company or group song is a manifestation of groupism, how does one explain the fact that Japanese sing their national anthem much less often than Westerners sing theirs? On the basis of this argument, then, one would have to say that the Japanese are not group-oriented in terms of the State, but that they are in terms of the company. There are serious doubts, however, about whether an '-ism' so conveniently altered can stand the test of being supported by a consistent psychological framework.

In contrast, several arguments can be made to support the claim that Japanese are not group-oriented.

For example, Japanese tradition is based on the feudal system. In feudal society (for the *samurai* class only), the individual had to prove himself to the limit. In feudal times, wars were waged between groups assembled to fight individual battles. The *samurai* announced themselves before the battle began, found *samurai* on the other side of a similar rank, and proceeded to fight. The battle was won or lost on the basis of the outcome of personal encounters between those *samurai*. In the twelfth and thirteenth centuries, *samurai* engraved each of their arrows with their name, because individuals were rewarded on the basis of personal performance.[10] Until the Meiji Restoration in 1867, revenge was officially sanctioned in Japan, a practice unheard of elsewhere in Asia.

Any number of similar examples can be found. The view that Japanese are essentially group-oriented is not an opinion originally formulated by the Japanese themselves, but was, instead, something that was heavily influenced by Western opinions of Japanese. This point is important because, for many centuries, Westerners have displayed a tendency to adhere to an image of the countries of the Orient as places inhabited by faceless masses. The expression 'billions of ants' has been used to describe China, and the same has also been applied to Japan. The following comment is but one example of this type of thinking.

Japanese workers may certainly be enjoying prosperity.
However, in the ignorant eyes of those in the West, they look

very much like bees – bees that are not working for the honey, but for the beehive.

This whole scenario is just like the society depicted in George Orwell's spine-chilling novel *1984*. It would appear that people are watching out for 'Big Brother' everywhere they go.[11]

The various phenomena found in the contemporary economic society of Japan result from the sometimes conflicting and contradictory multidimensional activities of groups and individuals. However, those who do not understand Japan's internal circumstances tend to imagine that such activities are carried out according to a consistent plan by people with united wills. Many Westerners accept this scenario, probably because even if they do not make serious efforts to understand the complicated reality, they have the 'advantage', especially regarding Japan, of being able to feel that they have somehow understood.

In any case, there is no evidence that Japanese are group-oriented. That does not mean, of course, that they are not. In fact, the word groupism itself is vague, and it is difficult to expect such an obscure concept to explain the complex, well-structured Japanese system overall.

The lack of individualism theory

Like the groupism theory, the theory that Japanese workers are lacking in individualism is widely accepted in the West, particularly in Europe. This theory asserts that Japanese-style management can be implemented only in a country where there is no individualism as it is perceived in the West, and where individual awareness is underdeveloped. This is the obverse side of the group-orientation theory, but contains many more passive aspects.

Nevertheless, the fact remains that, in global terms, Japanese-style management is found only in Japan, and cannot be seen elsewhere in East Asia such as in Korea, Taiwan and Hong Kong, the Southeast Asian region, or in the Middle East. The corporate management employed in these countries has strong colorings of capitalist control, but fundamentally is about the same as in the West. There is generally no career employment system, so-called job-hopping is quite common, top management has much authority, and relations beween management and labor are generally rather cool. Workers show very little sense of belonging to a particular company; neither do they display a positive approach to their work.

Since it is clear that Western-style individualism does not exist in the countries mentioned above, and if the reason for the existence of Japanese-style management is given as the lack of an individualistic ethic, then it would be expected that at least one of those countries display a style of management similar to Japan's. But, in fact, none do.

The stereotypical image of Japanese workers that is held by Europeans depicts them as 'always obeying company orders, working silently under dehumanized conditions, a mass of non-individuals'. If Japanese workers really were nothing more than an easily manipulated, submissive labor force which never asserted itself, one would be hard put to say that the description of them as having no sense of individual awareness was wrong. But if one observes the shop floor of any Japanese plant, one will immediately discover that this assertion is clearly mistaken. Among the more prominent characteristics of Japanese workers are aggressiveness, initiative and an active nature. They do not perform their work simply as they are told, according to the rules; they use their own judgment and approach their work positively in a way that they feel will benefit the development of the company. There can be no denying that European capitalists of the nineteenth-century industrial revolution preferred a labor force that simply obeyed commands submissively and endured sub-human working conditions. But if Europeans attempt to impose their past experiences on an image of contemporary Japanese workers, this action will only reveal the extent of their ignorance of the real conditions of contemporary industrial society.

In contemporary industrial society, the greater part of the value-added component of products emerges as a result of constant improvement of product quality and production process, the quickness with which changes in market trends are grasped, and R&D and other intelligent and creative forms of labor.

Under these circumstances, if workers simply do their jobs as they are told, according to the rules, it will probably not produce good results. In industry, it is important not to try to regulate and control those who are working, but rather to give them enough freedom to display their initiative to its fullest extent. The success of Japanese industry today can be attributed to its creation of a fitting labor structure for realizing the use of intelligent labor, which is indeed the key to competitiveness in contemporary industry.

At any rate, when Europeans say Japanese workers have no individualism, it is difficult to understand what they mean by the word 'individualism'. It is difficult to believe that the many phenomena commonly found among European workers – disinterest in corporate management, unwillingness to think creatively to improve their work, absenteeism and a desire to receive as much compensation for as little work as possible – could signify moral achievements; nor is it conceivable that in any way they could be the products of individualism, an ethic. Individualism essentially signifies positive behavior based on criteria which exist within an individual, and is totally different from egoism, which does not attach value to ethics.

Even if the criteria in question happen to be based on thinking that evokes allegiance to a group, such as nationalism, for example, this is not proof for denying that someone is an individualist.

Europeans cannot deny that a person can be an individualist and a nationalist at the same time. After all, nationalism itself is an ideology produced by modern Europe. And if this is true, why is it impossible for individualists, in terms of their basic nature, to be – if such a word can be coined – 'corporationalists'?

As long as one remains faithful to the original meaning of individualism, it is completely possible for a Japanese-style labor structure, which emphasizes positive contributions to the group, to be in harmony with the individualism ethic.

The so-called small-group activities in Japan, for example, firmly embody Japanese organizational principles. They resulted from reflecting on shortcomings in the pyramid-style of organization, which is more suited to standardized control based on commands and regulation. One of the original aims of small-group activities is to allow each person to develop his or her initiative and individuality to the greatest potential. One cannot say, therefore, that such a management technique is not suited to essentially 'individualistic' Europeans. The core of the problem is the European corporate structure which makes it difficult to cultivate a positive interest among workers in corporate management.

The features of Japanese management are also explained at times using theories which relate to Japan's rice culture, its old feudal system or traditional ethics related to, say, Confucianism or the *samurai* code. Some people say, for instance, that because the Japanese are a rice-growing people, they are accustomed to the close communal labor. necessary for producing a rice crop, and this has in turn led to the emergence of group-oriented management in contemporary Japan. Others say the Japanese corporate system is a carry-over from the feudal *han* (clan) system of the Edo era. But such theories are far too conceptual; the basic problem is that they tend to emphasize only those features of Japanese management that relate to labor. For example, as far as the theory about the influence on the Japanese due to the fact that they are rice growers is concerned, it has already been pointed out that Korea, which is also a rice-growing nation, has a corporate management system that is much closer to the Western system, invalidating this type of argument.

It is easy to display individual initiative in Korea, but group activity is generally not as successful as it is in Japan. This lack of success relates to the absence of a career employment system, thus allowing individuals to join or leave a company at their own convenience, which means no group consciousness has been formed in the company. The general unwillingness to pass on one's experience and knowledge to others relates to the same institutional reasons. In the Korean situation, highly skilled workers could be invited at any time to join another company for higher wages. The company already employing the worker would have to offer him a sufficiently high pay raise to make it worthwhile for him to refuse the new offer, thereby differentiating him from the other workers. Because the system is one which ranks workers according to their degree of skill, the difference in pay between workers is equivalent to the difference in their skills, and it is thus natural that workers do not want to teach their skills to colleagues.[12] It is also natural, therefore, in the Japanese system, where such conditions do not exist, that workers cooperate with each other more effectively.

As far as Confucianism is concerned, moreover, observers in recent years have noticed the outstanding economic progress of countries in the East Asian region which formerly had Confucian cultures, including Korea, Taiwan, Hong Kong and Singapore, and any theory which they have created has included Japan. Although this seems to be where Confucian theory evolved, not even a fragment of Japanese-style management can be found in any of these countries. Thus it would appear that this view of the region is in itself fundamentally mistaken. Confucianism originally had no relation to physical labor or business, but instead comprised the ethics observed by the cultured bureaucracy of the ruling class in old China. It is inconceivable, therefore, that features of Japanese-style management such as a bottom-up style of decision-making, a positive approach to work and equality could have emerged from Confucianism.

There are probably many other cultural theories or psychological approaches for explaining Japanese-style management, but in general, most of these fall short of the mark because they only explain specific aspects of Japanese management. In particular, they fail to offer a systematic explanation for the following two phenomena:

1 Not only is there no trace of Japanese-style management in the West or in West Asia, but neither can it be found in East Asian countries that in terms of cultural and religious traditions bear some resemblance to Japan.

2 Japanese-style management was formed after Japan's industrialization had already significantly progressed, paralleling the weakening of traditional ethics and social elements.

A link between the system and local conditions

As discussed thus far, it is difficult to give much validity to claims that the elements characterizing Japanese management can be linked individually to unique conditions relating to traditions or natural features of Japan. The author, however, is not attempting to go to the other extreme by claiming that Japanese-style management as a whole is totally unrelated to the traditional mentality or social nature of the Japanese.

Japanese-style management was not created by some profound thinker, nor was it systematized and introduced through legislation: it simply evolved naturally. It is not even appropriate to say that this management style is linked to the Japanese reality. Rather, it *is* the Japanese reality. It is, so to speak, nothing more than a systematic structure found in the midst of reality.

Given this situation, one has to use prudently such assertions as 'unrelated'. The author prefers to say that the whole structure can be adequately explained under a given set of systematic conditions, with the rest resulting from the rational behavior of the company and its employees. He does not attempt to assert anything more than this point.

What needs to be rejected here is the arbitrariness which is inherent in explanations that try to link the features of Japanese-style management separately to parts of the Japanese psyche or other circumstances chosen at random. And yet it cannot be altogether denied that the structure of the overall Japanese management system may indeed be connected to these things at the deepest level.

Democracy, for example, has a clear ideology and a systematic structure which is rooted in that ideology. It is obviously impossible, however, to explain the individual elements which make up democracy, such as why the Prime Minister is nominated by Parliament, or why the Lower House has supremacy over the Upper House, by saying that they are linked to the ideological and religious traditions of the West. Traditional ideologies of the West, such as Christianity, are certainly linked to tenets of democracy such as the basic equality of individuals, but it is clearly inappropriate to explain the reason for the Prime Minister being nominated by Parliament in terms of a connection with Christianity. These matters should be explained as a logical evolution of the principles at the core of democracy. This same attitude should also be adopted when explaining the structure of Japanese-style management.

2 The Core of the Japanese Corporate System

The elements at the core of the Japanese corporate system are the integration of management (or the company as the organized expression of management) and labor, and the independence of that integrated management from the control of capital (and, it goes without saying, from State control). Therefore, Japanese management is no longer 'management' in the ordinary sense of the word, that is, linking it to capital and conflicts with labor. In

Japanese management, the relationship has been reversed and broadened to cover, in effect, the activities of workers.

The goals of management are concerned with pursuing the interests of the group of employees, and labor takes on management functions. The burden of risk has been shifted to the side of labor, and with it the overall body of employees has accepted the responsibility for organizing production and carrying out innovations and other managerial functions. The functions of management and labor have thus merged, creating an inseparable, unified whole. The autonomy of the management of Japanese corporations was achieved in two ways: (1) By severing – with progress in the securitization of capital – the control of management by capital that had moved outside the corporation, away from management; (2) By pulling labor, originally in confrontation with management, back into the corporation and unifying it with management.

The 'autonomy of management' in Japanese corporations, therefore, does not simply mean freedom from control by stockholders and labor unions. Other essential elements of this concept include employees taking initiative and participating positively in management.

What about the West in regard to these areas?

> Whenever you talk to supervisors about how production could be increased, they say, 'You're not an engineer.' So what? I know a better, cheaper way to do what I'm doing. Why shouldn't somebody care?[13]

As this comment by an American worker suggests, the corporate system in the West works in an organized manner to repress and distort any manifestation of management functions within the ranks of workers.

In Japanese corporations, then, those equivalent to the president, plant director (president in Chinese), general director (president in Yugoslavian), managers, *gangbu* (manager in Chinese), and workers are integrated through a common corporate employee awareness, and the corporation pursues its own goals, goals that cannot be broken down into the goals of stockholders, labor unions or the State.

The features discussed in Chapter 3 as the foundation for the progressiveness of the Japanese corporate system – the fact that there is virtually no conflict or dispute between management and labor, the existence of functions which support the self-initiative and morals of employees, the development of employee skills, the smooth conducting of job rotation, and the ability to structure an organization that depends on spontaneous organizational activities by employees – are nothing more than manifestations of the autonomy of management completely integrated with labor. These surface as features of Japanese corporations only when compared to Western corporations, because when they are viewed from the eyes of Japanese management they appear natural, so much so that pointing to them one by one as 'strengths' seems almost strange, in the same way it was strange to refer to 'spontaneity' as one of the features characterizing entrepreneurs in the earliest days of capitalism.

For example, one of the essential features of quality control in Japan is Company Wide Quality Control (CWQC). Foreign countries tend to see QC circles as being at the nucleus of Japan's QC activities, but, as Kaoru Ishikawa points out, QC circles are nothing more than one of the elements which make up the CWQC system. CWQC refers to QC activities conducted in an organized manner, not only in manufacturing, but in design, product development, buying, sales and every other division in a company, from top management down to direct workers at every level.

First, based on the leadership of those in senior positions, education and training in QC is carried out in an organized manner in every section and department of the company. At the implementation stage, an annual plan is prepared for improving quality, and that plan is used as the basis upon which all employees strive to improve quality. The company forms a QC assessment team composed of the president and other company executives, who visit each plant and each department to check that the plan is being implemented correctly and to make recommendations where necessary. In order to encourage employees in their QC activities, there are internal and external awards systems. Internally, for example, a company might have a President's Award; externally, one of the most famous awards is the Deming Prize. The suggestion system and small-group activities also have a place within the overall scheme of CWQC.[14]

When Japanese are asked about CWQC by foreigners, they naturally offer an explanation similar to the one above. And understanding the explanation, at least understanding it as knowledge, is much easier than understanding, say, linear programming or operations research. So the foreigners return home convinced they understand the system. But then come the problems because this system cannot be easily introduced using knowledge alone. CWQC requires that management embrace labor, for example, which is the most direct manifestation of Japanese management. Metaphorically speaking, little more than 10 percent of what happens is due to technique; the remaining 90 percent is due to Japanese management features manifesting themselves in terms of QC. It is unlikely that something can be implemented if one only understands 10 percent of it.

But the Japanese do not explain the remaining 90 percent which encompasses the real essence of the CWQC system. Although it is systematic and complicated, CWQC represents something that is taken so completely for granted that the Japanese are unable to easily explain it, in much the same way that the ordinary, yet complicated and systematic movements of the human fingers when writing cannot be easily explained. That is how a gap in perceptions emerges.

CWQC is a typical example, but there are many other Japanese management techniques which can be regarded as more of an automatic expression of the system rather than of technique.

The single-step arrangement and suggestion system are other such examples. The contents of the single-step arrangement are not so difficult, and it is thus relatively simple to understand it as knowledge. Implementation, however, is a totally different matter. In the West, die setters are usually clearly separated from the press operators who change the dies, and die setting is only carried out during the periods when work is suspended between shifts. If dies were changed during regular work hours it would clearly save time, but it would also threaten the jobs of the die setters. As a consequence, it is very difficult to change dies during working hours.[15]

Of course, it is probably not impossible to break through the resistance of the workers and restructure job positions so that the functions of the press operator and the die setter are integrated into one. The problem does not rest essentially with the system of the single-step arrangement itself, but rather with the fact that the innovation function, i.e., the conscious effort by the workers at the work site to review their jobs and to initiate and accept innovations, must rest with labor itself. In other words, even if job positions are restructured, the only result would be the conversion of the previous form of fixed labor into a new form of fixed labor. The reason one can see innovations relating to production control technology so clearly is closely related to the nature of the Japanese corporate system, under which management and labor are integrated.

The suggestion system, meanwhile, is also not quite as simple as generally thought, and a great amount of know-how is required to make it function properly. Nevertheless it relies much more on the features of the Japanese corporate system than on technique to function.

For a suggestion to be clear, for example, the worker who initiates it must be able to view the entire production control system from a broad perspective. Moreover, the following two conditions must be met in order to ensure that a suggestion does not become isolated from the reality in which the company finds itself. Those conditions are as follows:

1 Knowledge and technical information which can be used to upgrade the quality of improvements should be supplied continuously even as it is processed into a form that is most easily accepted by the average person making suggestions.
2 A system of mutual enlightenment and mutual help should be established so that information is passed to the lowest levels of workers in the most understandable form possible through the energetic activities of work site groups.[16]

Because Western companies do not know when workers will leave the company, however, it is difficult for them to undertake the type of planned job rotation system that helps to develop in Japanese workers the broad perspective with which they view their jobs. Also, the Western corporate system structure does not provide workers with enough company information on a daily basis to make such a plan feasible.

Much of the credit for making the suggestion system functional in Japan must go to the group leaders, the frontline supervisors of the production work sites. They encourage suggestions, make the initial assessment and forward good suggestions to the next highest level of supervision. They are thus not only leaders at the production work sites but also fulfill the role of conveying to the production team members what the company really needs at any given time, and which direction improvements should take in order to be of the greatest benefit to the company. Their contribution in ensuring that suggestions have significance for the entire company is most important.

In Western companies, however, the foreman is not a member of the labor union. He belongs to management, has a separate office in the plant, and, unlike his counterparts in Japan, does not spend much time on the production shop floor. As a consequence, he does not have a good understanding of the floor situation, and in that sense would not be able to encourage workers to submit suggestions or make the initial assessment of suggestions as the group leaders in Japanese plants do. Another crucial barrier, which has been mentioned before, is the very weak connection between the interests of the workers and those of the company under the Western corporate system.

A productivity increase has no direct tie to workers' interests because the volume of employment is determined by dividing the total volume of work by the standard task. When the volume of work decreases in bad times, the volume of employment decreases, but when the standard task increases due to technological innovation, this also results in a reduction in the volume of employment. Actually, there are times when this does not occur, mainly due to intervention by labor unions, but the basic principle still applies. The workers thus resist technological innovation and attempt to minimize its effect on the volume of employment to the greatest extent possible through a process of demarcation.

Unlike Japanese workers who are guaranteed employment on a company basis, Western workers are keenly aware of the relation that exists between improved productivity, a subsequent increase in the standard task, and a corresponding reduction in employment. This is why the United Auto Workers (UAW) insists that QC circle activities be introduced only if resultant increases in productivity do not lead to layoffs. Given that backdrop, and the fact that workers are, in effect, tying a noose around their own necks by suggesting improvements in productivity, it is difficult to imagine Western workers embracing the suggestion system with the same enthusiasm and positive spirit of Japanese workers.

The same can be said of wages. In Western companies, the higher the wage rate and the lower the standard task, the better off workers will be. Workers would probably feel it is unfair if they voluntarily initiate activities that result in an increase in the standard task and their wages are not raised accordingly. Wages, however, cannot be revised quite so easily. The difficulty lies in the fact that while both the submission of suggestions and QC circle activities take place in individual companies that reflect their results, wages are determined at a supra-company level through negotiations between labor and management. Thus, if wages cannot be adjusted easily, one is inevitably led to ask exactly what benefit such a system has for workers. Because of that system, disputes arise between workers and management over whether workers should conduct QC circle and suggestion system activities during working hours, and what sort of compensation should be paid to workers for these activities.

Companies in other countries finding themselves in such a situation will eventually be forced to realize that the suggestion system is more than simply a management technique. The reason they have been unable to breathe life into the suggestion system and make it work as it does in Japan up to now is because, in effect, they have been saying to the workers — who are really the ones selling their labor to the company — the equivalent of 'We'll leave the price of your labor where it is, but we want you to improve its quality voluntarily.' If the suggestion system is to function perfectly, these companies will come to understand that their workers must be like Japan's 'workers' and take a positive interest in management while at the same time believing in their own minds that their wages are separate from their specific daily work.

3 The Autonomy of Management

One of the problems of the corporate system in the West, especially that which exists in the United States, is that it has begun to stray from what was originally one of the ironclad principles of capitalism, i.e., that only those who bear risk may exert control. On the other hand, although it may sound paradoxical, perhaps it would be better to say that the development of capitalism has given birth to conditions that cannot support this principle.

There is no question that shareholders shoulder risk, but unlike entrepreneurs who establish companies with their own money, shareholders are only exposed to risk while they own shares – and they are free to determine how long they remain shareholders.

The risk borne by owning shares, however, corresponds in only a limited way to the risk a corporation has as an ongoing concern while it continues to develop its business activities. The principal interest of most shareholders is having the company pay them high dividends for as long as they wish to remain shareholders; they do not have any interest in what happens to the company beyond that point. Such shareholders probably look at companies as objects to be milked. It is clear that as long as they continue to have any authority to control the company, the company will remain subordinated to serving their capitalistic interests, and, as a result, the rational development of management will be impeded.

Moreover, even though labor was formerly outside the company, it did not harm managerial autonomy in any way. Years ago, the form of labor revolved around repetitious acts with almost no prospect for improvement. Thus, there was no need to encourage workers to improve their skills, to be innovative, or to adopt any other management functions. All that was required was for entrepreneurs to obtain labor from the market and use it in much the same way they used raw materials and fuel. But when employers were forced to become dependent on the initiative of workers because of changes that were taking place as industry gradually moved closer in nature to agriculture, management was left with no choice but to incorporate labor into the company in order to preserve its own autonomy. Because of such changes, a self-contradiction appeared in capitalism as it exists today. The fulfillment of one of the most ironclad principles of capitalism — that only those who shoulder risk may exert control — is effectively being obstructed by a second principle of capitalism, that control is based on ownership.

The right of private ownership was the basis for managerial autonomy during the earliest period of capitalism. At the time, the scale of companies, as well as the number of managers, was small, and entrepreneurs hired workers from the market and directly supervised their work. Corporate risk, equivalent to the entrepreneur's ownership risk, was unified in the person of the entrepreneur. Thus, it is clear that private ownership tied authority and the bearing of risk together. Private ownership today, however, as least as far as large corporate organizations are concerned, has turned into something that harms management's autonomy by giving rise to external control of the company by the shareholders and the separation of labor from management.

Facing that situation, Japan levied extensive restrictions on the labor market and risk-bearing capital in order to render a portion of private ownership non-functional and shift the burden of corporate risk to the side of labor, thereby paving the way for a new era assuring the autonomy of management.

Therefore, according to the existing concept of the economic system, especially as far as it relates to the large corporations that are the backbone of the economy, and from the point that private ownership related to stock in Japanese corporations has been rendered nearly non-functional, it has become difficult to say that Japan is capitalistic in the original sense of the word. And from the point that market principles in the labor and capital markets are rather restricted, liberal elements have retrogressed.

But if one understands the essence of capitalism to reside in control by those bearing the risk, which leads to managerial autonomy, rather than in private ownership, and if such autonomy is the source of a vitality never seen before in history, one can call the Japanese system a restructured form of capitalism that emerged in response to new conditions in a new age.

To the extent that one interprets capitalism in that way, the conditions now existing in Japan and the countries of the West can be described as follows.

Whereas Japan has sacrificed some liberal principles while preserving the essence of capitalism, Western countries have not so much a shortage of liberalism, (once again, viewed from the point that managerial autonomy is the essence of capitalism) as they have a shortage of capitalism. And if one looks closely at the securitization of capital, i.e., the infiltration of market principles into risk capital, one sees that it has undermined managerial autonomy, and one must say, therefore, that liberal principles are eating away the vitality of capitalism. Liberal principles do not necessarily lead to managerial autonomy; the two are essentially separate.

This point is clearly evidenced by reviewing the tenant farming system which once existed in Japan and is still widely seen today in many developing nations.

In many countries, the tenant farming system is considered to be hampering the development of the productive capacity of agriculture for the following reasons.

The competition between tenants that results from the scarcity of farmland gives rise to constant pressure from landlords in the form of increasing land rents. This rental income enables the landlords to obtain a high income from land revenue without having to work or become involved in farm management. Landlords thus become isolated from farm management, and they do not reinvest their income from rents into farming operations, but instead use the money to acquire more land, or for other commercial or financial activities. Meanwhile, because tenants live in fear of having their contract rescinded at any time, they are unable to take a long-term view toward managing their farms. Since it is pointless for tenants to invest in improving their land, given their situation, they often rush into destructive farming which does nothing to maintain the soil.

Since any increase in production will result in a rental increase from the following period on, there is little incentive for tenant farmers to increase production. As a result, technical improvements do not advance either. In prewar Japan, because tenant rents were generally paid in kind, tenants could not choose which crops to cultivate, and because they had little chance to contact the market directly, they had no opportunity to develop as farm managers.[17]

Thus, under the tenant farming system, even if landlords and tenants were completely free economic agents, and even if rents for farmland were determined by free market forces, 'farm management' would still be prevented from developing freely.

It is not the limited permeation of the market principle that has prevented the free development of farm management and the expansion of agricultural production capacity in many developing nations today, but rather the ownership relationship that has prevented the autonomous development of management.

Because the system in prewar Japan was one of payment in kind, and because the tenant gave the landlord a reduced volume of production in times of poor yield, the landlord bore considerable risk. In short, the landlord had ownership and assumed much of the risk related to it, and the tenant was responsible for all other functions.

The emergence of independent farming after the war greatly contributed to the steady improvement in the production capacity of agriculture, because the independent farmer came to embody and fulfil three roles at once: he bore the risk of ownership, he was the manager and he was the worker.

As Seiichi Tohata remarked, aside from its impact as social policy, the real significance of agrarian reform was its creation of 'appropriate management'.

> It is not a question of simply choosing between tenant and independent farming. Rather, the question at the core of the matter is whether either represents appropriate management. What tenant farming needs is not an immediate switch to independent farming, but appropriate management (size, freedom of choice of crops, tenure security, etc.)
> . . . The social significance lies in the subordination of both controls on and sanctioning of the two (ownership and tenant rights) to higher and more dominant positions, and appropriate management aimed at bolstering production capacity represents this very element. The significance of agrarian reform is directly attributed to the emergence of this element. The right to the appropriate management of production is greater than simple ownership or the right to cultivate.[18]

Because of agrarian reforms, those who must shoulder the risk of, and take responsibility for, agricultural management were given complete managerial control, and as a result, agricultural management has been promoted autonomously. It is inconceivable to consider the noteworthy rise in productivity of Japan's agriculture in the postwar period without those conditions.

It is clear that free economic principles alone do not guarantee the growth of production capacity. In addition to that point – rather than more than that point – managerial autonomy is necessary. It is only when managerial autonomy has been achieved that human energy and vitality can be linked to the progress and development of management. The close tie between authority and the bearing of risk creates a situation in which groups and individuals find that the only way to improve their own destiny is to further the development of management, and the responsibility for doing so rests with themselves. For both managers and workers alike, the further they are from the risk of management, i.e., the weaker the link becomes between the development of management and their own interests, the more their efforts will gradually become less related to promoting management, and at times may even begin to follow a direction which is contradictory to the aims of management. When managers put the development of management aside and become engrossed in producing higher dividends, not only will they be unable to expect from workers the energy needed to support management, but workers will use various restrictive practices to suppress the development of management and to promote their own interests.

If the corporation's affairs were seriously affected by government intervention, managers would probably invest most of their energy in trying to influence government decisions more favorably in their interests. Also, the greater the influence of labor union actions on the results of management, the more management will direct all its efforts to compromise with, repress or manipulate the labor unions – rational behavior in such circumstances.

But if the outside influence could not be resisted or manipulated, then everything would have to be left to fate and managers would have to hope for good fortune.

Managers who find themselves in a situation in which all their work goes for naught, despite detailed planning and the expending of great amounts of energy, because of some unexpected government ban, or perhaps a strike, will probably lose some of their willingness to continue making steady, diligent efforts to develop their company, and likewise, managers who find that their company, in imminent bankruptcy, has been rescued by government subsidies, may also lose their enthusiasm.

Apart from the inevitable economic risks, managerial autonomy minimizes all other artificially induced risks and creates the conditions for having those involved in management invest their total energies in promoting the development of management. The creation of such conditions is what leads to the brisk vitality that is characteristic of capitalistic economies.

These conditions are lacking in Western companies. Ownership is separated from management (this is less true in Europe than in the United States, but in contrast, there are many cases in which management in European companies is subordinated to the private interests of powerful families) and management is separated from labor. Shareholders are separate from management, and they view management simply as a resource to be milked. And just as tenant farmers, cannot develop a managerial sense if the landlord shoulders all the market risk, labor also exists outside the company and adopts the attitude of a bystander rather than a participant. Furthermore, the conflict of interests between labor and management can be described in exactly the same way, in that it encourages the emergence of a variety of restrictive practices which work to impede the development of autonomous management.

A free economy unaccompanied by managerial autonomy may indeed be superior in terms of its static effectiveness. And as far as the process in which innovations spread to all companies once they have been introduced is concerned, the market displays a superior degree of effectiveness. The situation is different, however, when viewed from a dynamic perspective.

In order for human beings to take all the energy and willpower they use for advancing themselves and concentrate it on attaining corporate goals, there must be a close bond of interests between the corporate goals and the persons supporting the corporation, with no external interference between the efforts of those persons and the results of those efforts. In that sense, one can say that although the market works best in a situation of static effectiveness, managerial autonomy is the driving force behind dynamic vitality and innovation.

This element, again, is an advantage inherent in Japanese management. As discussed in the previous chapter, the advantages of Japanese management realize their greatest potential in an economic environment of great uncertainty, where innovations can be constantly implemented.

If the economy is in a constant state, i.e., if the economy appears fixed because future conditions are not expected to differ from current conditions, the features of Japanese management given as advantages would no longer be considered such, and in many instances would be evaluated as being opposite to the features of Western management.

Because management that emphasizes ROI makes the most rational choice under conditions it knows about, it is probably more effective than Japanese management. If the content of the work to be performed does not change over time, there is absolutely no need for a company to develop its human resources in-house. Instead, a system of leaving education to outside organizations and hiring workers as needed will reduce the burden on the company and probably be more efficient. Also, since the make-up of jobs does not change under constant conditions, no merits are gained by rotating workers to different jobs. In a situation where there is no uncertainty and the work consists of pre-set and repetitive jobs, a dynamic organization dependent on the spontaneous activities of corporate employees will be less efficient than a static organization strictly controlled according to manuals.

In short, Japanese management realizes its innate advantages best in a wholly dynamic economic environment. This is a reflection of the fact that the superiority of the Japanese corporate system is that it keeps managerial autonomy, once the core of capitalism, intact.

The features of Japanese companies are reflected throughout the economy. In contrast to the American economy, which is more liberal and efficient, the Japanese economy is more capitalistic (in the sense of preserving managerial autonomy) and has a great dynamic vitality. The American economy is like a motor vehicle with a refined design and highly efficient internal mechanisms. The problem, however, is that in recent years something has started to go wrong with the engine.

In the Japanese economy, on the other hand, market forces concerning labor and risk-sharing capital do not always function effectively, and the market includes certain inefficient sectors, such as agriculture and the distribution industry. Nevertheless, if the Japanese economy were also likened to a motor vehicle, its engine would be a powerful one. Its engine's great power propels the economy further, without concerning itself with inefficient or outdated internal mechanisms. In the background of the different impressions that the economies of both nations give, one is confronted with a bare fact, i.e., the formerly united principles of liberalism and capitalism have begun to drift apart as a result of changes in the roles of capital and labor in economic activities at the economy's most basic level.

4 From Authority to Responsibility

At the core of the Japanese system is managerial autonomy made possible by independence from capitalist control and the integration of labor into management. In this system, the meaning of words like company, shareholder, director, management, organization, labor, worker, labor union and others, that are generally used to explain capitalist economies in their original form, have changed almost systematically.

The company has expanded to include blue-collar workers, and has been transformed from an organization owned by its shareholders into an organization of corporate employees. Shareholders have become like bondholders, and corporate shareholders mutually holding shares of other companies submit blank proxies for the general shareholders' meetings, thereby faithfully following the will of the company. For all practical purposes, the management trusteeship function has disappeared, and the board of directors has ended up merely being a part of the mechanism making decisions regarding policies of the corporate employees. Management has thus broken away from the control of capital to become integrated with labor. And as the burden of risk shifted to labor, managerial functions also began to penetrate the inner ranks of labor; labor also came to include the functions of innovation and the organization of production. Workers became corporate employees, and labor unions became corporate employee unions. Also, the structure of the corporate organization changed from one in which management, representing the interests of capital, controlled workers in a static, pyramid-shaped organization, to a dynamic organization that has process rather than structure as its essence, and that is dependent on the self-motivated teamwork of corporate employees.

Against the backdrop of all these phenomena, two facts stand out particularly clearly as being at the core of the Japanese system: first is the severance of management from capitalist control; and second, the integration of labor into management. As a result, the autonomy of management – formerly one of the essential features of capitalism – has been realized, with large numbers of the working masses as indispensable elements in its formation. From this structure comes the special features characterizing Japanese companies and the Japanese economy: all employees involved in dynamic innovativeness and vitality. It is difficult and inappropriate to explain this system by relating it to existing concepts of systems.

Japanese reality now requires a term that effectively describes this new system.

In the context of the discussion thus far, there is probably no better word than *kigyoism* for describing the new system. As explained earlier, some Marxists in Japan are already using the word *kigyoism* to point to an ideology that they say has warped the thinking of Japanese workers, who, as a result, no longer view themselves as 'workers' in the original sense of the word.

Although this same word is borrowed for this book, it refers to the corporate system outlined thus far, and to an economic system composed principally of corporations adhering to this system. In this book, in other words, the word refers to an objective structure, and is thus devoid of any value judgments.

The reason for limiting the definition by saying 'composed principally of corporations adhering to this system' is because the *kigyoistic* mode of production does not apply to the entire economic structure. Almost all of agriculture, for example, as well as a large percentage of medium-sized and smaller enterprises, does not fit this description. Still, the *kigyoistic* mode of production is the dominant mode in large and middle-rank corporations that are at the core of the Japanese economy and exert an ongoing influence on the economy, on society-at-large and on the formation of the social values and behavioral patterns of the average Japanese.

Even in those countries classified as having either capitalist or socialist systems, it is difficult to say that only one or the other mode of production is in use. Agriculture, for instance, regardless of the type of economy, often uses methods that are neither capitalist nor socialist. In capitalist countries, too, many people operate businesses just to maintain a livelihood for themselves and their families, and, in recent years, there has also been an increase in the number of State-run industries. Also, a free market exists even in socialist countries, whether officially recognized or not, and something close to private ownership can actually be found in the mode of production. The problem is deciding what a country's dominant mode of production is, and as long as one approaches the question that way, Japan is a *kigyoistic* country.

The core of *kigyoism* – Responsibility

The essence of *kigyoism* is the existence of management that is integrated with labor and that has managerial autonomy inside the company. When seen from a human viewpoint, this means that corporate employees autonomously promote corporate activities. If one follows Marxist terminology, which defines a capitalist something like being 'capital with eyes and ears attached', then a corporate employee is the personification of management integrated with labor, complete with eyes and ears.

Corporate employees are charged with managerial autonomy, and their relationship with the company is essentially one of participation rather than control. Such participation derives from their responsibility for corporate management as a group. Having such responsibility does not come from any psychological sense of 'feeling' responsible, nor does it have a legal or institutionalized meaning. Rather, it signifies that the interests of corporate employees are tied to the company's fortunes, and, based on that objective situation, employees are forced to accept the responsibility for management. By accepting that responsibility, and pursuing their own best interests as a group, corporate employees actually move the corporation by participating in management. In this system, therefore, the motive force is responsibility, not authority.

A problem, up to now, in characterizing various economic systems has been pinpointing authority.

The capitalist system has been depicted as a system in which capitalists control companies on the basis of the right to private ownership, and the system of 'joint decision-making' has been depicted as a partially amended version of capitalism, under which workers are given joint control. Socialism, on the other hand, has been portrayed as a system in which the working class has seized authority from capitalists. The system of self-management socialism, meanwhile, proclaims that all previous forms of socialism have actually degenerated into control by the State or the bureaucracy, and that as a new form of socialism, it has been able to achieve a reality in which control emanates instead from the workers themselves. Also, when the industrialized nations of the West are portrayed as having free economies, one of the essential features is that the system is regarded as giving the individual the right to make economic decisions.

At any rate, regardless of the system one studies, 'authority' is always at the core of the system's concept.

In contrast, *kigyoism* deals not with authority, but with responsibility. It is possible to portray Japanese companies as being 'controlled by corporate employees', a phrase used by the author in Chapter 1.

When explaining the *kigyoistic* system, however, one must realize that adhering to the concept of control means actually being influenced by existing concepts of systems, where, in fact, the core of *kigyoism* does not lie. This statement is evidenced by the fact that no one in Japanese companies clearly controls the company from anyone's viewpoint. The location of authority in Japanese companies has always been unclear.

For example, while there is one theory that says Japanese companies are controlled by 'managers who act as supervisory workers',[19] there is also a theory that says that companies are controlled mutually as a result of the mutual holding of shares by corporations.[20] Yet another theory says the companies own and control themselves.[21] So there are many variations on this theme. And, needless to say, many Marxists believe that, as before, Japanese companies are still controlled by capitalists.

Thus, it is obvious that there are myriad conflicting opinions regarding the situation. And the matter of who controls companies in Japan, a basic, simple question, is not at all self-evident. Such a phenomenon is not found in companies operating under other economic systems. The system itself clarifies the location of authority, and the reality almost exactly matches the theory.

In Japanese companies, however, the system makes it clear that the owners of capital, who are supposed to have authority, do not actually control the companies. Even more so, neither do the State nor the labor unions. Some companies are under the control of banks, but this is a partial phenomenon, and, besides, one would still be faced with the unanswerable question of who controls the banks, which are incorporated companies themselves.

The answer, 'management controls the companies', is a possible contender, of course, but that confuses internal control with the company's ultimate control structure. The persons heading governmental agencies, such as public corporations, commissions and public enterprises for example, and having the greatest internal authority, are the president or the board chairman. Therefore, although it may be appropriate to say that the president or board chairman of a public corporation, commission or public enterprise controls a particular entity in terms of describing its internal organization, that is clearly not a proper description for explaining the nature of that entity.

The essential nature of such organizations is that they are government agencies, i.e., they are under government control.

Similarly, although one might say that management controls Japanese companies, this answer can only be used to explain the organization's internal structure and does not explain the nature of the overall corporate organization. The authority of the president, for example, comes from his position as the top person in the organization, and there is absolutely no mechanism external to the company that guarantees his position. If he resigns and leaves the company, his authority disappears. Thus, the authority of managers comes from within the company. Although the company explains their authority, their authority cannot explain the nature of the company.

As mentioned in Chapter 3, *o-mikoshi* (free reins) management is thus an appropriate term for describing the Japanese management style.

The remuneration Japanese presidents receive is truly modest compared with that received by the presidents of corporations in other countries. Of course, some may point out that Japanese presidents have large entertainment allowances. Although that is true, the president is not the only manager with that type of allowance. Also, even if some managers tried to supplement their income with their entertainment allowance, the very fact that they would resort to such measures says much about the true nature of their position.

Some might point out that the prestige accompanying a position like president serves to replace material rewards such as higher remuneration, and, indeed, there may be some truth in that. But the strength of that point alone is not enough to support the argument that management controls the company. Regardless of the kind of prestige that accompanies a position, it is still true that there is no better reward than higher remuneration. This was true for company presidents before the war, and it is still true today. Although some presidents in prewar times are said to have taken half the total amount of bonuses for themselves, in practical terms, today's presidents would be unable to do so.

If, therefore, the theory that management controls the company is invalid, how does the idea of expanding the parameters of management to include supervisors and supervisory workers, thus having the overall management structure controlling the company, bear up? This idea suggests a situation in which the supervisory class of workers in Japanese companies sits as a group and controls all other worker groups below.

However, this theory also has flaws. As already pointed out, everyone in a Japanese company, from the president to the lowest ranking employee, is connected in a straight and continuous line, even though there are differences in pay, status and degree of participation in decision-making. There is even a system today that enables shop workers to be promoted gradually, even possibly rising to plant manager, clearly a supervisory position. The line from plant manager, to assistant plant manager, general manager, manager, assistant manager and line or shop worker, is unbroken, and there is no way of distinguishing those who control from those who are being controlled.

Although it is clear that both managers and supervisory workers have authority and perform a controlling function, neither can be seen as holding positions comparable to those formerly held by persons who had owned capital in the company.

The final scenario which comes to mind is one in which the definition of those in control is expanded to include all corporate employees as a group. This scenario cannot be challenged. It is obvious that corporate employees are moving the company, and if there is an element of control, it is strange to think that anyone other than the body of corporate employees is exclusively in control. If one uses this line of reasoning, the explanation is plausible.

Still, as was made clear in the discussion up to now, the process leading to this conclusion is one of gradual elimination. Possibilities are eliminated one by one until only one remains – the proposal that control rests with corporate employees as a group. Merely because that theory remains, however, does not mean a control phenomenon actually exists and has been substantiated.

Besides, if one were to ask what exactly was meant by the tentative conclusion arrived at that Japanese corporations 'are controlled by their employees', one would have to say that since the essence of a Japanese company is the united body of corporate employees, this is equivalent to saying that 'one controls oneself'. If this situation was considered in terms of the individual, one wonders if the same type of roundabout expression would be used to describe it. In extreme terms, it would probably be expressed by saying, 'I will not be controlled by anyone' or 'I am an independent human being'.

The situation in Japanese companies is similar. There is no need to say anything more than, 'the company is independent, and its management is autonomous'.

Just because Japanese companies have broken away from the control of capital does not mean someone else must take over the reins of control. Those who think that way are clinging too closely to the concept of the capitalist corporate structure, and there is no need to raise such an issue in the first place.

The nature of Japanese companies cannot be explained in terms of authority. This does not mean, of course, that the phenomenon of authority does not exist in Japanese companies, but its importance has been reduced because of the way the organization operates. In short, the significance of authority has been reduced, but authority, of course, has not disappeared altogether. Still, authority is wholly an internal matter and does not help to explain the nature of the Japanese company.

Meanwhile, what about companies which do not adhere to the *kigyoistic* system? In a word, those companies exhibit phenomena that are divergent with those in *kigyoistic* companies. For example, although the location of authority is clearly defined, the location of responsibility is not. In other words, it is extremely unclear who will benefit or accept responsibility, although not in a legal, institutional or ethical sense, and who will lose, depending on the company's fortunes.

In capitalist companies, investors who buy and sell a company's stock on the stock exchange can maintain their assets without being involved in any particular company. Workers, meanwhile, are nothing more than vendors of their labor, and if their company goes bankrupt, it merely means they have temporarily lost the buyer of their labor, and managers and supervisors are no more than employees who provide the company with specialized management skills.

Responsibility in socialist companies is borne by the State. But whether the bureaucrats who prepare and implement economic plans will consider the smooth management of one of the great many State-run corporations an urgent problem is a moot question. Also, workers in Yugoslavia suffer almost no loss when their corporation declines in the same way that they bear no responsibility.

In short, the location of authority is very clear in these systems, but the location of responsibility is blurred. This is a reflection of the fact that whether it comes from the owners, the workers, or the State, the common driving force behind corporate activities in these systems is authority.

The unique path taken by *kigyoism*

The view that the essence of capitalism lies in the authority held by those with capital, based on the right of private ownership, was itself a one-sided approach. Of course, entrepreneurs in the early years of capitalism used their authority over workers. But as part of their role in society-at-large they were responsible for managing their company.

It is clear that the economic power of entrepreneurs enabled them to organize labor and utilize it to achieve corporate goals. They harnessed the energies of labor through dismissals and coercive measures such as salary assessments. One might ask, then, what the driving force was that harnessed the entrepreneurs as innovators and as the organizers of production. Needless to say, the motivation could not have been authority, for the entrepreneurs already had authority and were not controlled by others. No, it was not authority that drove them on, but responsibility, i.e., the bearing of risk. If they did not make the necessary efforts, they would suffer losses. However, if they were successful in their efforts, they might reap great rewards – this was the source of their energy.

The situation subsequently changed in many countries. In some, people with capital turned into investors, thereby effectively removing themselves from any corporate responsibility. In others, workers became aware of the authority capitalists had, and took over part or all of that authority. Because they defined capitalism as 'a system in which people with capital have authority', the question of responsibility was pushed into the background.

Thus, in many countries, the former embodiment of authority and responsibility in a single person, the capitalist, was lost, as was managerial autonomy. That was because, to a greater or lesser degree, companies then came to be controlled by persons whose interests did not always match those of the companies.

Some countries are hoping in vain that authority will give birth to responsibility, but this is rather unlikely to happen. It is unlikely to happen because, to possess authority, i.e., to have the power to manipulate the destiny of an entity, and to bear responsibility, i.e., to have one's personal interests determined by the destiny of an entity, are two entirely different matters.

In fact, for a person with authority, the ideal situation is to have authority, but not responsibility, and realize as much personal profit as possible from those under his control while maintaining the status quo of his personal interests, no matter what happens to the entity.

The separation of authority and responsibility thus becomes fixed, managerial autonomy is impaired, and the company becomes a tool for servicing the interests of the group in authority, a target for milking.

Meanwhile, Japan has taken a completely different path from those of other countries. Regardless of what the historical facts are, if one were to position what actually happened in this framework, one would have to say that of the functions formerly performed by those with capital, Japanese workers have seized responsibility, not authority – that is, providing the word 'seize' is appropriate.

The function of the burden of risk, which formerly motivated people with capital, has now been distributed among the body of employees. At the same time, the employees have become responsible for performing a series of management functions, including promoting management positively, organizing production, and implementing innovations. Now, in the process there may have been a stage when a separation of authority and responsibility occurred between the employees who had assumed responsibility and the persons with capital who temporarily still had authority. But, unlike the scenarios discussed previously, in this case there was a strong contributing factor to have authority integrated with responsibility.

The reason is because a situation where the destiny of an entity affects a person's most vital interests but where the person has no power to change the entity's destiny, a situation, in other words, where a person has responsibility but not authority, is completely intolerable to the person who must bear the responsibility.

Naturally, persons placed in such a situation will probably try to widen their influence over such an entity. And although one may not doubt that the removal of capitalist control with the dissolution of the *zaibatsu* by the Allied Forces after the war contributed greatly to *kigyoism*'s formation, that kind of influence made the administrative reforms a firm reality and continued afterward, while under a capitalist system, to prevent capitalist control from emerging.

Maneuvering to obtain stable shareholders, mutual holding of shares by corporations, *sokaiya* – all these phenomena run contrary to the principles of capitalism, hold the capitalist system in contempt, and, even if they cannot be called illegal, are close to evading the law. But even though they may be worth criticizing from the standpoint of capitalism, they are expressions of an urgent desire by the group of corporate employees to hold their fate in their own hands. Let those who criticize the corporate employees according to capitalist theory do so. But the urgent wish of corporate employees was there before capitalism. And among the many wishes of humans, is there any more reasonable than realizing that while one cannot help being punished for one's own mistakes, one does not want to be punished for those of another?

However, desires, of course, do not always immediately become reality. But a market economy is such that, in the final analysis, those who willingly bear the burden of risk are given authority. This is because the more authority given to those who bear risk, the greater the company's advantage in competition.

In other types of companies, growth is twisted to meet the interests of owners, and inside the company, because of a dual conflict between labor and management, the energy of employees cannot be fully directed toward achieving corporate goals. Such companies cannot avoid being weeded out through competition, unless the company can restructure itself internally so that owners lose their authority, or unless the owner, on the basis of his personality, plays the complete role of an entrepreneur who has tied himself securely to the company's growth.

Honda Motor Co., for example, now the world's leading manufacturer of motorcycles, was a tiny company 40 years ago – just one small company among numerous other similar sized concerns. Why then, one might ask, did Honda develop so remarkably? At least one of the reasons is that the founder, Soichiro Honda, who had a small amount of capital, acted more as an entrepreneur than a capitalist. The owners of other companies controlled them and viewed them as family assets eventually to be transferred to their descendants. Many of them lost out in the competition and declined, or reached a point where there was not much hope for substantial growth.

Honda, however, did not worry about bearing risk or about losing his capitalistic control of the company, but always acted as an entrepreneur. Although the business developed, Honda's equity position within the company rapidly declined, and when the company went public in 1954, Honda personally owned only 13.2 percent of the total number of shares. Today he owns less than one percent.[22]

Similar scenarios also occurred in many other industries.

If a company has a system that forces responsibility on its employees, all that remains in moving toward perfecting a *kigyoistic* system is for companies still under the control of their owners either to be swallowed up in fierce competition or internally restructure themselves. Japan's period of rapid, high-level economic growth was also a period in which intense competition developed among companies. In this era of competition, authority completely shifted from owners to employees.

With the acquisition of responsibility by workers as a foundation, workers began participating spontaneously in their company's management, much as individual entrepreneurs formerly promoted management, only on an enlarged scale that included all corporate employees.

Companies organized along *kigyoistic* lines derive the driving force for their progress from 'participation' born of 'responsibility'. It is only under such a system that it becomes possible to expect the spontaneous participation of a broad spectrum of workers – not an individual or coincidental spontaneity, nor a spontaneity induced through 'technique' but an 'organized' spontaneity. This type of spontaneity could never be produced by authority, because although it is possible to order people to behave in a certain way, orders will never result in spontaneity. Human spontaneity is forever beyond the reach of authority.

Even if the principal entity controlling a company changes, and the company comes to be governed, perhaps, by a council of workers or a party committee rather than a board of directors, as long as that company derives its main driving force from authority, it will have to use control and coercion as the ultimate means for organizing large numbers of people and urging them to move toward achieving corporate goals.

Socialist nations, too, emphasize the uniqueness of their system in terms of resource allocation outside the company, but it is not coincidental that inside the companies they are firm believers in so-called scientific management.

At any rate, working people need a system that makes it possible for them to participate at the work site. No matter what beautiful and flowery phrases are used to describe a work site system, as long as it remains a system essentially reducing human beings to functions, it probably makes little difference to the individuals doing the actual work whether the company is controlled by owners, by the workers themselves or by an abstract notion such as the working class (or a Party or State that monopolizes how the wishes of the working class are interpreted).

A system that relies on authority as its main pillar of support will ultimately find that it is unable to elicit sufficient spontaneity from the people who work within it, an indispensable element for operating in contemporary industry. Such a system, moreover, would not really expect spontaneity from workers, i.e., the system does not allow for the development of such spontaneity or the directing of it toward achieving corporate goals. That is why, whether in a capitalist or socialist situation, the type of thinking that considers a lack or absence of worker spontaneity to be an ethical problem has spread so 'systematically'. Consider the following two excerpts:

> Regardless of the location, workers on the Continent are criticized for unwillingness to give an honest day's work for their pay, for restrictive practices, for absenteeism, for wildcat strikes or for bloody-mindedness in general.[23]

> According to official arguments of the Soviet Union, the Soviet economy has an unparalleled strength, but is impeded by the 'leftover traces of capitalism in people'. That is why the only way to increase the efficiency of the Soviet economy is to improve workers' morals. For decades, workers have been called out, mobilized and repeatedly told to aim for 'increased production, improvements and greater efficiency'. Whether under Stalin, Krushchev or Brezhnev; whether under Bierut, Gomulka or Gierek; whether under Gottwald, Novotny or

Husak, people always heard the same criticisms: workers have lost the will to work, investments aren't being used in the best ways possible, raw materials are being wasted, technology is not advancing, product quality is poor – the workers heard these complaints and were constantly made responsible for taking steps to improve the situation.[24]

The differences between *kigyoism* and other economic systems can be easily summarized. Of the functions assigned to owners during the early capitalist era, *kigyoism* has taken over responsibility that has led to participation; other systems have taken over authority based essentially on coercion.

This leads us to the present, where the various attributes of responsibility and authority have been carried into *kigyoism* and other systems as is.[25]

5 Impediments to the Development of Kigyoism

The structure of *kigyoism* as described in this book is logically derived from the bearing of corporate risk by employees, and, at the same time, depicts the reality in Japan. It is clearly not, however, a complete portrayal. There is a slight disparity between reality in Japan and the type of structure that *kigyoism* should naturally create. This disparity stems from a variety of institutional and ideological restrictions which impede the overall spread of *kigyoism*.

Hiroshi Arabori claims that the ideology of *kigyoism* conceals the Marxist situation in Japanese society in which companies are controlled by capitalists and an intrinsic conflict of interests exists between the workers and the capitalists, and says *kigyoism* prevents workers from directly facing this reality.

In fact, however, the reality is exactly the opposite of that viewpoint. Marxist thinking prevents one from directly realizing the true nature of Japanese companies. In this respect, not only Marxism, but the ideology of capitalism, which regards the company as the property of its shareholders, and liberalism, which stresses the independence of the individual from the company, are similar in that they impede the development of *kigyoism*. The institutional structures of the Japanese economy and Japanese companies are also capitalist, and likewise impede the development of *kigyoism*.

As long as one follows the reality in Japan and makes practical judgments about what is and what is not necessary for Japanese companies there is absolutely no reason for holding general meetings of shareholders.[26] Just as controls which ignore econometric reality give birth to black marketeers, an organizational structure that is removed from reality gives birth to *sokaiya*. Companies have to use many people and much energy to take measures against *sokaiya*, a task that essentially is not part of a company's original work.

Similarly, based on the real goals of Japanese companies, there is no reason whatsoever why a company's business results have to be evaluated using profit and loss statements. Profit and loss statements, in which total sales are listed, followed by a detailed breakdown of expenses incurred, which are then deducted from total sales to show the net profit resulting from the company's activities, are based on the capitalist concept of 'profits first'. In those statements, personnel costs are clearly regarded as belonging to the same dimension as the cost of raw materials. The profit and loss statements express the belief that a company's business results can be improved not only by conserving raw materials, but also by reducing wages.[27] A company made up of corporate employees, however, would find it very difficult to accept such a definition of business results.

Although the results of a nation's economic activities are evaluated either by dividing net added value by population to derive national per capita income or by computing the latter's growth rate, a completely different method – with preference given to shareholders – is used to evaluate corporations, the cellular units in a national economy.

Also, although a system whereby corporations can be merged or divided if the shareholders agree to it is natural in a capitalistic system, such action would not likely be unproblematical in a situation where the system did not give corporate employees the right to speak out when their interests and their destinies were being so critically influenced.

If this type of system and the thinking at its foundation are thought to be more correct, then naturally that will affect the behavior and the consciousness of everyone involved with carrying out *kigyoism*, which naturally will thwart the all-out development of *kigyoism*. Of course, a reality such as *kigyoism*, a reality that has a giant system rooted in the deepest recesses of the economy, will in the end totally defeat any system or ideology with some degree of retrogressive force. For example, even if the president of a company happened to have capitalistic thoughts and believed that companies belong to their shareholders, he would still know it will not benefit either his company or himself to lay off employees just for the purpose of paying high dividends, although how he would know is not clear, except that in Japan's 'special' economic environment that is the way it is. And labor union leaders who believe in the Marxist ideology also know that, in the context of the Japanese reality, carrying out wage increases which cause problems for the management of a company will not benefit the workers. So no matter what ideology these people believe in, the objective conditions in Japan's economic society force their actions to become, in reality, *kigyoistic*.

Up to the present, the reality of *kigyoism* in those ways has conquered the obstructive forces of systems and ideologies, but the separation between the system and the reality has become very large. Needless to say, it is meaningless and even harmful to try to match the reality to the system. Rather than leaving events to run their natural course, the time has come to intentionally create a new system.

It will not be long before the Japanese people create a new socioeconomic order which truly fits the reality of *kigyoism*.

Notes

1 Though often reported erroneously, the QC circle and other small-group activities were created in Japan.

   Dr J. M. Juran said in an interview, 'Japan should sell its excellence in product quality overseas.' See *Nikkei Mechanical*, 2 (1982), p. 14.
2 Masaru Ibuka, 'Ima no Beikoku Kigyo wa Nihon ni Katenai' (Today's American Companies Cannot Beat Japan), *Voice*, 10 (1979), p. 56.

3　Werner Meyer-Larsen, *Auto-Grossmacht Japan* (Europe Will Be Run Over by Japanese Cars) (Reinbeck bei Hamburg, Rowholt, 1980) p. 180.

4　Joseph A. Greenwald, 'Yukisugita Shudan Shiko wa Sozosei o Umanai' (Excessive Group-oriented Thinking Will Not Result in Creativity), *Manejimento*, 11 (1981), p. 92.

　　Despite his general theme, the author does not hesitate to affirm the following Japanese labor characteristics: 'Rather, the important point is that the Japanese are positive toward work . . . Many Japanese still have a strong interest and pride in work and are devoted to their company. Hence, I believe the basic thing is that a more assertive effort is made in work, and the work standard is maintained steadily and continually in Japan. This has had a good influence on work efficiency and quality.'

5　Japanese deadwood may have a title such as 'acting' something or 'special assistant' to someone, but they are actually a kind of unproductive middle-management limbo and spend most of their time reading newspapers and magazines. Very often, they are put by the windows – the corporate equivalent of wallflowers – to keep them out of the way of people who are working. So common is this that they have been nicknamed the *mado-giwa-zoku* (windowside people) in Japanese. Although the slump which followed the second oil crisis made considerable numbers of people redundant, they could not be fired outright. Instead, they were relegated to these window-side positions, and many have given into peer pressures and quit 'of their own accord'.

6　Gregory Henderson, *Korea: The Politics of the Vortex*. Cambridge, Harvard University Press, 1968, pp. 13–18.

7　Nikkan Seisansei Hikaku Chosa Iinkai, ed., *Nikkan Ryokoku no Sogo Seisansei no Hikaku ni Kansuru Chosa Kenkyu* (Comparative Study of General Productivity in Japan and Korea). Tokyo, Japan Productivity Center, 1981, p. 75.

8　Nikkan Seisansei, p. 14.

9　Yoshio Sugimoto, 'Nihon Tokushu Shudan Setsu no Kozui no Nakade' (Amid the Flood of Theories on Japanese Being A Special Group), *Asahi Journal*, 11–14 (1980), pp. 11–12.

10　Susumu Ishii, *Nihon no Rekishi (7): Kamakura Bakufu* (History of Japan – Part 7: Kamakura Shogunate). Tokyo, Chuo Koronsha, 1965, pp. 113–49.

11　*Oakland Tribune*, April 25, 1969.

12　Nikkan Seisansei, pp. 122–3.

13　Woodruff Imberman, 'Strikes Cost More Than You Think', *Harvard Business Review*, Vol. 57, No. 3, May–June (1979), p. 137.

14　On the characteristics of the CWQC, see Kaoru Ishikawa, *Nihonteki*

Hinshitsu Kanri (Japanese-Style Quality Control). Tokyo, Nihon Kagaku Gijutsu Renmei, 1981, Chapter 5.

15 Yoshiro Ikari, 'Nihon no Jidosha Kojo: Seisan Gijutsu Reberu wa Tashika ni Takai, da ga Jakuten mo' (Japanese Automobile Plants: Indeed, the Level of Manufacturing Technology Is High, yet There Are Shortcomings), *IE*, 10 (1980), p. 26.

16 Nihon HR Kyokai, ed., *Showa 55-Nendo Teian Katsudo Hokokusho* (1980 Suggestion Activity Report). Tokyo, Nihon HR Kyokai.

17 For the characteristics of the landlord-tenant system above, see Seiichi Tohata, *Nochi o Meguru Jinushi to Nomin* (Landlords and Farmers Arguing over Farmland). Tokyo, Kantosha, 1947, pp. 171–94.

18 Tohata, pp. 174–5.

19 Nishiyama, *Theory of Control*, pp. 66–8.

20 Hiroshi Okumura, *Hojin Shihonshugi no Kozo: Nihon no Kabushiki Shoyu* (Structure of Juridical Entity Capitalism: Stock Ownership in Japan). Tokyo, Nihon Hyoronsha, 1975, pp. 193–205.

21 Yoshikazu Miyazaki, *Kasen* (Oligopoly), Tokyo, Iwanami Shoten, 1972, pp. 67–9.

22 Tadanori Nishiyama, *Nihon wa Shihonshugi dewa nai* (Japan's System Is Not Capitalism). Tokyo, Mikasa Shobo, 1981, p. 208. Although the Honda family is believed to hold some shares, this does not alter the gist of the argument.

23 Einzig, p. 74.

24 Ota Sik, *Atarashii Keizai Shakai e no Teigen* (Arguments for a New Economic Society). Tokyo, Nihon Keiei Shuppankai, 1976, pp. 158–9.

25 Sik, Chap. 1.

26 Nishiyama, *Theory of Control*, p. 248.

27 Yoshimitsu Kagiyama, *Kigyo Oyobi Kigyojin* (The Corporation and the Corporate Man). Tokyo, Hakuto Shobo, 1977, pp. 112–19.

5 Kigyoism as a Social System

Japan rapidly industrialized after the end of the Second World War. Whereas in 1950, for example, the number of people working in the primary industries accounted for 48.5 percent of the country's total labor force, by 1987 this figure had dropped to 8.3 percent. Viewed another way, the industrialization process might even be called the 'corporatization' of Japan, because the number of persons working in corporations increased from less than 40 percent of the total labor force in 1950 to 75 percent in 1986.[1]

As Japanese society thus became more 'corporatized', the social relationships formed within corporations came to be directly reflected as is in society-in-general. In that sense, a *kigyoistic* society is a corporate society, and Japanese society-at-large can be called an accumulation of a great many large and small corporate societies, each held together by a strong cohesive quality.

1 Features of Japan's Social Structure

The essence of *kigyoism* as an economic system lies in the managerial autonomy attained in corporations through integration with labor, an achievement made possible by having those who work in corporations assume corporate responsibility. *Kigyoism* as a social system, on the other hand, is what can be called its social 'expression'. In other words, companies became the objects of a commitment by corporate employees internally, thus becoming strongly integrated, and they became highly self-sufficient social groups externally, a different existence from Western corporations, which had become little more than abstract economic structures.

It goes without saying that *kigyoistic* corporations are also different from their counterparts in socialist countries, where corporations are a part of the State and the State assumes all authority, responsibility and goals related to them. Osamu Hashiguchi, former chairman of the Japan Fair Trade Commission, expresses the unique quality of Japanese corporations as social groups as follows:

> In particular, in the nature of Japanese corporations – whereby companies provide their employees with greater benefits than what the government provides and guarantee career employment in return for a commitment – a strange existence that binds the fates of the corporation and its employees might indeed be above the State and the family. At the very least, this is true for medium-sized and larger corporations.[2]

Corporations with such a powerful integrated force give society features that differ from a simple liberal society and, naturally, from a socialist one.

The basic principle of a liberal society is that the individual is the unit of activity. Freedom is given to the individual, and he is responsible for pursuing his personal objectives on his own.

The individual's relationship with the corporation in a liberal society is a limited one, with the two only tied together via an intentional choice which the individual made in the labor market. Also, the relationship between the two is equal. The individual's acceptance of orders inside the organization, for example, cannot be separated from his market choice. It is inseparable because, since he is free to quit at any time, his acceptance of orders is tacit approval of his market choice, a decision to stay on the job.

Personnel matters in Western corporations are also carried out in market-like ways. Although Japanese corporations carry out uniform, well-planned personnel practices, Western companies, as already pointed out, view them as a way to fill vacant positions. If a job opens up, a notice is officially posted and personnel are initially recruited from within the organization. If no suitable candidate is available, a search is then extended to outside the company. Western companies also carry out promotions and demotions as market-like decisions. It is clear that essentially such companies can never win the allegiance of individual workers. If the idea of allegiance is brought up in Western companies, the individual will swear allegiance only to himself. Freedom, the one power that has complete control over itself, can be found only in the individual.

219

In the socialist system, meanwhile, there is almost no freedom of economic activity given to the individual or the corporation. We have already reviewed the situation regarding corporations, but, for individuals as well, although freedom in choice of employment, freedom of economic activities and various other freedoms may exist in theory, in socialism in real existence, they are severely restricted. Only the State has the authority to control itself completely, and individuals and corporations are not allowed to pursue goals based on either personal or corporate interests and profit, except within boundaries deemed permissible by the State. In terms of socialism's basic nature, the only freedom is the freedom to pursue the collective goals ascribable to the State's economic development.

In the Japanese social system, in sharp contrast, corporations exist in an intermediate area between the individual and the State, and, at least as far as production activities are concerned, they have almost complete freedom and responsibility.

Based on that, one can say the *kigyoistic* society lies in the intermediate area between the liberal social system of individual autonomy and the socialist social system where the State has autonomy. 'Intermediate' does not mean that Japan's economy has adopted a mixed economy with aspects of a planned economy in its market principle. Rather, the word is used to indicate that the high level of self-sufficiency found in Japanese corporations is the same as that found only in individuals in liberal societies and only in the State in socialist systems. Insofar as production activities alone are concerned, companies in Japan occupy the same position as individuals in liberal and the State in socialist countries.

Japan's social system thus has a type of duality. The relationship between the State and corporations appears, at a glance, to be liberal. The role and importance of private companies in economic activities in Japan are, of course, higher than in socialist nations and, even compared to the advanced countries of the free world, they are probably the highest; and the Japanese government has set few legal restrictions.

On the other hand, when one looks at the relationship between the company and the individual, one finds that, in effect, no equal relationship exists, such as in the private employment contracts of the West. The relationship is more like the one between the State and the individual. In fact, a great many of the activities considered by their nature to be the individual's responsibility in the West, based on personal initiative, are the corporation's responsibility in Japan.

In the Japanese system, in other words, a considerable portion of what in other systems is left to the responsibility of individuals or the State has been transferred to the corporation, and, as a result, the corporations have become self-sufficient.

The State and the Corporation

In comparison to the governments of other countries, Japan's is not large at all. This fact, however, is not necessarily generally recognized. Since the Japanese people themselves do not recognize it, how much truer it must be for non-Japanese. On this subject, the following remarks are interesting.

> Japan is marked by a degree of central investment planning and government control that would make any good capitalist cry.
>
> Elements of central planning are common. The Japanese have their MITI and the French have indicative planning. Government is often the principal source of capital investment funds, and can control as it lends. The most extreme example of this is in Japan, where most investment funds directly or indirectly flow through government channels.[3]

These remarks are from a book by Lester C. Thurow. Many other non-Japanese observers of Japan have stated similar opinions.

The reality in Japan, however, as will be seen later, is completely different, and it is hard to understand why such remarks, so obviously far from the truth, are repeated so often.

Perhaps they relate to the remnants of images formed during the postwar reconstruction period when the government closely controlled the economy. (Domestic controls on goods and materials were almost all lifted by 1950, and trade liberalization was almost completed by the mid-1960s. And even during the years of control, the ratio of government spending to total GNP was no more than about 20 percent, which is lower than today's figure.)

221

Or perhaps such remarks relate to fixed ideas Westerners have which force them, when dealing with Asian or Oriental countries, somehow to tie them to 'despotism' or 'totalitarianism'. With such fixed ideas in mind, it may be psychologically difficult for a person to accept the image of an Asian nation as being able to attain rapid economic growth by depending on the dynamic vitality of private corporations under a small but efficient government. At any rate, the reasons for such remarks are not clear.

Apart from that discussion, it is clear that Japan has neither a controlled nor a planned economy. Some proof of that can be seen if one looks, for example, at the small number of personnel MITI has assigned to its sections in charge of four important Japanese industries (Table 5.1). Certainly it must be clear that such a small staff cannot design and carry out major programs of centralized control that 'would make any good capitalist cry'.

Table 5.1 *Number of personnel assigned in MITI to selected industries (As of July 1, 1989)*

Industry	Section	Personnel
Automobiles	Automobile	11
Computers	Electronic Policy	13
	Data Processing Promotion	13
	Electronic Products (also includes home appliances, electricity generating equipment, etc.)	16
Steel	Iron and Steel Administration Division	13
	Steel Manufacturing	9
Petrochemicals	Basic Chemical Products (also includes inorganic chemicals industry, such as caustic soda, etc.)	23

Fiscal spending is a good index for measuring the degree of a government's participation in industry. Materials prepared by the OECD (Organization for Economic Cooperation and Development), *Public Expenditure Trends* (June 1978), for example, compare industry-related spending by the governments of selected countries. That comparison shows that the Japanese government's total budget allocated for trade and industrial policies, even when final consumption expenditures, transfer expenditures and fixed assets formation are included, is no more than about 0.2 percent of Japan's GNP, a much lower figure than the 0.51 percent in the

US, 1.83 percent in the UK, 0.79 percent in West Germany, and 1.10 percent in France.

A comparison of the total number of personnel in MITI and in its counterpart in the US, the Department of Commerce (DOC), is also revealing. MITI's entire organization numbers 12,000; the DOC alone has 35,000 employees, and if the Department of Energy is included, there are another 17,000 staff members, for a total of 52,000. This comparison reveals how few people there are in MITI.

Concerning guidance policy financing, too, loans are principally directed toward energy development and environmental protection, areas where it is difficult to attract private sector investments. The dependence on guidance policy financing by major industries such as electric machinery, electronic machinery and automobiles, is no more than a few percent, and interest rates are not much different from those of private financial institutions.

The low level of Japanese government participation in industrial activities is also demonstrated by the fact that there are almost no public corporations in the manufacturing industries. Compared to the EC countries, where there are public corporations in the mining, steel, chemical, automobile, computer and other industries, public corporations in the mining and industrial areas in Japan after the Second World War were generally found only in the manufacture of industrial-use alcohol, salt and tobacco, and today even those public corporations have all been privatized.

Compared to those of the governments of other countries, Japanese government controls related to industrial activities are also very limited.

In France, for example, comprehensive pricing controls have been in effect since the end of the Second World War, and as of January 1980 about one quarter of all consumer goods were the object of price controls. In the UK, too, until the Competition Act went into effect in April 1980, a system of prior application was used to control price increases.

In Japan, however, there has never been this kind of overall government interference in economic activities, except during the war and briefly in the postwar reconstruction period.

Also, although there are some restrictions on specific industries, their areas of application are extremely limited. Concerning the principal manufacturing industries, the ones in which restrictions can be carried out by law on new entrants to the industry, facilities, quantity and prices only affect alcoholic beverages, gun-powder, oil refining, aircraft, shipbuilding and weapons.

A look as well at the size of government in selected countries in terms of fiscal expenditures as a percentage of GNP puts the UK, France and West Germany, respectively, at 46 percent, 47 percent and 53 percent, the US at 37 percent and Japan the lowest at 34 percent. (Japan's figure is for fiscal 1987; other countries are for calendar year 1986.) The number of civil service workers per 1,000 population, even excluding those related to national defense, are 65 for the US, 82 for the UK, 79 for West Germany and 122 for France. The figure for Japan is 41, the lowest among the principal industrially advanced nations. (Comparison is roughly for 1985.)

According to the foregoing objective indices at least, the Japanese government is 'relatively small' among the governments of the principal industrially advanced nations. Although there is concern for the future because of signs in recent years of increased government spending in Japan and a corresponding expansion of the administrative structure, at least at present – relatively speaking, since it is difficult to believe that the size of the government in the developing nations and in socialist countries could be smaller, and except for special cases like Hong Kong – the Japanese government probably belongs to the category of smallest governments.

One reason for the relatively small size is that private companies in Japan perform many of the duties that are normally taken on by governments in other countries. In fact, Japanese companies do more in the area of social welfare than companies in the world's industrially advanced countries. For example, Japanese companies in effect carry out unemployment countermeasures, which is partly why, not surprisingly, the unemployment rate in Japan rarely rises above the 2 percent level, no matter how depressed business conditions are. When business conditions worsen, corporate employees become 'unemployed' inside the company. There are times when they are not working, but they will usually share the work load and work fewer hours per day. Wages, however, remain almost the same as before. In this way, corporations bear the cost of unemployment countermeasures.

Meanwhile, wage increases are, as a rule, paid within the limits of the capabilities that are made possible by a company's improved productivity. Unless wage increases are tied thus to productivity, a company's competitiveness will be weakened, thereby enfeebling it and endangering the basic interests of the corporate employees. This form of company income policy greatly alleviates the burden on the government's macroeconomic policies.

A large part of the industrial adjustment assistance normally accompanying shifts in the industrial structure is also carried out inside corporations in Japan. For example, prior to large-scale unemployment taking place, such as in Western countries when entire industries decline for one reason or another, Japanese companies will usually provide their corporate employees with in-house training and education and, at the same time, try to move into a more promising industry in line with the retraining provided. The situation in European countries, where important industries are nationalized when they begin declining, is almost never seen in Japan.

One of the reasons for Japan's low crime rate, too, is that Japanese companies, in effect, regulate the deviant social behavior of their employees. Besides this point, which will be touched on later, there are many other areas – too numerous to list here – where private companies play an overwhelming leadership role, such as in R&D activities, the development of export markets, and so forth.

All of the foregoing lighten the Japanese government's burden and help it to remain 'small'.

The Corporation and the Individual

This discussion concerning the size of the government would not be balanced, however, if it only passively treated the Japanese government's role. Although MITI's functions concerning industrial policy are not covered in this book, there are many points regarding those functions which should be mentioned. It needs to be pointed out, too, that most of MITI's functions do not result from infringements on the freedom of private companies, and in the end it is not possible to truly appreciate MITI's role if one sets it solely in the framework of freedom or control. Indeed, in the limited sense of applying such a framework, one must say that the Japanese government allows a greater latitude of freedom for corporations than do the governments of Western free nations.

Despite being able to make such comments about the relationship between the government and companies in Japan, this should not be immediately interpreted as meaning that Japan is more liberal than Western nations. In other words, the small role of the government in Japan is not a reflection of a larger role played by the individual.

Some of the actions which individuals can take of their own free will in the West, for example, may not necessarily be possible in Japan.

First of all, once an individual joins a particular company, it is very difficult for him to move to another. Even though it is not impossible, in almost all cases the worker must be prepared for less pay and other worsened conditions when he relocates.

Quitting one company for another in Japan, therefore, means more than merely separating from a specific company. It means, in effect, giving up all possibility of ever working in a corporation again. Once one leaves the corporate world, usually the only alternative is to go into business for oneself, e.g. by taking over a family business or perhaps opening one's own small business. This is called Datsu-Sara, which in effect means to drop out of the ranks of the salaried.

Inside Japanese corporations, job rotation of the labor force – viewed from the corporation's standpoint – is virtually unrestricted. In other words, once a person joins a Japanese company and becomes a corporate employee, he will then have almost no freedom in choosing his job. And an employee's refusal to obey an order rotating him to another job in the company is considered very serious. Moreover, a corporate employee may not be rotated to a job that is the same as or closely related to his previous job. As explained earlier, Japanese companies can even take production line workers, depending on the circumstances, and turn them into salesmen.

Apart from such extreme cases, it is still true that Japanese workers are often rotated from one job to another even when, in the Western sense, the new job is completely different.

In Japan, then, insofar as a corporate employee (a person seeking his future in a company as a corporate employee) is concerned, the situation is the same as if there were no freedom of job choice, just as there is none in socialist countries. Viewed in terms of the nature of a liberal economy, such a situation is completely unthinkable in common sense terms, and yet the Japanese do not consider this strange.

A well known Japanese scholar of labor economics wrote as follows about this subject:

> While in university, almost no Japanese student thinks about the kind of job he would like to have after he graduates. He only knows he will have to work and therefore he will try to find employment with as 'good' a company as possible. This is the only incentive driving a serious student to study hard. It is rare, however, for a student to know what specific company he will work for. In fact, not only the student himself but also his parents, his teachers and society-at-large believe it is the company that decides whether to hire him and determines what kind of working life he will lead. . . . And if the student is fortunate enough to join a good company, it is normal for him to have no idea of the type of work he will be asked to perform when he joins the company, let alone where he will be working or what he will be doing one year after joining the company, or certainly the work he will be performing 10 years in the future.[4]

Kimihiro Masamura says that in a free economy there must be the 'freedom to make things' and the 'freedom of job choice'.[5] Viewed from that limited standpoint, Japan does not in substance have a free economy, at least not as far as production activities are concerned.

Still, in any country, an individual's freedom to make items is restricted greatly by technological factors. Although the example may be far-fetched, obviously a person can easily prepare and sell noodles from a mobile shop he puts together, but it is absolutely impossible for him to manufacture steel or automobiles as a business. In our contemporary age, an individual's freedom to involve himself in production activities is thus essentially concentrated on the 'freedom of job choice'. In Japan, however, even this most basic of all freedoms is seriously restricted.

The Japanese system cannot be called a free economy in the pure sense of the term. An individual's market freedoms related to economic activities can be observed in the area of consumption but are woefully scarce in production. Workers are 'hidden' behind the corporation, and although market freedom exists in terms of production activities, it exists with the corporation as the basic unit.

As a counterbalance against the company's absorption of so much of an individual's freedom, an individual's responsibilities are also greatly decreased. Through the career employment system, for example, the individual is protected against dismissal from causes originating in the external market. The individual is secure, therefore, but the corporation assumes that much more risk in bad times because it cannot easily lay off personnel. In short, the corporation has assumed the individual's risk.

Education is also largely removed from the individual's area of responsibility. Americans will go to a vocational training school between jobs or after work to improve skills that will facilitate the finding of a new company that will offer better working conditions, including higher pay. In Japan, however, a company's personnel system considers the effects of education, and is structured so that employees become more skilled naturally, on the job. The company monitors an individual's vocational aptitude and assigns him to the most fitting post. (The system is not infallible, of course, and, as with individuals themselves, companies also make mistakes.)

Companies also offer employees various social welfare benefits, not only during working hours – their daily company 'lives' – but also afterward, in their private lives. They are thus blessed with a living environment that persons outside the company cannot enjoy. Even as corporate employees live their daily lives in Japanese society, therefore, they also live in a second dimension, in an environment their company has created directly and artificially.

Moriaki Tsuchiya quite aptly terms this situation a 'corporate capsule'.

When a person decides to work for a company, he is provided with a handbook which describes welfare benefits such as company housing, and rest and hospital facilities, as well as recreational and cultural activities in attractive terms. . . . An employee can enjoy yachting in summer and skiing in winter with his colleagues, using company facilities, and he can play outdoor sports such as tennis and baseball using company courts and fields. . . . Also, if he wants to improve his foreign language ability or his skill in a hobby, the company will assist him by paying for the major part of related costs. With the adoption of the five-day work week, the company will even tell him how best to spend the weekend with such slogans as 'one day for rest, the other for culture'. And when he gets married, there is, of course, a company house waiting for the newlyweds. . . . For saving money, the company has an internal savings system which pays a high interest rate. Some companies even have hospitals that are better equipped than ordinary university hospitals, which keep the employee and his family healthy. . . . And when he finally has the time and money to play golf, golf courses owned and operated by related group companies are waiting for him.[6]

Although such benefits provided for employees by a company may increase or decrease, depending on business results, they are not affected by an individual's direct efforts (or lack thereof). In other words, this pleasant environment is entirely outside the individual's responsibility.

A Japanese, living in an environment like the one described above, naturally has a different view on life than his American counterpart. The latter views life as an endless series of choices. As the result of a particular choice, he may meet with great success or be plunged into deep despair. Ideally, an American worker lives his life bravely challenging opportunities without knowing what the results will yield.

Once the all-important choice of the company for which he will work is decided, however, a Japanese will thereafter be given almost no opportunity to decide on matters that determine his future. To a Japanese, therefore, life is akin to climbing a mountain. Some persons may have the ability and good fortune to reach the summit, but most end their corporate lives midway up the mountain or even lower. Regardless, after choosing which mountain to climb, all they have to do afterward is keep climbing. There is no need to think about anything but work. In return for shouldering only a small amount of personal risk, however, an individual's freedom of choice is also proportionally limited. He has little freedom on the one hand, but at the same time he has gained lifetime security. Regardless of how it is described, such an environment clearly cannot be said to be based on principles of a liberal society founded on the self-responsibility of individuals.

2 The Company as a Source of Social Integration

One outstanding feature of Japanese companies is the strength of their cohesion as a social group. When one accustomed to Japanese companies looks at a foreign company, one gets the impression – although this is just a feeling – that its existence as a social unit is weak. In the sense that it is a collection of people, it undoubtedly is a social group, but it exists essentially as a system designed for earning profits, and human beings are merely arranged somewhere inside the organization. To the individual employee, it is not of such great significance whether success is attained from within the organization or whether human relationships are good or bad.

A company organized on the principles of *kigyoism*, on the other hand, is a closely integrated society that strongly influences the daily lives and ways of thinking of its employees. Employees not only owe their daily sustenance, but also a great part of their social position and trust to the company. One can even say they are indirectly connected to society via the company. In fact, depending on one's viewpoint, it is even possible to say that a company's influence on the livelihood and the lives of its employees is greater than the State's influence, which decreased substantially after the Second World War.

Even a person who is totally uninterested in government matters will show great interest in his company's managerial strategy, in who the next company president will be, and in internal shifts of power. And if the police should arrest a corporate employee for even a minor offense, he will be far more greatly concerned about the company learning of the incident than about any possible legal punishment. Also, if a company is involved in an incident related to, say, environmental pollution, and suffers wide social criticism as a result, its employees will unite to defend the company and refute the criticism. Moreover, if an employee is charged with, perhaps, bribery in his professional work but was acting in the best interests of the company rather than for private gain, the incident will often not be recorded internally as a black mark in his personnel records.[7]

Although an employee may be uninterested in Japan's position in international society, he shows great interest in his company's position in its industry. The ordinary foreign worker probably would not understand the sharp reaction Japanese employees show when their company's market share drops below that of a company that previously had a smaller share.

What all of these facts indicate is that a Japanese, or, more accurately, most Japanese who are members of corporate society, are more effectively governed by the company than by the State. The corporation is clearly stronger than the State when it comes to its hold on the individual and its ability to induce an organizational commitment. And, in contrast to Western corporations, organized as so-called 'rational, goal-oriented societies' (*gesellschaft*), Japanese corporations are organized as 'cooperative societies' (*gemeinschaft*). But it would be nonsensical to liken Japanese corporations to communal societies existing as villages. They are modern organizations established along lines that are as highly rationalized as those in the West. And although the two are similar when one views them as rationalized organizations, there is a particular difference when one views the two as groups of human beings. Western corporations, on the one hand, lack a tight cohesiveness, whereas Japanese companies – viewed in terms of their systematic structure – can be called closely governed small societies from both psychological and physical standpoints. The difference, then, is that Japanese companies are the source of a strong socially unifying force that gives their employees a feeling of solidarity and of belonging to society.

This is the fundamental reason why Japan is achieving both economic success and maintaining a relatively stable social order. Just as in the West, industrialization in Japan either weakened the regulatory powers of closely knit regional bodies or brought about their dissolution. In contrast to the West, however, that development did not immediately break society down into a mass society of alienated individuals. This did not occur because, in Japan, people who were separated from their traditional ties to provincial and other communal bodies were reintegrated into new, strongly cohesive, social structures – Japanese companies.

Mass society often uproots individuals from their traditional communal groups, and the individuals start behaving more selfishly because they have lost their social ties and support. They feel estranged, even helpless, and their behavior sometimes results in nihilistic and impulsive acts of destruction and an increase in urban crime. The fact that Japan successfully avoided much of this type of behavior, generally considered a feature of mass society, is due largely to the unique functions companies took on under *kigyoism*. That the crime rate in Japan is remarkably low compared to the rate in other industrialized nations and that its long-term trend is downward can be thought of as reflections of those circumstances.

It is clear that companies gained their integrating capabilities via restrictions placed on the freedom of choice of individuals in the labor market, i.e., via the sacrifice of partially abandoning the principles of liberalism. Consequently, there is room for pure liberals to criticize *kigyoism*, although in all fairness it must be noted that Western society cannot either be considered purely liberal. The basis for a liberal society is individual autonomy. An individual is free, in other words, but he must take responsibility for the results of the decisions he makes. That is a basic rule of a liberal society.

Despite the foregoing, when one looks at contemporary Western society one sees that it has taken the form of the welfare state, and that the important balance needed between freedom and responsibility has shifted one-sidedly toward a reduction in individual responsibility.

In a welfare state, a person can spend more than he earns. And no matter how wasteful a life he may lead, a person will never fall into hopeless poverty, for the State will support him in the end. In such a situation, an individual loses his sense of responsibility for controlling his own destiny, for planning his life from a long-term perspective. It is only natural that he will begin to adopt a less serious attitude toward daily life.

Also, although citizens in a welfare state tend to make increasing demands on their government, they shy from paying an equivalent price. This situation comes about not from a weakening of public ethics, but from the fact that the welfare state – apart from what its original idealistic motivation may have been – destroys the social mechanism of self-discipline maintained by having freedom and responsibility embodied in the same entity.

A State faced with a situation where its citizens demand more, but where it cannot impose the cost of satisfying the demands on those citizens, will probably have to decide to, in proportion to the extent to which it has had to assume its individual citizen's responsibilities, extend its authority over those individuals. If that is done, freedom and responsibility are once again joined together

– not in the individual, but in the State. Just as the State absorbs responsibility, so also does it absorb freedom.

These facts lead one to conclude that a welfare state can never be a stable system. Although it is based on the idea of individual freedom in everyday life, the end results contradict this premise. It may be described as a transition stage where the daily lives of individuals are eventually placed almost totally under the State's control. Among liberal proponents in the West, there are many, like Friedrich August von Hayek, who assert that a welfare state leads ultimately to a 'road to slavery'. In the final analysis, however, it is anachronistic to believe that a return to true liberalism is possible. Not only in economics, but in society-in-general, liberalism alone is no longer enough. Various side effects thus accompany a welfare state, but it was still definitely one solution to contemporary problems, especially those faced by highly industrialized societies. It may not be difficult to eliminate severe poverty in today's affluent society, but a system that requires an individual to present himself unprotected in the market has become unrealistic in today's constantly changing, complex, and enormous economic society.

Freedom in the labor market may indeed be the basis for individual freedom, but that freedom does nothing to guarantee security. In fact, the labor market today tends to trifle unfeelingly with the fates of individuals.

To illustrate, assume there is an individual who had decided he would like to be a lathe operator. After going to a trade school and studying basic technical training, he joins a company. There he spends several years working, and acquires sufficient experience to qualify as a skilled worker. He is then confident that he has acquired the background to provide himself with a stable income, and he begins planning for the future. But suddenly, one day he is informed that a new technology has made his skill obsolete. The market, in effect, has taken his job away, and he becomes unemployed.

A liberal, or, rather, a person who calls himself one, would probably say something like the following to that individual.

The economy is always changing, and technical skills that have high value today may not have the same value tomorrow. You should have taken the possibility of such changes into consideration and made a correct judgment. Of course, information about the future is not always completely available, but everyone in society must face such uncertainties and make responsible decisions on his own. We must all accept the results of such decisions, whether they lead to success or failure. You can only accept the consequences arising from your mistaken judgment, because that is the one rule of our society.

In Western Europe of the nineteenth century such thinking may have been common, but today it seems quite unfeeling and inhuman. This is because the emergence of various objective conditions made strict adherence to the tenets of liberalism no longer practical. In the new context, a decrease in individual responsibility became unavoidable. Western society has fallen exactly into this contradictory dilemma. Ideally, liberalism and collectivism concentrate freedom and responsibility, respectively, either in the individual or in the State, thereby keeping the two together, an essential element for self-discipline in society.

Although pure liberalism has thus become unrealistic, collectivism, on the other hand, is against the basic philosophy of society. And a welfare state is 'a halfway house straddling the border between two towns. No one thinks that it is a noble and inspiring ideal.'[8]

Without a self-disciplinary mechanism the welfare state is a 'halfway' system clearly lacking the qualifications to become the third way.

There is, however, a theoretically consistent system that has a built-in self-discipline mechanism and reduces individual responsibility without turning to collectivism.

That system is *kigyoism*, which, in a sense, might even be called a pluaristic welfare system having corporations as its basic units. Under this system, individual responsibility is reduced, and the corporation provides a wide spectrum of welfare benefits and full employment – at the corporate level – via the career employment system. And although *kigyoism* reduces individual responsibility, as in a socialist country or welfare state, it forces the individual to assume the heavy burden of corporate risk. The market does not judge an individual's mistakes very severely, but it harshly punishes the mistakes made by a company as a group of individuals, completely apart from the skills or past accomplishments of the individuals in the company. Under this system, then, an individual's responsibility is definitely reduced. On the other hand, however, the individual's overall burden, in terms of society at large, has not been reduced in the least.

Therein lies the difference between *kigyoism* and a socialist or welfare state.

Because *kigyoism* does not merely unilaterally reduce an individual's responsibility, but also imposes corporate responsibility on him, the individual does not turn into a dependent and passive member of society, as in a welfare state, but acquires an active and autonomous ethos inside the corporation, which, though small, is a clearly defined and unified society.

In a sense, *kigyoism* is a system in which a number of people, not an individual, join in a group to face the dangers which the market might otherwise direct toward individuals, and they do so without government help. During bad times, when work becomes scarce, employees divide what work there is among themselves. And if new technology reduces the value of an individual's particular job skill, the impact on the individual is minimized because the company can see the new technology coming and can thus retrain the affected employees early and give them new skills. The company also protects its employees from the risks accompanying sickness, accidents and other untoward events, and bears the cost of that protection. Actually, it is the corporate employees, as a group, who bear the cost. The individual is protected, but as a member of the group, he also provides the protection.

A citizen may make unlimited demands on the State, but a corporate employee can never do the same toward his company. Because of that type of relationship, freedom and responsibility are borne together by the group of corporate employees, and the self-discipline so essential for the existence of society is realized.

The Japanese corporate system reorganized many people who were uprooted from their traditional communities in the unavoidable turbulence of industrialization, fostered within them a positive will to participate, and created a fitting *espirit de corps* for the situation now in place in contemporary industrial society, thereby attaining a powerful social integration. This Japanese experience should be viewed not only for its economic significance but also for what it may offer to the world's many other countries that are facing similar problems.

3 Equality within a Kigyoistic Society

In a *kigyoistic* society, the structure of corporations – the units comprising the society – is directly reflected in society, and thus there is almost no social-class distinction between capitalists and workers. Of course, some managers of small businesses can still be called capitalists in the old sense, and there are temporary contract workers and workers on loan from subcontractors who can be called 'workers', but it goes without saying that it would be inappropriate to select them as typical examples to explain the special features of Japanese society.

Persons at the top level of medium-sized and larger companies forming the core of contemporary Japanese society cannot generally be called capitalists. In large companies, in particular, it is the exception to find people at the top who control the companies through their stockholdings. Rather, top level managers tend to have backgrounds not so different from those of ordinary employees. They attained their positions only by succeeding in the long-term competition for promotion inside the company.

Ordinary employees also, as mentioned already, do not have the typical features of workers. The consciousness of so-called 'factory workers' is not much different from that of white-collar workers, and it is extremely difficult to cultivate a feeling of horizontal class unity among them.

In this manner, the classical confrontation of capitalists and workers has lost most of its reality in Japanese society, and a class consciousness has been replaced in individuals by a strong awareness of being corporate employees. In fact, most people define themselves in terms of the company for which they work rather than the class to which they belong. And since there is marked equality, uniformity and vertical mobility within the group of corporate employees, Japanese society assumes the same features.

Equality of income distribution

When comparing equality of income distribution in selected countries, measured using Gini's Coefficient of Concentration, Japan proves to have the lowest income differential (Table 5.2). Even

Table 5.2 *Income distribution in selected nations*

	Gini's coefficient	
Japan	0.2055	(1978)
Spain	0.3470	(1974)
UK	0.3796	(1986)
Canada	0.3829	(1974)
US	0.4110	(1973)
	0.3660	(1986)

Source: Economic Planning Agency, *White Paper on Daily Living*, 1979 and 1988.

when viewing the incomes of the lowest 10 percent and the next higher 10 percent of income levels, the percentage, compared to the overall income, is higher in Japan than anywhere else. This comparison also indicates that income is distributed more evenly in Japan.

As is already widely known 90 percent of all Japanese consider themselves as belonging to the middle class.[9]

Viewed globally, meanwhile, Japan's ratio of transfer expenditures against gross domestic expenditures is on the low side (Table 5.3). That fact means that the even distribution of income does not come from government intervention, but occurs naturally from the economic mechanism; it is another product of *kigyoism*.

Table 5.3 *Comparison of government expenditures and transfer expenditures in selected countries 1979 (compared to gross domestic expenditures) (%)*

Country	National expenditures	Transfer expenditures
Japan	16	11
US	20	11
W. Germany	23	15
UK	23	13
France	18	23
Sweden	33	22
Finland	22	12

Note: Government expenditures are comprised of final consumption expenditures and general total capital. Transfer expenditures include subsidies, social insurance payments and social grants.

A look at the so-called 200 families of France shows that if a family has enough capital to control companies, its income is also vastly higher than the income of the average citizen. And in countries like the United States, too, where institutional investors wield a strong influence, some people earn substantially higher incomes than the average citizen. Institutional investors can find talented individuals outside the corporation and place them directly into managerial positions. Markets for management talent are formed in those circumstances. Individuals who are able to assume the management of companies that operate at a loss and make their operations profitable in a short period are hard to find, thus making such talent very expensive.

It would not seem strange in Japan either if a group of share-holders in a major Japanese corporation, like their American counterparts, were to pay a large sum of money to a manager who was able to raise dividends in a short period to, say, 15 percent of par value rather than the current 10 percent. The reality in Japan, however, is that Japanese shareholders, despite the fact that they 'own' a company, have almost no power to place people of their choice into managerial positions in that company. In the end, Japanese 'capitalists' have to accept the managers selected from inside the company. Consequently, there is no system for evaluating such management talent, nor has a talent market formed.

Also, since there is no market for determining the remuneration for the officers and directors of Japanese companies, the compan-ies acquire their services at prices that are substantially lower than their market evaluation. In effect, companies can 'beat the prices down'. And although the officers and directors stand at the top of the group of corporate employees, they are still nothing more than first among equals and must place the operational rationality of the corporate organization before their own economic interests. Paying a selected few excessively high salaries can negatively affect the overall morale of the group of corporate employees. These factors combine naturally to keep management remuneration low.

In general, directors in Japanese companies get paid at a level that is 'a little higher' than department managers.[10]

If the remuneration of officers and directors of large private corporations is kept at low levels, the salaries of other manage-ment personnel in the organization must follow suit. Salaries paid to civil service workers are adjusted along levels established in private companies, but even if they were not, it would still be impossible to pay government ministers and upper echelon public officials salaries that were much higher than those of the presidents and officers of large private companies.

Among the industrialized nations of the free world, Japan has the highest percentage of workers with salary income. The very small disparity in salaries, therefore, relates directly to the overall equality in income levels in Japan as a nation.

The striking equality of income distribution in Japan is brought about by the corporation. And at the starting point of every mechanism leading to that equality is the Japanese corporate system, which prevents the infiltration of market principles into the company.

Other areas of equality

Homogeneity among Japanese is also great in areas other than income. In a country where the average remuneration of a company president is only about seven times that of a new employee, there is almost no base for developing a lifestyle for a few very wealthy people that differs greatly from that of the general public. Another factor contributing to this homogeneity was the elimination of social status discrimination between white-collar and blue-collar workers after the war. In prewar days, career employment systems were often not applied to blue-collar workers, and wages were paid those workers on an hourly or daily basis, compared to monthly salaries for white-collar workers. Bonuses to blue-collar workers, moreover, were limited to nominal amounts at the year-end, and blue-collar workers were not included in the severance pay system. In addition, other forms of discrimination existed in the company between the blue- and white-collar workers.

In Europe, a movement has recently appeared that seeks to reduce the disparity in pay and other work conditions between white-collar and blue-collar workers, and to apply white-collar working conditions to blue-collar workers as well. Japan has moved much further ahead in this area.

(a) Vertical mobility

The degree of vertical mobility in Japanese society is an indication of how Japan is essentially no longer a class society.

When families own and control companies, they try very hard to produce managers from their own families, going outside only when proper talent cannot be found inside. Even then, family members occupy all positions of trustee management, thus retaining supervisory control over management.

In Japan, at least as far as large corporations are concerned, family-type capitalist controlled corporate structures have been eliminated and the way is open for any employee with ability to attain a top management position.

The elimination of discrimination against blue-collar workers has raised vertical mobility. In prewar days, the highest position that a factory worker could hope to attain was line foreman. Today, introduction of a 'job chief system' is being promoted, whereby a factory worker can climb through the stages of job chief and assistant section manager and continue all the way to become plant manager.

A system that bonds an employee to a specific company also has the effect of raising vertical mobility. If a middle-sized or smaller company happens to belong to a growing industry and develops into a large company, it will raise the social level of all corporate employees as a group. As the company grows, the social position of all its corporate employees also rises (and, of course, falls if company fortunes decline). Social position in Japanese society is constantly shifting with the rise and decline of companies accompanying changes in the industrial structure.

(b) Diversification of value distribution

The diversification of value distribution is another facet of equality in Japanese society. The fundamental factor that brought this about is that wealth and authority do not necessarily go together in a *kigyoistic* society, where ownership is no longer tied to control. High social prestige originates mainly from an affiliation with a large corporate organization, but the persons in the top positions in these organizations are not always wealthy. And, conversely, just being wealthy is not enough to give a person high social prestige or position.

In the United States, social class rankings are generally related to level of income. Also, in urban areas, people live in separate locations according to income level, and merely knowing where a person lives gives one a general idea about which class he belongs to and his level of income. Higher social standing is also gained through a higher income level. A person's social standing will be heightened, for example, if he moves from the 50,000-dollar to the 100,000-dollar income bracket.

In Japan, however, income is not considered such a serious matter. The main factors determining social status are, first, the kind of company a person works for, i.e., whether it is a large company with high prestige and considerable influence, and second, his position in that company. A person's social standing can generally be considered as a multiple of these two factors. If two companies have about the same standing, a section manager in one has a higher status than an assistant section manager in the other. Likewise, a section manager in a large company has higher social status than a section manager in a medium-sized or smaller company[11]. These circumstances also explain why competition to enter higher schools of learning turns into such a ferocious battleground of entrance examinations. This cannot be explained from the standpoint of economic motives, because the ratio of income returns attributable to educational investments is notoriously low in Japan. In short, there is not much relationship in Japan between educational background and the total income a person earns in a lifetime of work. Japan is one of the few countries in the world where this holds true.[12]

College entrance competition is fierce because one factor that determines a person's social standing is the status of the company in which employment is found, and that, in turn, depends greatly on the college from which a person graduates. Graduates of prestigious Japanese universities seldom seek employment in a medium-sized or smaller company. They are much more oriented toward larger companies than their American counterparts, probably because choosing to work at a medium-sized or smaller company means a person is placing himself in a greatly weakened position on his first step up the ladder of social standing.

(c) Equality created by corporations

The marked equality in Japanese society is not a traditional condition. It was finally attained only after the maturation of *kigyoistic* society. In Japan's feudal Edo period, which ended in 1867, society was much like traditional European society, with strict distinctions of social class and position. In comparison, the traditional societies of China, Korea and even Vietnam had less distinct forms of classes than Japan. In those countries, even a person who was born as a lowly peasant farmer could, at least in theory, attain a lofty position as a civil servant by passing government civil service examinations. Such vertical mobility did not exist in feudal Japan, except in very restricted forms.[13]

Equality is not a Japanese tradition. Even the Japanese language contains a complicated and detailed system of honorifics that is not found in the European or Chinese languages. In conversation, therefore, a Japanese is always conscious of and must make a judgment concerning whether the person he is addressing is of higher, lower or equal status. Even the Japanese language, therefore, is not conducive to creating an equal society.

Neither is democracy an adequate explanation for equality in Japanese society. Democracy originated in the West, and the fact that Japan is democratic does not explain why its society should be more equal than Western society. The postwar reforms that eliminated the peerage system in Japan may have provided preliminary conditions for creating an equal society, but it actually only provided grounds for equal opportunities. It cannot sufficiently explain the amazing 'equality in the end-result' seen in contemporary Japanese society, as evinced by the equality in income distribution, homogeneity of lifestyles, ease of vertical mobility and diversified distribution of values.

It is difficult to state, therefore, that Japanese society by nature is an equal one. The marked equality seen in contemporary Japanese society is the product of *kigyoism*. This belief can be confirmed by the fact that those areas of Japanese society where aspects of inequality and remnants of feudalism still remain are almost the same areas which *kigyoism* has yet to penetrate.

Some say the equality that exists by nature in Japanese society created the equality found in companies, but, as seen above, the opposite appears to be true: in Japan, society does not explain companies; companies explain society.

4 Freedom in a Kigyoistic Society

In a *kigyoistic* society, the freedom of market choice of individuals involved in production activities is severely restricted. Once a person is affiliated with a company, it is difficult to change to another company or occupation. A society based on *kigyoism* takes away much of the freedom an individual has in a liberal society. As explained earlier, however, this cannot be construed to mean that a *kigyoistic* society is not a liberal one. For example, freedoms similar to those seen in liberal societies can be found in areas other than production. Furthermore, Japanese society gives working individuals greater freedom in actual working processes inside the organization as compensation for restrictions on their freedom in the market. As previously explained, these two factors are intimately related. Restrictions on freedom in the market make freedom inside the organization possible.

A *kigyoistic* society has organizational freedom, which more than compensates for restricting an individual's freedom in the market.

There are those, of course, who interpret these matters differently.

Let us compare these two freedoms, therefore, and see which of the two ultimately brings freedom to the individual. One is a situation where a person can make a relatively free choice among non-liberal organizations; the other is a situation where a person is rather tightly tied to a relatively liberal organization. A person with confidence in the variety and future promise of his personal skills and potential will choose the former type of organization and strive to grasp opportunities for rapid advancement. For the majority, however, the situation will not greatly change even if they switch jobs or move to different companies. This claim is borne out by the fact that even in the United States, the majority of middle-aged or older workers, except for executives, tend to remain in familiar jobs. As well, there are times when freedom in the market will place almost unbearable risks on the individual.

When these circumstances are taken into consideration, most people would probably realize that organizational freedom has more substance.

The freedom that *kigyoism* gives to individuals is the most significant type of freedom for large numbers of average human beings.

A quote from Alexis de Tocqueville is fitting here:

> When one passes from a free country into another which is not so, the contrast is very striking: there, all is activity and bustle; here all seems calm and immobile. In the former, betterment and progress are the questions of the day; in the latter, one might suppose that society, having acquired every blessing, longs for nothing but repose in which to enjoy them. Nevertheless, the country which is in such a rush to attain happiness is generally richer and more prosperous than the one that seems contented with its lot. And considering them one by one, it is hard to understand how this one daily discovers so many new needs, while the other seems conscious of so few.[14]

A person looking at his surroundings in Tokyo may not find the city beautiful nor see that it has character, but will have to admit that the city exhibits vitality to the highest degree in the world. And those who compare countries around the world will recognize that Japan most clearly represents the special characteristics of a free nation as described by de Tocqueville.

Rather than listening to thousands of words and phrases about ideological theories, the presence or absence of freedom in a society can be intuitively grasped through de Tocqueville's way of immersing oneself in the society and experiencing it. Even if freedom exists in the theoretical world, for example, society would in fact already have lost its freedom, or freedom would be about to be lost if there were only lethargy and stagnation, the absence of an adventurous spirit, and indolence and self-satisfaction.

The two systems of liberalism and socialism existing in the world today have both declared their societies to be free, each basing its views on its unique philosophy. The situation in socialist societies needs little argument, but even in societies under the so-called liberal system, freedom has already been lost to a considerable degree. To state this more accurately, the ideals and the system may have been adequate in the past to ensure freedom, but this is no longer true today.

The deterioration of freedom in liberal societies is not because of loss of freedom per se, but rather because new organizational structures have formed in which liberal ideals and the liberal system cannot effectively exert their strengths.

When liberal societies were still basically agricultural societies, or when industrial, even if they comprised chiefly cottage industries, the principles and systems of liberalism were adequate to maintain them as fundamentally free societies. With the advance of industrialization, however, and as the period becomes one in which a vast majority of the population passes its working life within large organizations, the kind of system that cannot provide practical forms of freedom inside those organizations will begin to lose more and more of the qualifications it needs to call itself a free society.

A European may say that freedom of choice in the labor market guarantees freedom to workers. His grounds for this claim include the argument that because workers are always free to leave a company, regardless of how strictly they are controlled inside the organization, the situation is the result of a choice they freely made, thus attesting to their essential freedom.

But if he quits his job, where on earth will he go? No matter where he goes, he will find the same kind of work site. When placed in a situation like this, can a person really be called free to begin with?

With disappearing class distinctions and a decline in the influence exerted by regional communities, an individual's working life is becoming almost the only manner in which he can find his position in society. Where in the past it was sufficient for a person to say 'I am a *samurai*' or 'I live in such and such a village' to identify himself, today it is becoming more necessary for him to identify himself by saying what kind of work he does. For the individual, his working life has become almost the only means by which he can ascertain that his is not a meaningless existence; his work has also made it possible for him to direct his daily attention to something higher than himself.

No matter how working hours may be shortened, it can be said that a person's working life has become more important now than in the past, both as a tie to the community and as a means of determining his general social awareness. In the West, however, this critically important living area has been left to autocratic controls. A person who is forced to live under a system which binds him with restrictions and rules that make him feel like nothing more than someone being controlled, without at the same time allowing him to feel the significance of his existence, which is almost the only tie between him and society, will find it difficult to maintain the special spiritual qualities of a free person with a proper attitude toward life, no matter how much freedom he may enjoy in other areas of his life.

If one looks closely at Western society, it becomes obvious that persons who are self-content because the society existing in their country is free are actually limited to the so-called elite. These people enjoy to the greatest extent the benefits presented by various areas of freedom, such as freedom of speech, economic freedom, and freedom to choose their work. Such freedoms are important, of course, but these people cannot see the plight of the masses who have lost their freedom in the work process, which to them is the most keenly felt freedom. Western politicians, businessmen and the intelligentsia shout about the over-dependence on others, the selfishness, indolence and lack of public morals of the general public as unbecoming to liberals and attribute those failings to moral decay. Such problems may indeed be tied to morals to some degree, but the major problem is with the system. If the general masses in the West show features unbecoming to liberalism, it is more a reflection of the fact that Western society itself is no longer a free society.

The Japanese system is the most fitting for meeting the demands of contemporary industrial society, and it essentially provides the most meaningful organizational freedom in the greatest quantity for the majority of Japanese citizens. Our contemporary period is one of organizations and a mass society. In such a period, the basic task facing a country's economic and social systems is simultaneously attaining organizational efficiency while enabling the many average people working in the organizations to find a purpose in life in their work. Therefore, for that reason alone and regardless of whatever other merits they might have, the social or economic organizations that cannot attain this task must be called failures. The ancient Greeks were essentially political citizens who depended on slave labor to support their material lives, but citizens living in the twentieth century are, first of all, 'working people'. Also, the existence of a society is greatly dependent on how working people can find purpose in life and constantly maintain their morale. In such a society, political democracy alone is clearly inadequate. Even if contemporary society is called a mass consumption society, the situation remains unchanged, for it is clear that consumption alone cannot maintain either an economy or a society.

In the Japanese system, the above task is being undertaken in a relatively ingenious manner by artificially creating a relationship in society in which the interests of the organization and the individual coincide. Apart from the question of how to evaluate the Japanese system from the standpoints of liberal and democratic theories, the system can certainly be called a new method for solving problems in contemporary society.

5 A System for the Masses

Young talented Americans fired by ambition take full advantage of freedom in the labor market. The success they attain in one job acts as a springboard for advancing to another position that is more important and promises greater remuneration. They meet such challenges over and over. And if they are blessed with good luck and ability, they can win great wealth and glory in a short time. In Japan, however, the same type of person cannot readily hope for the same scenario to occur.

In return for the freedom that corporate employees forsake in Japan, they obtain greater security for planning their lives and they participate in specific work processes in their daily corporate lives. The security they receive is not only freedom in the career employment system from the possibility of dismissal due to causes not of their own making, but also stability in their employment environment. Position and pay will be determined, more or less, by the seniority system, and competition between individuals will be based on results accumulated over a long period. There is almost no chance of rapid and high promotions from a relatively low level, but neither will there be sudden demotions. The situation possible in Western companies, where a person's subordinate yesterday can turn into his boss today, is unimaginable in Japan. In the Japanese employment environment, stable human relationships are formed within the company. In short, corporate employees are provided with a stable life pattern which is predictable over an extended period of time.

Young people in Japan often liken joining a company to getting on an escalator. This statement is not made in a positive sense but rather in a negative one. Once one gets on the escalator, there is no stepping off along the way. With the passage of time, there will be increases in pay and promotions, but one knows exactly what to expect. The newest employees see those retiring, usually between 55 and 60, as reflections of themselves 30 years in the future. In the eyes of some young Japanese joining a company, the system may seem as though it will take their ambitious hopes for the future away and enclose them within a petty framework that will turn them into minor citizens.

And yet, on the other hand, this system makes it possible for an individual to plan his entire life by placing him on a stable course. Because stability in the job environment is quite high in this system, there is little chance of someone attaining wealth and authority in a short period through good fortune, or of suddenly losing his current position due to circumstances for which he is not responsible. In the end, success in life can only be attained through steady efforts, and although it may not thus be possible to have grandiose ambitions, the Japanese system makes the cultivation of a solid attitude toward life possible.

When workers too often have things given to them and taken away for reasons beyond their control – by the State in socialist countries, and by market forces in capitalist countries – they will gradually lose the feeling of being securely in control of their own lives, and will turn into fatalists, depending on luck and chance and adopting a despairing attitude toward life.

These are general statements, of course, and there certainly is a small number of talented and ambitious Westerners who think nothing of a few risks lying in their way and do not even consider them as factors that can possibly endanger their self-dependence. They may even consider such risks as necessary costs for attaining the great success for which they are aiming. These persons will evaluate the American type of freedom more positively because it provides them with greater latitude to exercise their potential than the Japanese type of security and freedom. American vitality is created from the ambitious activities of such talented people. For the great masses of people, however, the situation and the evaluation probably differ.[15] For them, too, there is no doubt that freedom is desirable.

Although freedom in the market may be available on an equal basis to all, there are large variances in the ability to utilize this freedom. Economic freedom, for example, is important for large companies conducting large-scale business operations, but probably has little significance for an individual with neither capital nor credibility. Freedom of job choice, meanwhile, gives talented individuals the opportunity to push their potential to the maximum extent, but for those without any particular skills to offer, such freedom is not that important. It cannot be denied that freedom in the labor market brings greater rewards to talented persons. The average person, however, more keenly feels a need for greater security in his work and daily life and for a work site that lets him find a purpose in life, and thus he would probably prefer the Japanese type of organizational freedom because it meets those needs. And he probably feels that if a certain degree of limitations on freedom in the labor market is tied to meeting those needs, then it's better to accept those limitations.

The Japanese system is not one that makes it possible, nor does it rely on making it possible, for a small number of talented persons to realize their potential to the maximum degree. Rather, it provides a stable environment to a large number of average people, it turns work into a meaningful activity for those people by giving them greater freedom at their work sites, and it relies on the resultant group vitality that emerges. In short, *kigyoism* does not necessarily reward the small number of talented people to a great degree. However, it is a system that is more beneficial for the large number of average people. The system was created from reality and refined, not by a small number of thinkers or legislators far removed from the level of the common people, but by the unnamed masses, and the results the system brought about are indeed appropriate.

The growth of Japanese industry was achieved, after all, by drawing out the vitality of the working masses, which explains why it is difficult to identify specific individuals whose contributions were the key to the achievements of overall industry. If one had to credit any specific factor for the great achievements of Japanese industry, it would be found in the common activities of common people. Worded more accurately, under a *kigyoistic* system elements appear in the common activities of common people that tie it to greatness.

Notes

1 Management and Coordination Agency, Statistics Bureau, *Statistics on Japan, 37th Edition*, 1987, p. 72.
2 Osamu Hashiguchi, 'Kigyo to wa Kokka Ijo no Mono' (The Corporation Is above the State), *Hogaku Seminar Special Issue*, Series 14 (1980), p. 107.
3 Lester C. Thurow, *The Zero-Sum Society*. New York: Basic Books Inc., 1980, pp. 7, 139.
4 Tanaka, pp. 344–5.
5 Kimihiro Masamura, Jiyu Kigyo Taisei no Shorai (The Future of the Free Business Corporation System). Tokyo Diayamondosha, 1976, pp. 17–18.
6 Moriaki Tsuchiya, *Nihonteki Keiei no Shinwa* (The Myth of Japanese-Style Management). Tokyo, Nihon Keizai Shimbunsha, 1978, pp. 26–7.
7 Asahi Shimbun Keizaibu, ed., K.K. *Nippon Shindan* (Diagnosis of Japan Inc.). Tokyo, Asahi Shimbunsha, 1981, p. 16.
8 William Alexander Robson, Welfare State and Welfare Society: Illusion and Reality. London, G. Allen & Unwin, 1976, p. 13.
9 *Kokumin no Seikatsu Teido ni Kansuru Ishiki Chosa* (Awareness Survey on National Living Standards). Tokyo, Prime Minister's Office, August 1980.
10 'Yakuin Hoshu wa Kokimeru' (This Is How Executive Compensation Is Determined), *Nikkei Bijinesu*, 6–15 (1981), p. 47.
11 Ryushi Iwata, *Nihonteki Keiei no Hensei Genri* (Structural Principles of Japanese-Style Management). Tokyo, Bunshindo, 1977, pp. 232–9.
12 *Showa 55-Nendo Kokumin Seikatsu Hakusho* (The 1980 White Paper on National Living Conditions). Economic Planning Agency. According to this paper, the cumulative income of university graduates surpassed that of high school graduates at age 36 years and two months in 1965; this figure was 40 years in 1978. For comparative study, see Morikazu Shiogi, *Gakureki Shakai no Tenkan* (Transition in Academic-oriented Society). Tokyo, University of Tokyo Press, 1978, pp. 157–62.

13 Edwin O. Reischauer, *The Japanese*. Cambridge, Mass., Belknap Press of Harvard University Press, 1977, pp. 157–66. In this book, Reischauer compares Tokugawa Japan, in which a uniquely strict and oppressive hereditary system was meticulously practiced, with modern Japan, in which class consciousness is weak and little class difference exists.

14 Alexis de Tocqueville, *Democracy in America*, J. P. Mayer and Max Lerner, ed., translated by George Lawrence. New York, Harper & Row Publishers, 1966, p. 223.

15 On the hardships of American white-collar workers, see Makiko Yamada, *Amerika no Bijinesu Erito* (American Business Elite). Tokyo, Nihon Keizai Shimbunsha, 1976, pp. 159–62.

6 The Rise of Kigyoism

As demonstrated in the preceding chapters, *kigyoism* is a gigantic system that pervades Japan's entire economic society and is difficult to understand in terms of 'Japanese-style management' or other such concepts; it comprises both a new economy and a new society. In that sense, then, one must view the impressive achievements of the postwar Japanese economy not simply as the emergence of a single national economy, but as part of the process of the emergence of a new, more progressive economic system, i.e., *kigyoism*, a system that fitted the conditions of contemporary industrial society and proved itself with actual results.

Kigyoism liberated a great amount of human energy, energy which then could be turned toward attaining economic objectives to provide the national economy with a dynamic vitality. Society, too, took on such features as outstanding equality and vertical mobility, and an overall close integration emerged with corporations as the main standard-bearers. Changes that occurred in the corporate system at the base of the economy spread throughout society and the economy itself, resulting in the unique society and economy evident in Japan today.

Despite the essentially unique nature of Japan's economic society, it is not easy to grasp its overall image because we are still under the control of existing ideological systems, because we understand all phenomena by using terminology that describes the existing system, and because we cannot fully escape the method of thinking whereby the special features of our society are recognized by measuring it against the model society to which the existing system points.

1 Similarities in the Formation of Nations

The progressive nature of *kigyoism* as an economic organization lies in its acquisition of managerial autonomy under a new set of conditions; its progressive nature as a social organization lies in its all-out transformation of corporations from being the property of capitalists to being communal bodies of corporate employees.

Just as bourgeois revolutions changed nations from being the family property of sovereigns to being nations of citizens, so also did corporations change from being the property of capitalists to being organizations of corporate employees. Bourgeois revolutions changed people from being merely the objects of control to being citizens, each of whom felt he was a part of the country and who willingly bore the nation's destiny. Citizens who were aware of being part of an indivisible, unified body came to make up nations, and even if a country had a sovereign as its head, it was no longer possible for that sovereign to apportion the country among his successors nor to exchange part of the country's territory with another sovereign for territory in another country. Various systems and practices that restricted the freedom of citizens were abolished, and, at the same time, nationalistic feelings of allegiance to the State began to emerge.

These changes are most noticeable when one looks at how war, a form of national activity, was waged.

Wars in Europe during the period of absolute sovereigns were undertakings waged by those sovereigns. Military forces were simply tools of the sovereigns, and soldiers were mercenaries who fought only for money. They were not expected to show much initiative, and they were controlled only with the strictest discipline.

Rogier Caillois described some of the features of armies in those days as follows:

Soldiers were trained to line up in straight rows, with almost no space between them. They kept their shoulders square and chests and rifles thrust forward. They fought on foot, and there was nothing dynamic about their fighting: two opposing armies merely marched straight toward each other in textbook fashion, following orders strictly and mechanically, their every action determined in advance. No one suggested changing that style of battle either: it had to be that way, because the soldiers could not be depended on to show initiative.[1]

It is not surprising that military tactics in those days closely followed engineering-like principles. Armies did not pay attention to the soldiers' human attributes such as initiative, spiritual force and willpower, and had no expectations concerning such human qualities. Human beings were returned to their objective functions, and armies were thought of more as collections of functions rather than as collections of human beings. That thinking provided fertile soil for the development of the ruling military theories of the day, which were based on a mechanical approach.

Actually, one can say that military science up to then was limited to techniques and knowledge related principally to 'material', including the production, use and repair of weapons, the construction of fortresses and other defensive structures, the organization and arming of military forces, and forms of military maneuvers, which, in essence, are all related somehow to engineering.[2]

This general situation changed quickly with bourgeois revolutions.

States became nations comprised of citizens, military forces became the armies of nations, and soldiers became 'citizens in uniform'. Wars were no longer fought by mercenaries. Instead, in the words of Carl von Clausewitz, 'Suddenly war again became the business of the people – a people of 30 million, all of whom considered themselves to be citizens.'[3]

The changes in the nature of warfare related closely to changes in the makeup of nations, where the ruled masses were transformed into citizens who took the initiative in leading the nation. Soldiers likewise ceased to be fighting machines and took the initiative in participating in war.

Caillois commented as follows on the subject:

The French Revolution firmly established general elections and a system of compulsory military service. The military draft signified just one thing: in the same way that citizens participated in government, so also would they participate afterward in national defense.[4]

War methods also changed. Citizen armies could be relied on to take whatever initiative was required, and armies organized themselves into units that gave great freedom of movement to the individual soldier.

The victories of the French revolutionary armies 'completely demolished past systems of military science and threw out all material elements and geometrical factors that formed their foundation.'[5]

Up to that point, military theories considered war a game that was carried out using highly rationalized calculations based on known conditions and rules. Replacing those theories was the military science of von Clausewitz, which emphasized to the maximum extent possible the dynamic nature of war, the natural unpredictability of war's outcome, and subjective factors that overcame those two, such as human willpower, spiritual strength and initiative.

Paralleling the changes that took place with the transformation of states into modern nations were clear changes that took place in corporations. Although it is unreasonable to view nations and corporations in the same simple framework, and there were differences in the changes that took place, it still cannot be denied that there were similarities concerning changes in the relationship between individuals and groups that did not occur by chance. Individuals, instead of being ruled, became participants in the group, and the group, in turn, was able to draw out the initiative and energy of individuals and pull them together to attain group objectives.

Japanese industry, then, uses the liberated vitality of individuals and their pull toward their companies as its greatest 'weapon' in realizing great success in global competition. In contrast, although American industry has advanced technology, an immense home market, bountiful domestic natural resources and excellent management capabilities, it is falling behind or only barely holding its ground in competing with the powerful force of organized human energy displayed by Japanese groups of corporate employees.

2 Revolution based on Theory and Revolution based on Reality

Clearly, what might be called a 'corporate revolution' occurred somewhere along the way. Even as it was under way, however, it did not attract a due amount of attention considering its freshness and true significance. Although many reasons can be given for the lack of attention, the principal explanation is that no specific theory or thought system preceded it, and it emerged almost spontaneously from everyday business reality.

Past revolutions that brought about fundamental and cataclysmic changes in social and economic systems can be divided into two types: the first, as in the case of democracy and socialism, saw theories and thought moving ahead with reality, then being created accordingly. The second type, as in the case of feudalism and capitalism, saw continuous trial and error by countless numbers of persons – guided by invisible yet rational forces firmly grounded in reality – which eventually resulted in great economic and social change.

The roles played by Karl Marx vis-à-vis socialism and communism and Adam Smith vis-à-vis capitalism were not the same.

Although Marx, on one hand, created the 'reality of socialism', Smith, on the other, recognized the 'reality of capitalism' as it had developed before his eyes, and based on what he saw, formulated theories on capitalism and extracted its essential elements.

Revolutions based on theory from their very beginning embrace a grand vision of what the political, economic and social situation should be like in the future. The grandeur and logical consistency of the vision particularly appeal to the intelligentsia, and activist elements among them eventually take action to realize the vision. If the old form of rule degenerates and its powers of resistance wane, the revolution will succeed and overthrow it. Social agitation will then sweep a country with hurricane-like force and transform society into the new order overnight. Such swiftness of change is a principal feature of revolution based on theory.

Changes in revolution based on reality, in contrast, are slow, gradually materializing through repetition and cumulative efforts that are made in order to cope with necessities. One does not realize the nature of one's daily actions in terms of the changes taking place, nor where the overall results of those actions are leading. The existing ideological systems remain intact. And even as changes occur, one tries to comprehend the new realities, which are becoming increasingly difficult to explain, by applying old concepts that are no longer viable. As changes continue to occur in the surrounding reality, however, the new reality erodes the old concepts, and the vocabulary of the existing ideological systems begins systematically to acquire new meanings in daily usage.

Even in such a situation, during the interim until a theoretical framework is formulated that explains internally the newly emerged reality that has supplanted the existing theory, the new reality is often viewed as an irrational mutation of the natural state and often becomes an object of criticism.

However, since the new reality is verified through pragmatic application in daily life, it is supported by a surprisingly deep rationality in society and in human nature, which cannot be clearly understood from superficial observations.

If the principal shortcoming of revolution based on reality is the slowness of change, its principal advantage is its incomparably realistic qualities. One need not look very far to find examples of new systems which are created by revolutions guided by clear theoretical blueprints but which are sorely lacking in terms of reality.

The stronger a theory's attraction, the stronger the possibility that the development of reality will be retarded and warped. This situation results because theory serves the function of justifying a system, and therefore, even if problems occur for which the system would normally be responsible, ideas can be manipulated to blame the problems on mistakes made by administrators of the system, on poor public ethics or other external factors outside the system's area of responsibility.

In that sense, then, theories tend to lack the flexibility to pinpoint and creatively cope with problems related to the system itself.

Of the two general types of revolution, *kigyoism* is a spontaneous product of revolution based on reality. Its realistic quality is rooted in that fact.

Enterprises in Meiji Japan were based on capitalism, and corporations belonged to individual capitalists, such as the *zaibatsu* families. Labor was highly mobile, and labor–management relations were not close.

Concerning this point, the following description of the Meiji situation is revealing:

Japanese workers throughout Meiji and in the first half of Taisho had high labor mobility, almost higher than workers anywhere else in the world. Much evidence attests to this fact. Kojiro Matsukata, then president of Kawasaki Shipyards, for example, emphasized the magnitude of job changing by workers when he said, 'A look at length of service of our workers reveals some amazing facts. As of September 20, for example, the number of factory workers with less than one year of service is an astounding 9,200 out of 15,860 persons. For those with less than three years of service, the total is 13,470 persons, 85 percent of our entire labor force. When we realize we have only 2,390 persons with over three years of service, we know the rate at which workers change jobs is high.'[6]

Naturally, under those circumstances it was rare to find workers exhibiting the special features of the 'companified' employees of contemporary Japan.

A report compiled by the Ministry of Commerce and Agriculture in early Meiji stated that many factory workers lived only for each day, working during the day and drinking at night.

Ordinary factory workers have no thoughts of saving money for the future. Their only thoughts are getting as much money as possible for each day's work. They don't particularly care about the length of the working day, about overtime or about night work; nor do they consider any work too menial or degrading.

Compared to other workers, factory workers receive relatively high wages. But their standard of living is poorer, because many spend their wages on drinking and carousing. Even those living in boardinghouses will often stay out all night on payday, and as a consequence their work suffers the following day. The foremen have to put up with such behavior because they can't find other workers to take their place. The workers realize their situation and do not consider their attitude at all shameful. The older workers influence the younger ones, who often follow the same path to leading wasteful lives.[7]

According to Ryohei Magota, some presidents staggered pay-days to try to lower the high rate of absenteeism on the day after.[8]

At any rate, management in those days was not 'Japanese-like' at all; nor did workers resemble their current counterparts.

Although theories abound pinpointing when the situation in Japan began to change, all generally agree that the change began in the 1920s in the heavy industries. Unlike in the light industries, where work centered on simple operations and unskilled workers with low work ethics could still be managed using 'carrot and stick' methods, workers in heavy industries were highly skilled and management had to create a special environment to induce them to work with zeal and initiative.

Japan, however, was sorely lacking in social systems for cultivating skilled labor, systems corresponding to the apprenticeship or *meister* system in some other countries.

After much trial and error, the following changes took place:

In the waning years of Meiji, a radically new system began to spread in Japan. Companies introduced a system for educating and training unskilled workers in order to produce a large number of skilled workers in a short period of time. In effect, they established in-house schools for producing skilled workers.[9]

To realize effective results from this new system, companies had somehow to ensure that the workers remained after having been trained. The career employment and seniority systems were thus introduced. Although companies originally applied these two systems to only a small percentage of workers, as has been stated earlier, after the Second World War the systems quickly became much more common. It goes without saying that companies with these systems were superior to others in terms of the effectiveness of their education and training programs. That is not surprising, of course, since those systems were established with that objective in mind. But when developed to their logical conclusions, they were destined to lead to the introduction of a certain new principle in corporations, one that would force a fundamental change in the corporate system, a change turning corporations from 'being controlled by capitalists' to becoming 'corporations with participation by corporate employees'.

Kigyoism, therefore, originated and developed as a necessary innovation for overcoming the disadvantageous situation in which Japan found itself because it was a backward nation without the favorable circumstances that existed in the developed capitalist nations of the time. This form of adaptation was forced on the companies because of Japan's backwardness: *kigyoism* was not based on complicated theories, nor did it have the praiseworthy objectives so often associated with the emergence of other systems. In fact, in contrast to the high and noble objectives behind the creation of so many others, the motives of the unknown creators of *kigyoism* might even be termed petty and insignificant.

But whatever the original motives, it became clear that the resultant corporate system fitted closely with the realities of industrial society in the twentieth century.

In a limited sense, then, one can say that the 'backwardness of Japan in the past' contributed to forging the 'progressiveness of Japan in the present'. If one gives an example, that development might be compared to the evolutionary process during which some species of marine life made their way ashore to become land dwellers. Japanese companies, denied a favorable environment, were like fish forced by destiny to live in muddy water. In the struggle for survival, the fish gradually had to develop the faculties necessary for living in the environment in which they found themselves, such as, for example, having their fins evolve gradually into foot-like shapes. Viewed from the standpoint of the fish, the foot-like shapes were terribly unbecoming, but as the eons passed and the oceans began to recede, the fish that once swam in muddy water looked at other fish swimming in the open sea and made the necessary efforts forced on them in order to survive and took on the nature of experiments with a universal significance.

The fish developed a type of new faculty, and basic changes that continued afterward in their internal structure provided these fish with the potential for tremendous development in a new living environment on land. It then became clear that 'outstanding' fish without the same faculties could not expect their species to develop if they continued in the same form while the world changed.

Something like this occurred in the corporate systems of Japan and the Western nations.

That Japanese companies introduced education and training systems is significant only when presupposing the various conditions existing in backward Japan at the time. As the ability of religion to encourage individuals to be diligent began to wane, and as the fear of unemployment began to diminish with the formation of a more affluent society, systems to support and expand the work ethic inside corporations came to be well regarded and seen as universally acceptable advantages in many other societies as well. Systems for developing skills may have been unnecessary years ago in companies in the advanced capitalist countries, but today, when rapid technological advances occur almost continuously, those companies find themselves in a position similar to the one faced earlier by Japanese companies in heavy industries. This factor added further significance to the universal nature of *kigyoism*. With the securitization of capital – a natural result of capitalism's development – and the accompanying pulling away by stockholders from corporate risk, *kigyoism* turned employees into corporate members, forcing them to accept a role as responsible corporate managers, in place of individual shareholders. By placing the reins of management in their hands, it became possible to maintain management autonomy.

Another great advantage held by Japanese companies today, against the backdrop of the elasticity lost in the labor market because of the development of labor unions, is the ability to rotate workers from one job to another, thereby making greater organizational flexibility possible.

That it became possible to create a system allowing greater organizational freedom also meant that it became relatively easier to have employees satisfy, inside the organization, their increasingly diverse and sophisticated needs – needs tied to higher levels of education and a generally higher standard of living. This move also prevented the growth of an aversion to labor in Japan, similar to the one that is gradually spreading in other advanced industrial countries.

One can say, too, that the noteworthy equality seen in Japanese companies exactly suits society's demands for 'real equality'. These related features indicate that *kigyoism* is more appropriate for the various conditions of contemporary industrial society than other systems.

As outlined above, therefore, the strength of *kigyoism* lies in its realism, a realism clearly rooted in the process of spontaneous generation in which the system developed.

In contrast to various systems around the world designed by thinkers, governments, 'great leaders' and others that have achieved results far below their original intentions, *kigyoism* is a system that did not voice idealistic goals but instead developed with practical soundness and applicability in everyday situations as its sole guideline, which is why it has easily achieved that which no one at the outset could even have dreamed.

3 A Reality that Surpassed Theory

Kigyoism took the first country in which it sank its roots – Japan, fundamentally an agricultural country with seeming minimal conditions for supporting industrialization – and within a quarter of a century or less enabled Japan to stand in the ranks of the world's most advanced industrialized nations. In 1950, nearly 50 percent of Japan's working population was employed in the primary industries. That percentage had dropped to nearly 10 percent 25 years later. Despite such accelerated and wide-reaching industrialization, however, which led to urbanization and rapid changes in lifestyles and social values, *kigyoism* gathered the Japanese people – who faced a solidarity crisis in the immediate postwar years – beneath its corporate wings and created a vibrant spirit that formed the foundation for a healthy society.

Despite its notable achievements, *kigyoism* has no theory to support it. On the contrary, *kigyoism* is rare in that it is a system that has been condemned from so many quarters. Economists said it interfered with the mobility of workers, thus preventing optimum distribution of the labor force; Marxists criticized it for warping the class consciousness of workers.

If such criticisms were valid, then certainly one might say there must have been supportive arguments from advocates of capitalism. But those people also criticized the system, saying it created a distorted form of management that ignored shareholders.

Up to now, the Japanese system has been continually harassed by persons waving the banner of established foreign thinking that was divorced from the true sentiments of the Japanese people. No matter how much criticism the system came under, however, it did not budge, because its foundations were rooted in reality rather than in theory.

In this way, reality got the better of theory; or, rather, reality outpaced theory.

The fact that theory was outpaced by reality means that rather than saying reality simply proved theory wrong, it decisively rendered theory meaningless. That is because inquiring about whether a theory is mistaken indicates that some kind of basic corresponding relationship still remains between it and reality.

Marx's argument concerning 'the increasing pauperization of the working class' in a capitalist society is one example. One sees today that workers in capitalist societies are growing increasingly wealthy, and normal scientific processes for determining accuracy, therefore, disprove Marx's argument. Also, what happens if workers themselves, by turning into corporate employees, cease to exist? If that happens, Marx's argument no longer applies at all, and there would be absolutely no reason to discuss its validity.

Today, it is extremely unrealistic to consider companies merely as material points for turning input into output and to treat labor as one factor of production. Labor productivity is not a constant; it is a variable. It varies, depending not only on technical training, but also on human factors, such as volition and willpower. And most of these types of changes occur inside the company, which means that the work ethic and level of technical skill, essential elements of the labor force, are created internally. Given such a corporate structure, one has to question how realistic theories up to now have been.

Such is occurring in Japan today. Situations that cannot be understood within the framework of existing theories are emerging. *Kigyoism* is still evolving and its latent possibilities are yet to be realized. Of course, its progressiveness is relative.

Just as feudal systems contained feudalistic problems and capitalism contained capitalist problems, *kigyoism* will breed its own set of problems. At the very least, however, those problems will certainly not be capitalist ones. And their solutions will require a totally different approach and thinking process. For that reason, there is no longer any great significance in considering Japan within the conceptual limits of a capitalist society.

Notes

1   Roger Caillois, *On War*. Tokyo, Hosei University Press, 1974, BELLONE ou la pente de la guerre (Renaissance du livre, Bruxelles, 1963) Vol. 1, Chap. 3.

2   Tokutaro Sato, *Tairiku Kokka to Kaiyo Kokka no Senryaku* (War Strategies of Continental and Maritime Nations). Tokyo, Hara Shobo, 1973, p. 128.

3   Carl von Clausewitz, *On War*, edited and translated by Michael Howard and Peter Paret, Princeton, Princeton University Press, 1976, Vol. 8, Chap. 3-B.

4   Caillois, Vol. 1, Chap. 5(3).

5   Sato, p. 128.

6   Fujiyoshi Sakamoto, *Gendai Keieisha no Ishiki to Kodo – Kigyo Kakumei no Atarashii Nami* (New Wave in Corporate Revolution – Awareness and Behavior of Contemporary Managers). Tokyo, Nihon Sogo Kyoiku Kiko, 1979, p. 381.

7   Bureau of Commerce and Industry/Ministry of Agriculture and Commerce, *Shokko Jijo* (Condition of Workers, Vol. 2). Tokyo, Shinki-gensha, 1976, pp, 19, 79, 129.

8   Ryohei Magota, 'Nihonjin wa hatarakasugi ka' wa sakkaku ni suginu' (The Saying 'Japanese Work Too Hard' Is Nothing but a Misconception), *Nikkei Bijinesu*, 5–5 (1980), p. 113.

9   Fujiyoshi Sakamoto, *Nihon Koyoshi (Ge) Nenkosei e no Nagai Dotei* (History of Employment in Japan – Part II: The Long Road of the Seniority System). Tokyo, Chuo Keizaisha, 1977, pp. 98–9.

Index

Note Names of firms and organisations etc. are mainly Japanese, except where otherwise specified.

265